RUDOLF STEINER

The Way to Healthier Thinking and the Demands on Modern Man

Ten public lectures held in Stuttgart between
March 2 and November 10, 1920

Translated by Hanna von Maltitz

ANTHROPOSOPHICAL PUBLICATIONS
FREMONT, MICHIGAN, UNITED STATES

HEALTHY THINKING
Copyright © 2022 by
Anthroposophical Publications

Cover designed by James D. Stewart

Rudolf Steiner Portrait by
Peter Gospodinov

Translation by Hanna von Maltitz
Cover painting
"Chakra Dance"
by Hanna von Maltitz
https://go.elib.com/ChakraDance

Thanks to the Basil Gibaud Memorial Trust for their support in the creation of this translation.

The e.Lib, Inc.
Visit the website at https://www.elib.com/

Printed in the United States of America

First Printing: October 2022
Anthroposophical Publications
https://AnthroposophicalPublications.org/

ISBN: 978-1-948302-37-1 paperback
978-1-948302-38-8 eBook

Table of Contents

About the publications from Rudolf Steiner's lectures

Rudolf Steiner always gave his lectures freely, that is, without a manuscript. He recorded many of his preliminary considerations in his notebooks merely in keywords, sometimes in short sentences, diagrams or sketches, without elaborating them further in writing. Only in very few cases are there prepared written summaries that were intended for translators. He did, however, agree to the publication of his lectures, even if he himself was only able to prepare a few for print.

The lectures published in the Rudolf Steiner Complete Edition are usually based on transcriptions of stenographic notes made during the lecture by listeners or expert stenographers consulted. Occasionally — and this applies to the early years of his lecturing activities, up to about 1905 — written transcriptions by listeners also serve as the basis for the text. For printing, the transcriptions in longhand or audience notes are thoroughly checked by the editors, especially with regard to sense, sentence structure and accuracy of the reproduction of quotations, proper names or technical terms. In case of complications, such as undecipherable sentences and words or gaps in the text, the original stenographs are consulted for clarification, if available.

Further information concerning the specifics of the textual basis, the editing, and the history of the lectures published in this volume can be found at the end of the volume.

The editors

SUMMARIES OF LECTURES

FIRST PUBLIC LECTURE, MARCH 2, 1920
Spirit and Spirit-void in their Life Effects

The hopes of John Maynard Keynes for a transformation of the intellectual condition of man. The scientific foundations of contemporary thought; its scope. The prophecy of John Scherr and its fulfilment. Spiritual-scientific method as a basis for a real knowledge of man. The world domination of the phrase in spiritual life. Independent spiritual life as a prerequisite for the development of human abilities. Herman Grimm as a symptomatic phenomenon. Today's state life under the influence of convention. Precondition of a real democracy. Routine as a characteristic of contemporary economic life. Revival of economic expertise through denationalization of economic life. Overcoming the triple rule of phrase, convention and routine through the realization of the social trinity. Forgery of letters as a means of political denunciation. Spreading of untruths by representatives of the Catholic Church. The alleged Jewish origin of Rudolf Steiner.

SECOND PUBLIC LECTURE, March 4, 1920
The spiritual demands of the coming day

Laws of development of man and mankind. Recourse to the unconscious. The necessity of a conscious shaping of social life. The idea of social threefolding as a healing contribution of spiritual science. The importance of research results from the supersensible for the comprehension of social reality. Denationalization of the school system as a necessary social measure. Resistance of the religious confessions against the living grasp of the spiritual world. Independent spiritual life as a prerequisite for the development of a consciousness of the spirit. Knowledge of the supersensible as the basis for a vitalization of the legal system and a need-orientation of economic life. The great goals of English politics arising from the unconscious. Their experimental character.

Criticism of the spiritual-scientific understanding of Christ. Christ not merely redeemer of sins, but resurrector for the progress of mankind.

THIRD PUBLIC LECTURE, MARCH 10, 1920
The Peoples of the Earth in the Light of Spiritual Science

The Development into a Single, Worldwide Economic Area. The opposing of national egoism. Prerequisites for a real knowledge of peoples. The roots of the peoples in the supersensible reality. The organization of man as a tripartite being. Three main types of man. The oriental man and the orientation towards the metabolic life. His connection with nature. The development of the emotional life as his ideal. Central European man and the importance of the rhythmic system. The comprehension of the human as his concern. The whole man as a summary of the peculiarities of the individual peoples. In what the true Germanness consists. Western man and the special development of his system of thought. His special relationship to the economic. The longing for the cosmic. The striving for cosmopolitanism at the time of German idealism. The abstractness of Marxist internationalism. True internationalism springs from love for all peoples. Spiritual-scientific knowledge as the basis for overcoming mutual hatred.

FOURTH PUBLIC LECTURE, MARCH 12, 1920
The History of Mankind in the Light of Spiritual Science The Absence of Great Points of View in the Writing of History.

The emergence of the democratic spirit as a fundamental fact of modern history. Spiritual knowledge helps to understand the history of development of mankind. The basic bio-genetic law and its application to history. Necessity of a reversal of this law for the spiritual course of development of mankind. The ancient Indian culture as representative of the first period of development: material life as manifestation of the spiritual-divine. The Greeks as representatives of the second period of development: material life from the point of view of the human. The blue blindness of the Greeks. Today's educational task in the light of the historical laws of development. Different views of the starry worlds in the course of time. The consequences of the reversed biogenetic basic law. The present time as the third period of development: material life in separation from the spiritual. Social tripartition as a necessary result of human development. The further development does not depend on the institutions, but on the people.

FIFTH PUBLIC LECTURE, JUNE 8, 1920
The path to sound thinking and the life situation of contemporary man.

Charles Eliot and his belief in natural science as the foundation for a religion of the future. Today's powerlessness against the social conditions of life. The materialistic world view and the missing bridge from the natural to the moral world order. The law of conservation of matter and power and its social consequences. New situation through attempts to implement the natural scientific world view into the social reality. The concern of the Russian philosopher Vladimir Soloviev about the fate of a technicized Russia. Russian socialism as the last consequence of Eliot's views. The incapacity of theoretical socialism for a humane social organization. The emergence of scientific thought from medieval scholasticism. Scholastic thinking as an outflow of seeing into the supersensible world. The necessity of a rebirth of thinking out of the spiritual world. In the spirit-recognition lives the world-future.

SIXTH PUBLIC LECTURE, JUNE 10, 1920
Education and Teaching in the Face of the Present World Situation

History lessons in the Waldorf School as an example of the be fruitful effect of spiritual science. Gap between contemporary education and the proletarian masses. The efforts to found folk high schools. Necessity of fertilizing the life of civilization with a new spiritual knowledge. Today's abstract science does not suffice. Two significant events in the life of the growing human being. The

5

change of teeth as the first life event. The progression from the abstract to the concrete as a concern of spiritual science. Sexual maturity as the second life event. The child's play and its meaning for later life. Preconditions of a real art of education: the artistic-image-like view of man. The pedagogical-didactic idea of the Waldorf School. What the present demands from people: Sunniness and readiness for action. The discussion about the introduction of the gold standard as an example for the missing sense of reality of the people. The demand for an associative organization of economic life. The whole of life as a school.

SEVENTH PUBLIC LECTURE, JUNE 15, 1920
Questions of the soul and questions of life.

A Contemporary Speech A central contemporary problem: the lack of correspondence between the needs of the soul and the facts of life. How the "philosophy of freedom" poses the question of freedom. The objectives of Jesuitism. Anthroposophically oriented spiritual science as a continuation of the "philosophy of freedom." Clarity of thought and social trust as basic ideals for the present. Why to be a materialist. The two great goals for inner training: the liberation of thought from corporeality and the seizure of the body by the will. The necessity of overcoming Kant's categorical imperative. The statement of Georg Gottfried Gervinus about the end of German poetry. The consideration of the occidental culture from the scientific point of view. "The Decline of the Occident" by Oswald Spengler as an example of such thinking. The rejection of a pre-existence of the soul by the Christian confessions. How the fulfilment of Spengler's prophecy can be counteracted. The resistance against a new spirituality. The necessary connection of science, art and religion.

EIGHTH PUBLIC LECTURE, JULY 29, 1920
Who May Speak Against the Decline of the Occident?

A Second Contemporary Speech Two important phenomena on the book market: "The Decline of the Occident" by Oswald Spengler and "The Economic Problems of the Proletarian Dictatorship" by Eugen Varga. How far Spengler's conviction of the inevitable downfall of the Occident is justified. The particular historical methodology of Spengler. The deepening of this methodology by spiritual science. Spengler's influence by the old scientific thinking. A New Spiritual Life as a Necessity for Development. Varga's attempt to translate Marxist ideas into social practice. A surprising statement for a Marxist. The Waldorf School as an example of the social fruitfulness of the anthroposophical approach. Various oppositions to anthroposophy. Spiritual science addresses itself to the will of man.

NINTH PUBLIC LECTURE, September 20, 1920
The great tasks of today in spiritual life, legal life and economic life.
A Third Contemporary Speech

Another important appearance on the book market: "The Economic Consequences of the Peace Treaty" by John Maynard Keynes. The failure of statesmen at Versailles. How influence was exerted on the American president Woodrow Wilson. The Darwinian way of thinking of Wilson. The necessity of a spiritual knowledge of the world. Increasing displacement of full humanity by specialism. The scientific courses at the Goetheanum and their objectives. Understanding of the spiritual-emotional development of the child as the pedagogical basis of the Waldorf School. The economic needs of the Waldorf School. The three currents in the course of human development: spiritual, governmental and economic thinking. American pragmatism as an example of contemporary economic thinking. The three great tasks in the present: the comprehension of the human personality, the cultivation of democratic coexistence and the solution of the price problem. The social threefolding as an answer to these tasks. Creation of true social unity through the lively cooperation of the three independent social elements. What constitutes the real practitioner. Ways to realize the threefold social structure.

TENTH PUBLIC LECTURE, NOVEMBER 10, 1920
The Spiritual Crisis of the Present and the Forces for Human Progress

Hopelessness in overcoming the prevailing state and economic crisis. The implementation of anthroposophical university courses as a response to the present spiritual crisis. A first objective: the detachment of spiritual life from state and economic paternalism. The attitude of the church representatives as proof of the lack of creative power of spiritual life. A spiritual life in free self-government as a prerequisite for the development of the individual abilities of people. Modern economic thinking since Adam Smith. The dichotomy between science without a worldview and science without a worldview. The effects of this dichotomy on Central European man: the example of the philosophers of Scholasticism and German Idealism. Intellectualistic science and its limitation to the mathematical-mechanical-technical. The practice oriented to mere routine as a counterpart to it. The necessity today to develop a world view from science. Mathematics as a starting point for the methodology of knowledge in the humanities. Perspectives for a way out of the threefold crisis of civilization.

Introduction

> We are thinking of a renewal of the whole scientific and spiritual worldview of the present into the near future.
>
> (Rudolf Steiner in the public lecture of June 10, 1920 in Stuttgart)

In 1888 Rudolf Steiner published in the "German Weekly Bulletin" a diagnosis on "The Spiritual Signature of the Present" (in GA 30). It was not very reassuring for him, since he had come to the conclusion: *"With all the progress that we have to record in the most diverse fields of culture, we cannot deny that the signature of our age leaves much, very much to be desired. Our progress is mostly only in breadth and not in depth. But for the content of an age only the progress in depth is decisive."* It was this one-sided insistence on experience with simultaneous contempt for everything ideal that made the young Rudolf Steiner take up his pen. The forgetting of the basic ideas of German idealism, whose outstanding representatives included such personalities as Fichte, Hegel, and also Goethe and Schiller, was a particular alarm sign for him. What, then, was the central concern of German idealist philosophy? Rudolf Steiner: *"Breaking with dogma in the field of thought, breaking with commandment in that of action, that must be the unalterable goal of further development. Man must create happiness and satisfaction out of himself and not let it come to him from outside."* When Rudolf Steiner wrote these words, European humanity had narrowly missed the outbreak of a great war. It was the great Balkan crisis of 1885 to 1888, the struggle for the delimitation of the spheres of influence in and around Bulgaria, which almost led to a war between Austria-Hungary and Russia and whose pull the other great European powers could hardly have escaped. Fortunately, the prudent forces working to maintain peace still retained the upper hand.

Years later, in an intimate circle of members in Vienna, Rudolf Steiner again expressed his concern about social developments. On 14. April 1914 (in GA 153) he warned, starting from the lack of coordination of production with consumption: *"He who has a spiritual view of social life sees such a cancer formation; he sees how terrible tendencies to social ulcerations are sprouting up everywhere. This is the great cultural concern that arises for the one who sees through existence. This is the terrible thing which has such an oppressive effect and which, even when one could otherwise suppress all enthusiasm for spiritual science, [...] leads one to cry out, as it were, to the world for the remedy for what is already so strongly in the offing and which will become stronger and stronger."* What Rudolf Steiner foresaw in anxious foreboding was to become reality in the next few weeks in the most comprehensive way: On June 28, 1914, the Austro-Hungarian heir to the throne, Franz Ferdinand, was assassinated; the ensuing July crisis ended on July 28 with the Austro-Hungarian declaration of war on Serbia. Thus the fate took its course. As a result of the existing alliance relationships, most of the European powers became involved in the gruesome warlike carnage of the following years. The First World War and with it the *"primordial catastrophe of the 20th century"* became reality.

The primordial catastrophe of the 20th century

Not only did World War I develop into a total war with millions of victims at the front and at home, but the social upheavals it triggered, in the face of the political lack of ideas in the democracies, led to the establishment of fascist and communist dictatorships and finally, in 1939, to the unleashing of an intensified apocalyptic warfare. Especially the view on Germany seems to more than justify the nowadays almost common phrase of a primordial catastrophe. The irresponsibility of its political leadership had steered the country into the abyss; with the peace treaties negotiated in the Paris suburbs, the sole blame for the outbreak of the war was placed on it and its allies.

The defeated Central Powers were to be weakened politically and economically so that no warlike threat could emanate from them any longer.

Rudolf Steiner saw in the whole event first of all a threat emanating from the periphery of Europe to the spirituality germinating in German idealism, the central basis for a renewed spiritual world view. Rudolf Steiner in *"Thoughts during the War"* (previously in GA 24, in the future in GA 255), published in 1915: *"The fact that the time must come when, in the spiritual sphere, the world-view of the German being, which is based on the spiritual, will have to conquer its world validity — of course, only through a battle of spirits — against those which [...] have their representatives from the English being: the fact of the present war can be a warning for this. But this has nothing to do directly with this war."* Even if Rudolf Steiner at first ruled out a direct connection with the events of the war, he was nevertheless convinced that *"England saw herself threatened by the development which Germany had necessarily to strive for in the latest period."* It had to undertake everything *"that could contribute to removing the nightmare that Germany's cultural work was causing it."* In the course of the war Rudolf Steiner's point of view broadened — clearly perceptible in his *"Contemporary Reflections: The Karma of Untruthfulness"* (GA 173 and 174), which he held in Dornach at the request of members of various nationalities at the turn of the year 1916/1917. Long-term, occultly supported Anglo-Saxon striving for world power in conflict with the world mission of German spirituality — in this he saw the deeper background of the unfolding primordial catastrophe. The legitimacy of the German position seemed to him unquestionably given.

Increasingly, however, the failure of the German leadership, the entire ideological nullity of the German elite and the resulting dangerous irresponsibility of the policy of the Central European powers came to the fore for him. Thus, for example, in the Dornach members' lecture of November 16, 1918 (in GA 185a) — days after the fall of the Empire in Germany and in Austria-Hungary: — he said: *"You* see, everything that has been done wrong, if I may use the expression, by the central powers, what the various rulers have sinned, what untruthfulness there has been in the events, that will come to light. The events have developed in such a way that the world will find out in the relatively not at all distant future everything that has been sinned against by the Central European rulers." And in the Dornach discussion evening of July 19, 1920 (in GA 337b) on the question of who had actually been in charge in pre-war Germany: "Wilhelm II? He really could not rule, but it was a question of a certain military caste being there, which maintained the fiction that this Wilhelm II meant something — he was only a figurehead with theatrical and comedic airs, who acted out all sorts of things to the world in a comedic way. It was a kind of theatrical play, maintained by a military caste, which now acted not exactly out of mere 'nature' and out of 'voluntary subordination and trust', but out of something quite different, out of all kinds of old habits, comforts, out of the view that this is just the way it has to be — a view, however, that was not rooted very deeply in the human breast. So this whole lay, and it was more held than it really governed. [...] Then, in addition to what held together this comedy play out of the military castes, there came, in the last decades, the still much more repugnant big industrialism and big trade, which thus added up and which so thoroughly inwardly, out of mendacious impulses, maintained this monarchical principle."

In view of this complete failure of the leading strata, Rudolf Steiner wrote in the "Preliminary Remarks" to the Memoirs of the German Chief of Staff at the Outbreak of War (previously in GA 24, in future in GA 255) — the records of Helmuth von Moltke were to be published in 1919 in connection with the agitation for the threefold idea, but this was then not possible: "One must point to these things if one wants to speak of the 'guilt' of the German people. This 'guilt' is, after all, of a very special kind. It is the guilt of an entirely apolitical thinking people, to whom the intentions of its 'authority' have been veiled by impenetrable veils. And which, out of its apolitical disposition, did not even suspect how the continuation of its policy had to become war."

But Rudolf Steiner was not concerned with exonerating the German people, but with clarifying as truthfully as possible the actual events that had led to the catastrophe of the world war. For him, the failure of the people — especially of the Germans — lay in the lack of understanding of the actual social necessities of development. Hence Rudolf Steiner's conclusion in the Dornach member lecture of September 30, 1917 (in GA 177): "*The present is a time [...] of which one can say that much will have to change in the thinking, in the feeling, in the willing of people. The directions of the soul will have to become different. This is what time will demand.*" He saw the prevailing of destructive-violent processes on the outer physical plan as caused by the lack of spiritual life on earth. Rudolf Steiner in the same lecture: "*And from this we get the practical call to do all that is in us to promote the only thing that in the future will be able to take away from humanity — the destructive forces — spiritual life.*"

Signs of impending doom

At first, people were completely under the spell of the effects of the disruptive forces. The social consequences of the mass deaths and mass mutilation were indeed incalculable. A profound traumatization and destabilization of societies, combined with economic hardships and political violence, were characteristic of the years following the end of the First World War, the European post-war period. It became apparent that the abstract ideals proclaimed by the victorious powers — for example, the Fourteen Points of American President Thomas Woodrow Wilson — were unable to hold their own in the face of political and economic power interests.

The former Central Powers, headed by Germany, found themselves exposed to the will to annihilation of the victorious powers. At least, this was how the vast majority of people in Central Europe felt in view of the unilateral provisions of the Paris Suburban Treaties of 1919 and 1920. Political servitude and economic exploitation instead of the promised self-determination in freedom — this was the reality for the defeated Central Powers. Rudolf Steiner also lived in this feeling. He was all the more impressed by the writing of the English economist John Maynard Keynes, "*The Economic Consequences of the Peace Treaty*," published in German in 1920. In his writing, Keynes — who had participated in the Versailles peace negotiations as a member of the British delegation — accused the statesmen of the victorious powers of a one-sided representation of interests without a view of the whole. Ultimately, such a lack of ideas could only lead to the "*downfall of the West*," as the cultural philosopher Oswald Spengler had described it in his first volume, "*Gestalt und Wirklichkeit*" ("Shape and Reality"), published in 1918. However, there was a radical draft of the future in the form of the Marxist-Leninist utopia of a classless society, the realization of which was sought in the violent and totalitarian form of a dictatorship of the proletariat under the leadership of the communist party. Rudolf Steiner could not discover any future value in these attempts; it was precisely the abstractness of the principles, characterized by scientific thinking, to the exclusion of the living human being, that was bound to have a devastating effect on the foundations of social coexistence. Rudolf Steiner saw his view confirmed by Jenö Varga's 1920 writing, "The Economic Problems of Proletarian Dictatorship," in which Varga — as an authoritative figure within the communist council dictatorship in Hungary — described in all candor the difficulty in applying communist principles.

Rudolf Steiner saw these three writings as symptomatic of the social situation in the immediate post-war period: Behind the façade of the melodious abstractness of Western democratic ideals, in the end, only pure power interests were hidden. Even the Marxist counter-draft could lead to nothing other than the total disruption of social coexistence. This mood of doom settled in the hearts of the people; it was the end of the unbridled belief in progress that had prevailed before the war. What prevailed was the consciousness of living in a shattered and divided world — in a world of crises.

Speeches for the future

Rudolf Steiner wanted to fight against this general mood of doom. He was not only concerned with pointing out the conditions that had to lead to the downfall, but also with the prerequisites for a socially fruitful new beginning. And this could only happen on the basis of a truly sustainable — that is spiritual — world view. Thus Rudolf Steiner wrote in his appeal *"To the German People and to the World of Culture"* (in GA 24, in the future in GA 255a), which was presented to the public for the first time on February 15, 1919: *"In place of the petty thinking about the most immediate demands of the present time, there should now be a great train of outlook on life which strives to recognize the forces of development of the newer humanity with strong thoughts and which dedicates itself to them with courageous will. The petty urge should cease, which renders harmless as impractical idealists all those who direct their gaze to these forces of development. The arrogance and haughtiness of those who think of themselves as practitioners and who have brought about misfortune through their narrow sense masked as practice should cease. Consideration would have to be given to what the practitioners, who are called idealists but are in fact real practitioners, have to say about the developmental needs of the new age."* However, it was not only the idea of the threefold social structure — the idea of a horizontal federalization of society according to the three functional systems of intellectual life, legal life and economic life — which he hoped would lead to a new beginning in society, but also a fundamental public understanding of the humanistic approach he advocated.

This *"progress of the world view of spiritual science from the abstract to the concrete, from the merely thought-like, which imagines itself to penetrate into reality, to the truly reality-like"* (public lecture of June 10, 1920 in Stuttgart, in this volume), i.e. a vivification of the view — this was his great concern after the attempt to bring the idea of threefolding as an igniting idea among the masses had finally proved to be in vain towards the end of 1919; people had remained attached to their one-sided party thinking.

Rudolf Steiner, supported by a small circle of collaborators of the Tripartite Alliance and the Anthroposophical Society, felt all the more obliged to stand up in public for the spiritual upheaval he considered necessary. He wanted to speak about "*The Spiritual demands of the Coming Day,*" about "*The Spiritual Crisis of the Present and the Forces for Human Progress*" — these were the titles of his public lectures of March 4, 1920 and November 10, 1920 in Stuttgart (in this volume). In the course of 1920 he held lectures with this concern in various places. He was convinced (in the lecture of November 10, 1920 in Stuttgart, in this volume): "*We will see the thinking man of action, the feeling man of law, the brotherhood-minded man of will emerging from a real spiritually oriented world knowledge, and we will thus gain from such an anthroposophically oriented spiritual science a new force for the progress of humanity out of the spiritual crisis.*"

Rudolf Steiner's public "*Present Speeches*" organized by the Stuttgart Initiative Circle in 1920 prove to be particularly impressive — they are united in the present volume. They were held in a climate of increasing rejection of anthroposophical endeavors. This opposition was fueled by the many practical efforts of the anthroposophical movement to demonstrate the fruitfulness of its worldview. On September 7, 1919, the Waldorf School was opened; in the first half of the next year, economic associations were founded to financially support anthroposophical cultural endeavors — on March 13, 1920, "*Der Kommende Tag A.G.*" in Stuttgart and on June 16 the "*Futurum A.G.*" in Dornach. These were large-scale projects that, beyond their narrower purpose, aimed at a fundamental change in economic activity and thus at defusing the social question. The Goetheanum, provisionally opened on September 26, 1920, but not yet fully completed, as the seat of the "School of Spiritual Science," was a striking expression of the claim to a holistically oriented scientific methodology. It is not coincidental that this provisional opening was connected with the holding of the First University Course, which took place from September 27 to October 16 in the Goetheanum building. Already in the spring of 1920, from March 24 to April 7, a kind of precursor course had taken place in Dornach under the title *"Anthroposophy and the Specialized Sciences"* (in GA 73a), which bore witness to the fertilization of the sciences by anthroposophy.

This course was intended to bear witness to the fertilization of the sciences by anthroposophy. At this time, that is, on April 9, 1920, the participants in the first medical course given by Rudolf Steiner went public with a "declaration" in which they confessed: *"The Free School of Spiritual Science 'Goetheanum', which is approaching its architectural completion in Dornach, stands as testimony to the inner content and creditworthiness of this whole school of thought, for whose medical-scientific fruitfulness the undersigned specialists vouch with their name."*

In addition to these large public lectures, Rudolf Steiner also gave lectures for the members of the Anthroposophical Society, in which he illuminated the spiritual background of contemporary events in addition to his public lectures. They are summarized in the volume *"Spiritual and Social Transformations in Human Evolution"* (GA 196). In view of the darkness of confusing events, it was important for him to set points of orientation, to understand the fundamental developments. Thus Rudolf Steiner made it clear to the Stuttgart members on November 14, 1920 (in GA196), Rudolf Steiner made it clear to the Stuttgart members: *"And while the beings which man saw in the old times in the phenomena of nature were of a Luciferic nature, the beings which work in the machines, in the technicisms, are of an ahrimanic nature. So man surrounds himself with an ahrimanic world, which becomes completely independent. You see, what is the meaning of the development of mankind — out of the Luciferic world, which, however, still works into his consciousness and there determines his destiny, man sails, and indeed just in the present time with a certain rapidity, into an ahrimanic world."* It is precisely the lack of awareness of such spiritual backgrounds that Rudolf Steiner felt to be a great danger for human beings. In the same lecture: "*A great danger exists that this ahrimanic world, because it acts upon his will, which he cannot get directly into his consciousness through intellectualistic science, will seize the will of man and he will become quite directionless within the demonic powers of technicisms.*" This was Rudolf Steiner's depressing concern for the future of humanity. And hence his public commitment to directed action: "*We are thinking of a renewal of the whole scientific and Spiritual worldview of the present into the near future.*" Turning to spirituality as a means of shaping the social future — only in this way could one hope to do justice to the cultural legacy of German idealism, but also to set an effective counterweight to the Western claim to power. Rudolf Steiner was convinced of this.

Alexander Lüscher

The Way to Healthier Thinking in the Demands on Modern Man

LECTURE 1
Spirit and spirit-void working in life
Stuttgart on 2 March 1920

My dear honourable friends! An important phenomenon, within the sphere of our discussion on current public issues, is the book by an Englishman John Maynard Keynes regarding the economic effects of the peace agreement. Mentioning this book in public discussions can be done in the widest circles despite, on the one hand, with all its prejudices — I could define it as written with the prejudices of the English — while on the other hand it is drafted with an extraordinary significant expertise and an overview of contemporary public life. For a long time Keynes was a delegate in the English Treasury during the war. Keynes also represented the English Delegation at the Versailles peace treaty, up to the time he relinquished his appointment because he was most disappointed by the Versailles negotiations in 1919. One must say, when one looks more closely at the content of this work, something quite significant can be found for a judgement on the public circumstances of the present moment. As an introduction I would like to mention some characteristics from this book ahead of our reflections today.

When Keynes went to Paris he came along with a bag full of prejudices, so to speak — above all, prejudices regarding the possible results of this peace treaty, specifically from the point of view of an Englishman, but also with prejudices against the personalities involved in the course of current public affairs. I must say I was particularly interested in the verdict that an assessor at the Versailles negotiations was about that particular man, who the whole world had worshipped a short while before. If I repeatedly keep on coming back, I rebel against this judgement of the whole world — really rebel and not merely within Germany, but, where I have the possibility to do so during the wartime itself and until the end of the days of terror, and do so also in Switzerland — but here such rebellion couldn't really make an impression. People had to experience, even within Germany it happened briefly, that the majority agreed with the glorification of Woodrow Wilson — that's what I mean, and that's what Keynes means — a glorification that took place all over the world. Again and again attention must be drawn out of the observation which I have represented here in Stuttgart for a long time already, that when dealing with someone like Woodrow Wilson you must know that he is a man of phrases, a man whose words lack any real, substantial content.

Now Keynes describes the gestures of this Woodrow Wilson at the peace treaty in Versailles. He describes with what glory this man has been admitted to and with which prejudices he has been met. He describes how this man was far away from any insight into any reality taking place at the meetings he attended. He describes how this man was not once, with his slow thinking, able to follow the thoughts of others, how others already had progressed far with something when Wilson was still pondering on something which had been contributed earlier, or spoken about earlier. You have to admit, with extraordinary plasticity, the complete inadequacy and phraseology of this world famous personality is described here, by a person who really didn't have insight into the facts from a central European standpoint. Keynes also described other personalities, whose presence at the Versailles peace treaty attained a meaningful influence on the destiny of Europe.

About Clemenceau he said that this old man had completely slept through time since 1871, that it only mattered to him that Europe is to be restored to that state which existed before 1871, and above all, what was necessary was to apply to current world relations, that which the French had gained to ensure their own nationality since 1871.

Keynes described the statesman from his own country, Lloyd George; how this man only thought about immediate results, how with

20

his fine instinct had to a certain extent sensed the views and opinions of those personalities around him, with whom he had contact.

Then Keynes considers what is being traded. In his book he discusses with the skill and methods of an accountant, a strict accountant, which economic results can be achieved for Europe, concocted out of this so-called "peace agreement." Not out of some or other political ambition, not out of some or other sensation or sensitivity but out of accounting results he now arrives at, so to speak, the conclusion that what economic impulse this peace agreement must indicate would be the economic decline of Europe. Nothing less can be learned from this book, through exact accounting results as I've said, than that the authoritative personalities of the European Union met the institutions and that this must necessarily lead to the economic dismantling of the entire Europe.

I could say that if you read the undertones of this book, you'll notice how the Englishman speaks from an English point of view, how he actually still allows a feeling to work on one's soul: this decline of Europe will be so fundamental that England will be damaged. One could therefore say: Like so many current western statesmen even this Fellow of Cambridge University has little concern with fear, but the description of the situation and the current relationships one finds right in this book. Something like this quickly brings to light more than the rest of the discussions on the current international situations of the world.

The most important aspect appearing for me in this book is this: after this man with a meticulous accounting point of view has set out his observations and simultaneously in these observations mixed quite creative sketches of character judgements of personalities who took part in the institutions towards which this decline was directed, one doesn't see anything in this book which would somehow throw a ray of light on what has to be done, in order for the general destruction not to take hold, in order for the destruction to, instead, become constructive. It's characteristic of just this accountant to say something extraordinary in the last sentence of the last page of his book. He roughly says he couldn't imagine that out of all the old beliefs, just as they developed out of the Versailles peace treaty, he couldn't see anything favourable unfolding for the further development of the European civilisation. He said he could only and alone hope that a better time could arise through the combination of all the forces for the development and the imagination — "by setting in motion those forces of instruction and imagination" he termed it. This doesn't mean anything less, my dear friends, than this precise accountant hoping for nothing more than a transformation of the spiritual mind frame of the European people.

From this position the possibility is often mentioned regarding the transformation of European people's spiritual mind frame. It is no longer possible when addressing economic questions, to simply speak as a continuation of what took place in old relationships, in considering economic life today. Today one can't speak about the transformation of state relationships out of the imagination which was the traditional way of thinking in the 19th to the beginning of the 20th century. In addition, one can't speak about any of this if one doesn't point out how necessary it is for the move into inwardness in European humanity as a new way of thinking about public affairs. What has turned out to be a terrible disaster is not the result of some or other faulty institution but the result of the entire state of mind which has arrived in the European people from the beginning of the 20th century. What has been happening in the areas of legal life or state life, what has happened in the area of economic life — is nothing other than the spirit, rather I must call it the spirit-void (Ungeist) which in the course of this evening I want to emphasise, whose working is expressed in the living conditions of European people, the spirit-void which was brought in from the spiritual life, out of the so-called spiritual life, into the legal, or state life and into economic life.

This non-spirit needs to be grasped in its most significant symptoms. It must be grasped there where it has asserted itself within spiritual life itself. It is necessary, in order to attain a clear view of these relationships, to at least for once look around to what has been

22

developing since the beginning of the so-called newer spiritual life, since the last three to four centuries. It is necessary to gain knowledge about it, how it has slipped into this spiritual life in human experience and feeling life. We must gain further knowledge about how our economic relationships have gradually become an outer expression of our spiritual life.

However, what is the most important characteristic of this spiritual life? Again and again one must say that actually a right judgement about the spiritual life which had unfolded in the course of the last three up to fourth centuries, could only be one that is in the position to sufficiently appreciate the light side of this spiritual life, that is able to see through what namely science of the last centuries developed for humanity, that has been achieved by civilised humanity. Again and again it must be pointed out how the weaving of nature is grasped according to scientific ideas. Here one has to refer to how, by embracing the area of nature, the maxims, the drives and the impulses have been found to be great achievements of modern technology, which they are indeed, which have completely transformed economic life in the course of the latest history of human development.

Let's imagine that — and this hardly happens today — someone takes the trouble to hold his gaze on the usual branches of the scientific world view, while they were developing during the last centuries. Let's imagine that someone holds their gaze on the most important achievements in the processes of mechanics, physics, chemistry, biology, and so on. Let's imagine that someone like this was also in the position to judge the way of thinking, way of imagining, who have trained themselves in the admirable methods of physics, chemistry, biology, mechanics, which have been achieved for the knowledge of the anthropological in the development of humanity. Let's imagine how a person, from the basis of a scientific education, has been able to research how people have developed out of the original primitive conditions, to higher cultural conditions, how they gradually developed the social relationships up to now. Let's imagine how people, equipped with a scientific schooling, have endeavoured to gain sociological views about people's living conditions. When we take such a person of this universality of scientific knowledge, who, as we said, no longer actually really exists any longer; if we imagine such a person we still have to ask ourselves: how does such a person stand before the great human question of existence? How, above all, does he stand in front of the fundamental question which repeatedly rises out of hopeful people, to the question: What is man actually within the areas of the earthly-cosmic, the soul-spiritual world order?

The most extraordinary thing is the way in which this question has been answered by the scientific world view. This scientific world view accomplished a great feat, as it were, by its conclusion of the evolution doctrine and showed you how to imagine that the simplest to the most complicated organisms developed and at the pivotal point of this evolution, kind of like a summary of the living beings on earth, man itself stands there. What can be accomplished by this? One could answer this question by saying: How does man stand in relation to the animal? What is man's attitude to those beings who he must look at in the universe as subordinated to his own organization? — This question could be answered in an exemplary way from external sense perceptible facts. The moment the great human question arises: Who are you really, as a human being? — this approach fails.

I believe that those of you, my dear listeners, who have heard entire series of lectures I've given over the years, will have hundreds of proofs of what I'm saying. If one summarises all that has been achieved in this area, and finally pose the question: What is this human being actually, who you are yourselves in connection with the earthly-cosmic, in relation to the soul-spiritual universal beings? — then one must say to oneself, especially if one takes into account the achievements of the modern natural science which knows how to appreciate worldview sufficiently: As much as one can know in this direction, as much knowledge as one can have about Nature, all these findings say nothing about man himself. Because the minds of people were more and more steered by the spiritual — I could also call it an un-spiritual — scientifically opinionated authority as being in force, what had been conceived in thought about nature was stretched into the feeling life, into the life of will. The human doesn't really only want to get to know nature intellectually. The human being needs to experience, to feel what it is. The human being wants to be able to pour into his will, into deeds of will, his entire outer life and its effect that comes out of his own deepest being, letting it flow into the being of the world. He gets the feeling that he can't relate merely instinctively to his decisions of will, to his will actions; he needs to take something up which would create goals towards which he could direct his actions, his will.

These goals do not come about in order to satisfy his will in a penetrating way, if knowledge about the world and humanity is nothing other than what is presented by science. Just through the great achievements of the scientific world view, a desolation of human feeling, a helplessness of the human will has come about. People who wouldn't participate in a certain soul egoism presented by the achievements of science, leant on old religious or other such traditions. They basically made themselves blind to the fact that they no longer could live according to these achievements made in the knowledge of nature. Out of some kind of soul egoism they say to one another: I fill my inner being with one or other confession, I don't worry about whether this confession, today, can still give something to people who want to go along with the demands of their time, in contrast to the statements of scientific thought.

Current public life can be understood by a symptom pointing to the scientific foundations of today's thinking; it should be no more than a symptom regarding what I'm about to say. You must not forget that what one generation thinks becomes the disposition of the next generation in the impulses of feeling and willing. You may perhaps today still refer with legitimacy to certain extraordinary individuals who had spoken out around the first half of the (19th) century. There was someone, you can really call him a blusterer, who pronounced so many things back in the 19th century that he can be called a blusterer. I'm referring to Johannes Scherr. By calling him a blusterer, no one will suspect that I overestimate the man. Yet I must mention the following.

This man had a heart, a sense for what was being prepared for the civilization of Europe, and in his blustering speech one finds some extraordinary remarkable observations, in any case some observations which the sleeping souls among the people could perhaps only really judge today — if the works of such a chap will again be taken up; these turn to dust in libraries. At that time Johannes Scherr said how every way of thinking reached a specific culminating point which, although great and mighty things can be said about knowledge regarding nature, it is unable to tell man what he actually is — a way of thinking which was unable to give him feelings about the fact that he himself has his inner soul- spiritual being and that it is integrated into his will, to put mental and spiritual powers into it.

Johannes Scherr had seen enough to ask himself: How does a way of thinking flow if it is only about matter and not about people, how does such thinking flow into humanity if the focus is not merely on the present — in that time in the sixties and seventies — but what you will see in the following generation? He thought to himself: What happens when, one might say a "silent scholar," proclaims certain sensations and feelings from his lectern in a certain epoch, and when these proclaimed feelings turn over and penetrate offices, factories, banks and stock exchanges? He asked himself, what would happen if one would take his way of imagination as applied in the knowledge of nature, and assert this way of imagination in a dominant way in relation to the shaping of the financial and economic world?

Such questions aren't usually asked. One believes that what people think about in the economic sphere, what is speculated on the stock exchange, what is traded in the banks, is independent from what the quiet scholar proclaims from his lectern below. In life everything is closely related. This intimate connection is only hidden because a somewhat theoretic way of thinking can exist in a generation whose followers have the drive for outer action, the drive for a public sensory world. Under the impression of such thoughts, Johannes Scherr said the most extraordinary beautiful sentence. He said: When the spirit-void of materialism, which rules in all the circles, takes his course in the civilized world, when it asserts everything that it is predisposed to, in the financial economy of Europe, in Europe's economic constitution, then a time will come in which we will have to say: 'Nonsense, you have won!'

These words were spoken at the time. What lies behind these words? Behind these words lie all the hymns of praise for the economic upswing, for the way we have brought it so far, for the glorious achievements of modern life which has taken us from the 19th into the 20th century. So much could be heard from these kinds of hymns of praise. However, under the surface of these songs of praise something sprouted of which Johannes Scherr said: It must express itself in such a way that one must say: 'Nonsense, you have won!' — And nonsense *has* won!

Let's look back at the last five to six years. What, my dear friends, is the destiny of those who know how to calculate, out of the present, with an inner vision, an inner understanding of future circumstances? One hears what they say, largely as sensational, but don't take it seriously. We let go of the things, as one does by giving them to the sleeping soul, and we come to that attitude which we hardly notice, that with each week going by these things sink ever more into the abyss, yet we repeatedly say: Tomorrow it should be better already.

Something or other happens today and then tomorrow, again — yes, I don't know what — but we arrive at something. Where does this way of thinking come from? Where is the origin of what the blunderer Johannes Scherr called the spirit-void at that time? The origin lies precisely in the fact that a worldview has emerged in the course of the last three to four centuries, which is unable to say anything about man himself, or to make him feel anything, out of the ideas which are derived from this world view. What is the point of being compelled when one has been brought up with a world view that says nothing about people themselves, what they sense or feel? What are we then compelled to do? We are compelled to speak about the human being. Yes, we are compelled to speak about the human being, one can't avoid it, because actually everyone is in public life and since in public life people act and have to talk to one another about their affairs, we have to talk about the whole world. One can't avoid speaking about people.

What are the consequences if we have to talk about people, if we have to talk about what is to be treated as a legal state, as a spiritual cultural state, as an economic institution among people? What is necessary if one still wants to talk about people but has no documentation, because precisely that which comes with such a world view has no records — what does one need then? Today, with what is in the sphere of spiritual life, of public spiritual life controlling the world, what you need- because you are not in the position to put spiritual substance into your words from the inner experience of the spirit — what you need is: the **phrase**!

You see my dear friends, what firstly is meant by spiritual science is for people to once again arrive, in their conversations, in their words, that to which only words, and words exclusively, can provide authority: spiritual substance! Spiritual substance becomes words which are spoken, not out of scientific knowledge; spiritual substance is not conveniently found as ploughed in chemistry, in physics, in botany, or biology. Spiritual substance must so to say be gained in the way which is described as less convenient by spiritual science, than it is depicted here. Spiritual substance will be gained through the true insight of the most inner being of man. That is of course only possible when one has developed the already mentioned characteristic intellectual modesty. This is only possible if one arrives at being able to say: the great achievements of science shows me precisely that if I remain as if I've been born into a purely physical world, facing the great achievements of humanity will look like a five year old child confronted with a manuscript of Goethe's poetry: he rips up the manuscript in front of him. However, a child can develop so that what had earlier been something quite different can then take on its true essence. To apply this to the grownup, this is not something modern man likes. He doesn't want to say to himself: I must take my inner soul development in hand; I must go beyond what I've become purely due to my physical birth, through my own inner soul work; I must develop my soul towards heights other than what it might be, if I hadn't added my input.

When spiritual researchers say to people: in order to really recognise the spiritual, which is also within people, it is necessary to apply inner, spiritual methods, that thinking is transformed through soul exercises, as is depicted in my book "*Knowledge of the Higher Worlds and their attainment*" or in the second half of "*Occult Science*" or in other books, then people come and say: Oh, that's a fantasist talking. — When he says that there is a need for disciplining the will which does not otherwise occur in ordinary, outer life, in order to lift the soul out of the situation in which it had come through a mere physical birth, to develop it in such a way that man can achieve his own, inner management of his soul, then people come and say: Oh, that's a fantasist talking; that's someone speaking who wants to capitalize on the disappointments, the destroyed hopes of modern mankind, who pretends to make people believe in the possibility of supernatural knowledge!

No, my dear friends, a true spiritual researcher doesn't speak out of such records today. He really doesn't speak out of dilettantism regarding science, but he speaks out of a true knowledge of scientific achievements. He knows that scientific methods are necessary because science has a great deal to say, but not however, about what the being of man really is. He knows that clarification about the being of man can only be acquired through knowledge, through slow, tiring inner soul work and that this human knowledge must be reworked in order for the sense perceptible to really be lifted up to the supersensible. May the philistines regard this lifting up to the supersensible as something fantastic — for human knowledge this rising up to the supersensible is necessary, because sense perceptible knowledge point to that area which never can provide information about the nature of man. What is wanted by this spiritual science is an inner renewal from man's deepest being; this is the striving towards a possibility for gaining human knowledge which truly relates to experience, which indicates real goals and ideals which can flow out into the will, right into the reality of economic life. What kind of effects arise in a person's life who doesn't strive towards this spirit which is so unsympathetic for modern humanity, but strives for the spirit-void (Ungeist), which only wants to have a world view which gives information about the non-human, the alien — what kind of life processes does this result in?

The first of these effects on life appears over the entire civilized world, already rules the civilized world in the areas of spiritual life — people don't want to take notice of this, they close their eyes to it — as the first of these effects on life is the world domination of the phrase. If one doesn't have a spiritual view that the world flows as a living substance, then words remain empty. Words are then spoken which have meaning only as a phrase, which means they have no sense.

During the course of recent years while the non- spirits themselves had ad absurdum moved through outer world events, we can really observe the triumph of the phrase over the entire civilised world. Phrases have words so that there is no need to think about realistic foundations — characteristic appearances is all that's needed for remembering, like for instance the two British parties up to the middle of the 19th century called the "Whigs" and the "Tories." These words are used with of course no longer an inkling of the original meaning they had at one time. "Whigs," when the word first came up, was a swearword for Scottish revolutionaries against English institutions, and "Tories" was the derisive name for the Irish Papists. Just as these words in the English language of Parliament relate to their origin in the real world, so today the dominant statements of people relate to their real origins in life. As if over life, over reality, there wafts something which we, one can't call it think, but what we in words express out of ourselves.

The world domination of the phrase will become clear to people. Those people who do not want it to be made clear out of the observation of relationships, for them it will become clear that through an economic life which develops without a pervasive spiritual impulse, such an economic life will let them starve to death. Starving to death will present the real truth that our economic life is not controlled by the spirit but by the spirit-void because the spirit is no longer looked for in reality, because we adhere to the spirit-void which in the area of so-called spiritual life, is only uttered as a phrase about the human being.

Against this there is only one remedy, one remedy alone can overcome the rulership of the phrase: to emancipate the spiritual life from under this pressure that it had to become a phrase. A spiritual life which is not to be created out of its own foundations, a spiritual life which allows institutions to prepare its care from the economic life or allows boarding up the state life, a spiritual life that will follow and comply with the state guidelines or forces of the economic life — such a spiritual life can't unfold freely. A spiritual life can only unfold freely and through this unfolding really come to the spirit and thus beyond the phrase, if its own institutions are created out of its own foundations. There is only one remedy against the ever stronger triumphal march of the world phrase which is the independent development of spiritual life. Like the harvest of the fields perish under a locust swarm, so spiritual life becomes desolate when this spiritual life is dependent on factors other than itself, and that which is revealed to people from spiritual life, only becomes a phrase. The world dominance of the phrase will only cease when bearers of spiritual life order spiritual life, it will only cease when in the lowest to the highest schools, and all other areas of spiritual life, that those who are active in the spirit bring spiritual life into institutions, and when the principle of teaching is for the spreading of spiritual life, and also make spiritual life active in outer institutions. Only a self-created spiritual life will be able to be in the position to oppose the triumph of the phrase which works so erroneously, which has led itself to absurdity in the terrifying events of the last five to six years.

My dear friends, we can, when we honestly and sincerely take the evolution of spiritual life, the so-called spiritual life of the last years, and then look at what the last years have brought, find remarkable examples of how this spiritual life has gradually passed out when faced with the realities of life. It is most strange what one encounters when one looks at a personality that one reveres to the highest degree, a personality who is characterised for the highest achievements in spiritual life toward the end of the 19th century. Such a personality I see in Herman Grimm, the great art historian. Then again, I only want to speak about Herman Grimm as a symptom regarding the newer spiritual life. Greatness, real greatness was achieved by this art historian. When I look around among his rich essays which are available, I have to say: Something, so saturated with an rich inner spirit of the end of the 19th century such as both his essays on Iphigenia and the one about Tasso — these are real spiritual revelations which shows to the highest degree what a man at the height of spiritual life of modern times can achieve. They are characteristic, these intellectual achievements, for the kind of spiritual creation of someone who was actually the best. About Iphigenia and about Tasso of Goethe, Herman Grimm wrote treatises which show points of view of spiritual life which simply penetrate deeply, admirably, into the human being itself. However, he was writing about what already existed in spirit. He needed something like Iphigenia, like Tasso, which were already there. I've been looking into what such a symptom actually means, and I could find nothing other than the most beautiful, the greatest of achievements of our spiritual heroes at the end of the 19th century, which are exactly those things which are written about full of spirit, brilliantly written about what was taking place in the minds of those at the turn of the 18th and 19th centuries. Very characteristic, very meaningful. These observations can be made by anyone who is awake and doesn't look with a sleeping soul at the newer spiritual life.

Now this very same Herman Grimm produced a book on Goethe. This doesn't deal with Iphigenia, not with Tasso, not with the spiritual creations of man but with Goethe himself, the living person, Goethe. I read chapter after chapter — I have repeatedly and publicly spoken about what I thought about this book on Goethe — I read chapter after chapter; I tried to be objective about how this brilliant man, who was so great about Iphigenia, about Tasso, now wrote about Goethe, about who living people were speaking between themselves. Chapter after chapter I failed to find a depiction of a living being, I found shadow images which scurry over the walls, shadow images without depth, shadow images of Goethe, the living human being. What could have been produced as spirit was something Herman Grimm could do. The moment he stood in front of a depiction of a living person, the depiction was not about a living being but presented in shadow images which had no depth, only surfaces which scurry along which one can't touch, which you can't grasp when it comes to reality. This is quite characteristic in the life processes of the spiritual morale at the end of the 19th century. This spiritual frame of mind was strong enough the moment it was about judging spiritual output of human beings and to put that down, even with numerous side glances regarding human life, but it fails the moment the reality of the spirit which is before us, is to be penetrated.

This is what is meant by what spiritual science is really striving for: linking up the human soul condition to the real spirit, so that we are again in the position to find spirit in reality. It strives for, not shadow images being painted of reality, but for really grasping the spirit in reality. This way we will not have these abstractions, this intellectualism with rises today in knowledge of nature, but we really gain a true insight also in the weaving and being of nature. Continuing from this point as a start we acquire an attitude towards the human being's true being, the human being's own dignity, that corresponds to the human being's own significance in the earthy-cosmic, soul-spiritual context, that this being, this dignity of the human being really corresponds with. Only by penetrating reality with the spirit in such a way, can we defeat the phrase, can we again establish the living word which empowers actions, during encounters with people, giving power again to the economic life. Whoever believes today that he succeeds better in economic life through the mere improvement of old institutions, who does not want to convert to a complete renewed way of thinking, indulges in insubstantial illusions. Today we don't stand in front of small, but today we stand within the biggest thinkable questions of mankind.

Just when it comes to establishing outer social relationships from one person to another, then it is necessary for each person to encounter his neighbour in such a way that the person sees the spirit within the other. It is necessary that with each encountered person you can see what a special case this soul-spiritual being is; it is necessary to penetrate into each encounter with another person with all the feeling and sensation which can only come about through impulses, internally empowered, through a spiritual world view.

Because we have no independent spiritual life, we develop materialism on a large scale; we develop in the area of spiritual life the world domination of the phrase, which is still hidden from many people whose souls are asleep. When the spirit-void penetrates into the areas of feeling life, of sentient life — not the good spirit which fructifies everything coming out of human beings — when feelings and sensations are immersed by the spirit-void, what happens then? No living relationship comes about between one person and another which can provide the foundation of a structure for the social organism; what then comes about in the non-spirit's input into relationships between one person and another, is **convention**. I would like to say, we Germans can be lucky because if we want to describe the present domination of spiritual life, we must say 'phrase' because we don't have a real word for it in German. Once again we are in an awkward situation to use a German word for something which in this newer time has come from the spirit-void controlling the life of feeling; we have to say "convention." Convention is something which has been determined purely from outside; it is what we can only see outwardly, which is not grasped by the inner being and inner experience. However, in those people in whom there is no flow of thinking, of the awareness of how the phrase can be permeated with spirit, in those who also can't penetrate sensations and feeling being permeated with spirit, no social interaction, no social relationships can develop which could be worthy of human dignity and human value. Under the influence of convention, under the influence of outward appearances they have developed in two areas, which have become the modern state life and political life. Just as spiritual life is ruled today by the world domination of the phrase, so state life is completely and utterly ruled by convention.

Only when true democracy is revealed among men, a democracy actually founded on the living relationships of one person to another, then convention will be replaced by something which develops in a lively way between one person and another. This depends on one mature person standing opposite another mature person when those human conditions come into consideration which are independent from the more powerful capacity, the ability of the mind, and are independent, because these are legal relationships of the strength of economic power. When it is freed from economic life on the one hand, from spiritual life on the other hand, and the legal or state territory and the legal or territory of law or the State, only what is asserted comes from the equality of all persons who have come of age, then when thus freed from the economic life on the one hand and spiritual life on the other hand, the legal or state territory then in the place of world domination of convention, will arrive at what has been developing in a lively way within people. Today people stride towards the phrase habituated world which they don't understand: the right that can only be born out of the lively feeling, the enlivened experience in exchanges between people, the right which never again can be born out of convention. However, we live in this area under the world domination of convention. Convention is everything which is asserted as sensation, as disposition during public relationships through the spirit-void, just like the phrase asserts itself in public relations when in the areas of spiritual life not the spirit, but the spirit-void determines the realities of life.

Now let's look at the third area of public life. Because there really was no humanly inclusive, human experience and feeling engendering spiritual life in this age of materialism, economic affairs could not be saturated with goals enkindled by the spirit. Out of the economic life no real living practice could develop because a real living practice can only unfold when people, as bearers of this living practice, carry into every grip of the hand, into every accomplishment, that which they gain from the context of their soul with the soul-spiritual essence of the world. Something different develops in the area of living practice when instead of the spirit, the spirit-void rules. When the spirit-void reigns then a person falls into a Routine (he uses the English word for routine) on the base of outer, economic life because if the economic measures are not imbued with what comes from the spirit, the person falls into a Routine. I notice again, that I'm not using a German word. People fall into a Routine. This is characteristic in the economic sphere, that we have increasingly, as real living beings, aware of goals, having been born only out of the spirit, have arrived at a Routine.

Just like we have in the sphere of spiritual life arrived at the phrase, like in the area of state and legal live arrived at convention, so in the area of economic life we have arrived at Routine.

Today, as economic people, we stand in a Routine! How proud we are of our Routine! How come he only asks afterwards: how do you do that? How do you endeavour to educate everything in this business of economics so things will happen mechanically? How can you regard the economic life as something great for not containing people who have ideas, but rather to have people who are capable of gradually continuing their life's practice in the most mechanical way? Out of this it has come about that people — while stuck in a Routine and finding no creative satisfaction in it — want to be released, as soon as possible, from what they have in outer practical life and then strive after sensations which are as different as possible from what they are professionally involved in.

Does spirit exist in outer economic life? Are people welcomed in economic life who uphold something, because something occurs to them? They are more uncomfortable towards economic life than those in a routine. However, when people, who can think of something, are welcome, then economic careers will blossom, and they will not adopt egotistic characters but will become altruistic, of humanitarian character. Why is this so? Now, when a person merely follows a routine, then it provides no other drive than selfishness, than the satisfaction of

36

instincts. When you insert something into outer life which has come from someone under the influence of a spiritual education, then this, what is introduced in this way, because it originates in the spirit, has a very special peculiarity. It has the peculiarity that it isn't applicable to each individual person but that it basically applies to all, what the one may think or the other one may think; it has the peculiarity that it works as a fact which brings something about, which all people can bring into the realities of life.

All of this, my dear honourable friends, is now really not said to be disrespectful, to go from above down to the spiritual void of the modern world; it is said with a completely different goal. This is said so that a sense can develop for perusing those foundations formed from what is inextinguishable in human nature and yet still leads from the spirit-void to the spirit. This is said to bring the soul's present sleepiness to wakefulness, so that those depths of human life can be searched for in the reality of mankind, from which alone we can help the dismantling and arrive at construction.

The practical Keynes, with whom I started, said: what people don't know, what they can't give a solution to, is what depends on combining all the hidden forces — he calls these forces "instruction" and "imagination" — to come to a new opinion of the world. —

Spiritual science wants to give this in an all-inclusive sense; spiritual science wants to bring what precisely the insightful people are crying out for, but which they consider to be a fantasy the very moment it comes before their souls. Today it's preferable to say to people: There is once again someone who speaks about the astral body, who speaks about spirit and immortality — than it is to say they need to really deepen themselves, sink into that which in the area of spiritual science the exact methods can be said to be used as in the way which scientific knowledge itself is acquired.

If one notices however, on which grounds the here indicated spiritual science rests, then, my dear friends, one is also made aware that this spiritual science has a particular stamp: it doesn't only work through that which man knows as a result of it, but it changes the manner and way in which people think. It brings people to another conception of themselves. It brings people to a different feeling about themselves and as a result a different feeling about their neighbours. Spiritual science enables people to fructify economic affairs again from out of the spirit. It leads to demands being made: The economic life must stand as an independent third member within the social organism in such a way that economic affairs form an economic objectivity and economic expertise is ordered only by personalities who have grown into this economic life. All economic life institutions must be established on the facts of economic life being based on expertise and knowledge, not through parliamentary decisions, nor through majority decisions. Decisions of the majority make no sense when the issue involves human interactions, mature people being equal.

In the area of economic life, expert knowledge, expertise and experience are decisive. In the area of spiritual life, facilities and skills are decisive. Both these areas promote their independence. In the middle of it all, is a third member of the social organism with its independence, and all that happens in public relationships in minds, experiences and feelings, need to be kindled by the spirit, not the spirit-void. Everything depends upon the spirit, and not the spirit-void, taking place. Spirit in spiritual life will itself vanquish the rulership of the phrase. Spirit will penetrate the sensory and emotional life so that we really gain a state life, a legal life. Spirit would fructify economic life in such a way that this independent life can really unfold differently than under the influence of the spirit-void, under the influence of tricky, abstract Marxist or other theories. To make these theories a reality, what will happen is what has happened in Eastern Europe as the most outer, most radical phase of destruction — destruction, not construction.

In a tripled way people have to face, not by exercising criticism, but by really searching in a threefold way into the depths of human beings and their humanity, which can really lead towards constructiveness. These three things are: the phrase, convention and routine. To take the place of the phrase, would be to take care of a true spiritual life. To take the place of convention has to be living sensation which can only exist when we, kindled by spiritual imaginations, as people encounter people in the legal and state life; otherwise we end up, while the spiritual life is still the most fruitful of them all, also in the area of legal life, with the mere phrase. Otherwise we get into the position like a person who is worshipped by the whole world and says strange things, for example, about the law. I'm referring to Woodrow Wilson, at whom I took a closer look so that I don't speak about him like a blind man about colour. There I found, for instance, in his thick book about the state, the actual compendium of modern phraseology, the definitive phrase: 'The Law is the Will of the state towards the bourgeois conduct of those who stands under its authority'.

Now, my dear honourable friends, those who are used to reality and knows how the living will proceeds out of a living person — I would like to know, what he has to think when this historian of the state argues: 'The law is the will of the State'. — In the time in which people are nothing more to the state than an outer institution of economic life, it is argued, without one really knowing about the will of the State — in serious books for the truly serious, are inclined spirit compendia in the modern life of phrases. Now, when we regard the modern economic life, we find there is much discussion about it. However, this life of economics itself is still basically not being controlled by what is being said about it. Also here the phrase goes over it like a breath, while below it the real economic life takes place. So much do phrases smother it that the phraseology of Marxist socialist teaching experiences it in a phrase called "ideology." To a certain extent they sense that the spirit-void controls economic life, but they don't realise that instead of replacing the spirit with the spirit-void, they replace an ideal, and in place of the spirit-void which has ruled up to now, another spirit-void replaces it which will rule in future.

Truly, whoever wants to consider what can become constructive must know precisely what the threesome rule of phrase, convention and routine have brought about, yes, what horrors of the last five to six years they have brought about. What we need to find out, in order to look in a healthy way at this threesome rulership, I will try to speak about the day after tomorrow. However, this lecture today had to precede others for the reason that then only can one see what is necessary for the coming days, to be able to realize exactly what this destruction has brought about. It is really not enough today to merely indicate that somehow the forces must evolve into a new "instruction," a new "imagination." It is today already necessary that reference is made to living fountains of spirit.

Now, because I've already been talking for some time, I would like to add perhaps in the next few minutes, a small addition to what I've said today. It is something that shows in an obvious example, how today's humanity has to take up what they strive for by observing simultaneously the conditions which could lead to excluding destruction and strive towards some kind of construction instead. If I go into detail about this, which I want to say in a few words, then I'll have to give a long lecture because there is very much to say.

The last time I travelled away from Stuttgart I heard, at my leaving, all kinds of slander in circulation about me personally and about those who are connected in their objective work with me. It soon became apparent that this slander was being spread with extraordinary refinement by informers at a particular chosen moment in time. I was able to then learn that this denunciation, this slander was thus created in letters which were fake, which could be conceived as if they had been written by myself; with these letters they wanted to prove things came from me or from those people of the Federation for the Threefold Social Order initiative. Yes, they didn't even once feel ashamed of the slander that was to claim that one of my measures contributed to delivering the Germans to the Entente, referring to letters written by me.

My dear friends, for me personally this is only an example how people are treated today who earnestly strive towards the search of truth and are not frightened away, that is to say, what today leads from destruction to construction. It is of course inevitable that such filthy finches who put such things into the world, ought in some way to be put in their place. But, you can't get to them. There are no legal means; refutations are valueless because people themselves know that they are spreading lies. They don't spread lies out of the foundation of coming to the truth, but in order to get, what causes them discomfort, out of the way. It does not involve people claiming something in which they believe, but to raise something which is as close as possible to the person in question, who will be harmed in the eyes of those who have no judgement. I have experienced this for many years, even without this refinement which has come to the fore in recent years. I have no pleasure in getting involved with such dirty people and to handle their dirty laundry.

I also don't like when from a certain clerical side — this certainly among people who do not base it on the truth — I am a priest originating from the Catholic church. Such people then had, after telling such big fat untruths, no other words that those which the gentleman in question had written in a respected clerical journal: The claim that Dr Steiner had once been a priest, can no longer hold, due to recent inquiries. — With this people believed that what had caused damage to numerous souls could now be put right. You can't make it good this way. The fact of the matter is that in the face of such conduct, the attitude is what happened years ago in the Austrian parliament when Count Walterskirchen countered the government by saying: 'Once a person has lied, no one believes him again, even if he says the truth a hundred times over.'

So, this is an example. Those people who place such things in the world are nothing other than representatives of objective lies, according to my suspicions — because I believe, you know as well — they are liars. One day it has to be announced publicly: All this slander is nothing other than a complete bogus from start to finish.

The second thing which is being peddled over and over again today is warming up the Jesuit lie, which started many years ago. I certainly don't want to say something for or against anti-Semitism. I don't want to say anything about his world view. However, over and over again, certain people, because they know that they are getting their money's worth, spread the lie that I am Jewish; in some way or other it is again mentioned from some corner. I had my baptism certificate photographed at the time, when this system was still practiced by Jesuits, and today still I have a very small photo of my baptism certificate which I can show anyone who wants to see it. However I don't believe that such a document can oppose the relevant party.

Among those people who have created this silly story about my Jewish origin, there was also the "Literary Lexicon." My whole biography is so cooked up that it is supposed to show that I am somehow of Jewish descent. The only ancestors I'm able to research are those of my mother's and father's sides which came about from the Lower Austrian peasantry. My father served a truly non-Jewish institute, namely the monastery and diocese of Geras in Lower Austria, which is a Premonstratensian diocese. The people of the Premonstratensian diocese liked him very much and even gave him a scholarship to do the training of the first classes of the grammar school. Later he became an Austrian railway official, not a state official but a private official. Just as well as it can be proven that these paternal ancestors were hardly Jewish, or servants of a Catholic monastery, just so can it be proven on the side of the maternal forefathers, as far as they are accessible to me. I don't for a moment think that one can make a difference with such things against these parties who work with such lies. Among these personalities who are listed under the "Literary Lexicon" as Jews, there is a personality who recently did approach Jesuitism, namely Hermann Bahr. His biography is also so cooked up that one can just about believe he somehow is from Jewish descent. Now he could come up with the fact that twelve of his ancestors were real Upper Austrian farmers, not Jewish or something like that. When this possibility was proved with documentation, the editorial staff of the "Literary Lexicon," which is definitely the series from which such things come, turned on it by saying: Well, yes, good, we want to believe that the twelve ancestors consistently were far from Judaism.

Then we also believe in reincarnation and we believe that Hermann Bahr was a Jew in an earlier physical incarnation.

You see, with thoughts, with refutations you can't come to terms with this party. Quite different ways must be found. I don't believe, however, that another, really goal orientated way can be found other than that the number of rational and decent thinking people will constantly grow in contrast to those who want to slander their contemporaries, to wade in dirt. I don't believe that indecency can be defeated by anything other than decent thinking people. Neither with court hearings, nor with counter refutations will you win, but only through finding many people who have a sense of decency.

It has often been said in public: such things which I have now presented also belong to what comes about through the penetration into the realities of life, of the spirit-void instead of the spirit. With everything that's going on today as terribly destructive to humanity, it can be summarised with the words: Mankind is much in need, but particularly the German spirit is in need of putting the spirit in the place of the spirit-void, in the place of the materialistic spirit-void, because the spirit-void must be conquered, if we want to become constructive, if we want humanity to progress. The spirit-void can only become spirit through the spirit defeating it.

LECTURE 2
Spiritual requirements to face the future
Stuttgart on 4 March 1920

My dear honourable friends! With a sensitive, unprejudiced judgement of present events, I believe it quite relevant to speak about these events with regard to the coming days.

When I refer to what I was allowed to speak about the day before yesterday, I can perhaps add that such depictions about the frame of mind of present day civilized humanity, express a kind of evening mood. Events of humanity's evolution over the last three to four hundred years up to the present must be depicted within our present day, and what must be shown is how, in the most varied spheres of life, despite the enormous progress and triumphs – which, however, as has been pointed out, also exists – the horrific events of the last four to five years have befallen humanity. It has not only become possible that these shocking events have befallen humankind, but it has become possible to confront the helplessness in a certain way, with: What now? – Yes, in many connections we must admit: If we want to build only on what has resulted from our knowledge, from our developmental will forces, then we have to reckon with hopelessness. This is like an evening mood. This evening mood is to some extent close to what can be observed from the opposite side: the morning mood, speaking about the coming day.

However, when one wants to speak about the coming day, then it appears that one can't simply look back at events, how they contributed, how they developed up to the present moment in time, in order to derive reasons for some random things one can only hope for. Out of the foundation of helplessness of the present, there is little chance of finding such hope. For this reason, for those who want to speak about the coming days, they must find another approach rather than the depiction of possible effects of events up to now, or only observe what can emerge from general relationships in culture and civilisation.

45

No, my dear friends, if someone wants to speak about the coming days, they must speak about what has to be done so that these coming days may come closer. To point to some destiny outside humanity alone will not raise hopes today. It must point to people themselves, to their possibilities for action, what it is which can ignite deeds within them, that they become those who, as the world may be in flames, can bring about the day to come. It is not an initiative to only observe helplessness and hopelessness in destiny of the outer world, it gives in addition the initiative to observe somewhat deeper into the becoming of humanity, which one can certainly see from the point of view of the here-mentioned spiritual science. Most people today are accustomed, when the subject is human evolution, to only follow the line from cause to effect, in such a way as if everything consecutively happens to clarify previous events, which are then called causes.

This is just as little the case in the historical development of mankind as it is the case with single human individuals. We can't possibly be satisfied in the course of individual human development for which we can state: Now, if we look at a person, when he is thirty years old, we declare that as a thirty year old he is the result of what he was as a twenty nine year old, as a twenty eight year old, as a twenty seven year old. – Such a statement would be external, abstract, and couldn't enter into the real being of the person. If we want to grasp the real being of the individual, then we must enter into the individual stages of his development. We must be clear that we, as human beings, when we are children, are subject to certain developmental laws which aim at roundabout the time of the change of teeth. Then one has to be clear that after the change of teeth, in the entire human being's organism, some law is allowing the inner being to ascend, which can't be explained by simply tracing external facts of evolution from around the 9th year by referred back to development in his 5th or 6th year. One needs to repeatedly look back to the moment of adolescence in the fourteenth or fifteenth year. Here again something rises in the inner being of a person which one must call on to help if one wants to come to an understanding of to total human being.

Likewise, in the following periods of human individual development, during these periods the turning points are less clear in human nature; it can emerge quite clearly for someone with insight.

Just as it is with single individual development, so it is with the historical development of the evolution of humanity. It is not enough that one merely, as has become customary, always explains it as a result of a previous event. One must clearly understand that big turning points also appear in the historical evolution of humanity; epochs come about where out of the depths of human development, laws rise up so that the essential, which is expressed in humanity, appears different from that which appeared in the epoch preceding it.

If you now look back at what I called, being under the surface of what I described, regarding three to four hundred years ago and want to work your way up – because it first wants to only work from the depths of the human being upwards – then you must say: Everything indicates the tendency, the goal, for every member of humanity to develop his full awareness, complete full awareness in every area of life. For the expert who knows historical becoming, who does not only consider external history as it is taught today which is basically just an agreed fable, but who goes into inner human development – as one has to enter right into single individual people, into their natures, if you want to understand them – for them it shows that around the 15th century the first facility of this new kind of humanity came which could lead to understanding, in full consciousness, what was going on in the world. Only one fact about human evolution is available which masks, obliterates, what I have just characterised. From old epochs some developmental forces always remained behind as conservative elements in the whole human evolution – forces which continue working and which actually, for that part of the human becoming which is really the task of the time epoch, do not only let this retreat go into the background, but in a way, fight against it. So in the previous epochs from the 15th century onwards and in our epoch, what has remained is what I would like to call the unconsciousness in all spheres, first of all the unconsciousness of all things in the realm of spiritual life itself.

So strongly has this unconsciousness in the realm of spiritual life remained, that today we have broad spiritual currents which see in the unconsciousness, what the deeper, the essential human being is. For instance we see in America the rise of a spiritual movement connected to the name of William James (1842-1910), which under intellectuals in Europe have quite a few followers, who say: 'Only a part of what man's soul contains, comes into full consciousness. Out of the unconsciousness everything rises which for instance is the content of artistic creation; out of the unconscious ideas rise which are then subjected only to the judgement of science. Out of the unconsciousness rises all that ensoul people in religion.'

That which spreads from educated spiritual streams, taking on grotesque forms at times, like psychoanalysis for example, has something different as its counterpart. How often can you still hear it being said today that anyone is well-meaning in relation to the supersensible, to a spiritual world which he presumes, but his good intention stops the moment when spiritual science steps in, which out of the signs of the time want to, in full consciousness, with sight, penetrate the spiritual world. Such a well-meaning person often says: What you can consciously absorb from nature and man, into the soul, beyond that, there must be something. – However, then he is happy to say: That which exists there, is an unknown, it is something which one can't research; it is something which can't enter completely into full human consciousness – artistic creators takes fright, has a fear of elevating the impulses of their artistry into consciousness. To do so, they believe, would be to lose the elementary power, the naive power which they require for artistic creativity. Some people also certainly do not want impulses of social life to be brought to full awareness, because they want to refer to something unconscious, unknown, as relevant in their exchanges between one person and another. Out of the unconscious the person is to create impulses of his social relationships, and it will be disturbed in some way, when consciousness is brought into it, in the same way as dew, which is refreshing, is taken away from him.

So in a certain way the unconscious, the unknown is presented in the most varied forms, which you can see even in enlightened circles. The result is that, against the spiritual science which is meant here, reproaches arise again and again, namely what one misses within this spiritual science regarding the spiritual world and its content which really mean something and not merely point to what lies beyond the borders of mankind, as an unknown super sensibility. This is confronted with the so-called "simple, plain faith" which doesn't insist on the content of spiritual life but only refers to spiritual life out of a certain general feeling, from out of the most primitive part of human nature. This faith, which wants to ignore the signs of the times, which rejects a certain content of spiritual life for which spiritual science strives for, this faith is only the remains, left by what had ruled in human evolution as the unconscious. What is this unconsciousness?

In earlier stages of evolution, humanity was different to what it can be today. This unconsciousness was in earlier evolutionary epochs of humanity, a living elementary thing. The further we go back in human evolution, the more we find how it rose up in people – in any case not in the way which consciousness today must be ours, but in the way of unconscious perception – how it ever more rose up not only as the content of their spiritual life but also enabling them to understand surrounding nature.

One only has to look, my dear friends, at the last foothills of this ancient vision of mankind and what came out of that unconsciousness, and you discover glorious myths, delightful mythologies, through which earlier human beings were enlightened through their unconscious mind about themselves and surrounding nature. We find the spring of artistic creation rise out of this unconsciousness. When we really and not purely through conventional prejudices want to teach, then we also find indications that earlier man searched for impulses in his social will and his social relationships in circles of his fellow men which rise up from the unconscious. It is still inherent, not as everything but as part of what connects people socially out of their unconsciousness, in human language – in this human language through which we become sisters and brothers to other people, in whose circle we live. We take ownership of human speech in our earliest childhood, during a time in which we first dream ourselves into life, in the time in which no full state of awakening can be spoken of. What is this which we carry, this which is born out of the childlike sphere of life, into later life?

We stand under the influence of the genius of language. Language gives us so much. It connects us socially with others, but the social driving force which permeates language is hidden even in earliest childhood; this is not born out of consciousness but born out of unconsciousness. So we can say: social life is often developed out of the unconscious. The state of unconsciousness had given humanity something other than what it had, up to the time of human evolution, up to the 15th century, than what it gives today. Just as little as developmental forces in single individuals are present before they reach puberty, in the same way in which they must appear after puberty in a different relation and power, just so in human development, in the place of earlier unconsciousness, it must now become consciousness in our time. The element to which I drew your attention the day before yesterday, which permeates our present day civilisation, the Phrase, is what intensively prevents full consciousness form coming out of the depths of the human being. What had been penetrated in all liveliness rising out of the unconscious is no longer living today: it has been killed by the Phrase.

I also had to draw attention to this the day before yesterday, that the glorious scientific worldview hasn't found a way to tell people about something other than the outer human being, and about what is present in inanimate nature. I must point out that whoever wants to include everything which comes as scientific knowledge and is confronted with the question: Who is the human being actually? – will remain perplexed. About the question: Who is man actually - practiced science of today gives no solution. Why does this happen?

50

It is the result of science not having been created out of full consciousness, because this science, despite its glorious results, is the continuation of what during that epoch of unconsciousness came from quite other sources than those existing today. So you see this science is in quite a strange situation.

Recently I received a, not quite a worthless brochure regarding general social concepts and ideas. I must stress that I saw a lot of value inside it. However, in conclusion something was expressed which, for such an observation, is extraordinarily characteristic today. There, in conclusion, it states that the author has considered the social condition purely scientifically, that is, in accordance with the scientific conventions of the present. While the writer wanted to be scientific, he could not somehow make any scientific ideas draw a conclusion of any kind regarding the moral, the artistic or the political, or cultural life, because science doesn't have the job of drawing any conclusions for these different branches of life. Whether that which he depicts purely scientifically – so says the creator – whether they treat ulcers or disturb suns, that is completely indifferent to science – that is not what science is interested in.

Don't we see, by us looking at an expression of such a view – which doesn't only stand by itself but is typical for what is often today called "scientific" or "scientific knowledge" – don't we see the continuation of a certain life asceticism before us, which doesn't recognise itself as a sequel; don't we see this again as the asceticism which in earlier centuries had a contempt for outer life, which had withdrawn into mankind's inner soul, which doesn't care about what is in the outer ethical, moral or social world of facts but only, to a certain extent, to the affairs of the soul's inner state, alone? Other forms were taken on through this ascetic striving, but it appeared again in this scientific mindset which is admirable in its strict and conscientious methodology, but whose greatness is precisely in what it confesses: I have nothing for the moral, artistic, political or cultural life which I present out of myself as an impulse or drive.- Against this sentiment which not only occurs in scientific life, but which – because scientific life is controlled by education – spreads over our entire public lives, against this sentiment is spiritual science which wants to rise in its fullest protest.

The moment the great question about the future arises today in the sad relationships of our present civilisation, then there must come about – as if by implication - out of spiritual science, the true spiritual science as it is meant here, the inner human being kindled by its flame, then insight about social life, about the continuation of social life will come about. It is not through a whim or arbitrariness of single personalities that this Three Fold Social organism has been added to what has already been represented here for decades as Anthroposophically orientated spiritual science – that has come about as a matter of course. It has come about in such a way that people had to feel the lack of truth, sense dishonesty, and pretend to strive with their souls towards spiritual science but have no heart for what shakes all of humanity as a social question, or what at least should shock and shake them all. So there is no longer a search according to outer natural wisdom but according to spiritual wisdom, which, through it being experienced in the human soul, offer direct power also to social will.

To mention one more thing – I could also glance at other areas of life but want to mention one more thing. In our building in Dornach we have created something which does not count on some or other old building style, but that the forms of the building, the artistic element, consistently, right into the smallest detail, have emerged from the forces of our spiritual insight, resulting from our spiritual vision itself. That it would be right to allow the artistic element to be unconscious, not to lift it up into consciousness, that is what this spiritual science, which is meant here, objects against. Just as spiritual science itself wants to be perceived in full consciousness in the spiritual worlds, so it also wants to appear here as a new style of building, leading to new artistic forms, lifted out of what works in spiritual worlds. Because spiritual science wants to show the spirit itself, which people are acquainted with in their innermost being, it comes to the fore in the inner being of man in such a way that it touches the very kernel of humanity – there where the moral will germinates, where the moral will rises up. Spiritual science can't say it isn't concerned about what happens in moral will, but it can only be held responsible for – by its penetration of knowledge from the widths of worlds to the depths, most intimate soul realms – at the same time giving birth to the moral impulses out of which man shapes his will, his actions. This spiritual science can't say it isn't concerned with ulcers being healed or suns being extinguished. You can say it is concerned with its knowledge creating power for people, healing power to the outer course of world events which causes damage; it is concerned with introducing something which can be a sun to people and contribute to the well-meaning forces in human evolution. Doing things together, acting together, having combined intentions in the entire course of human beings' life historically, into a social becoming; that's what makes spiritual science not an abstract goal, but what it gives, from out of its own nature and being. It can't act in any other way than continuing in full consciousness with what earlier mankind had in a certain way, unconsciously.

Out of this unconsciousness, people of earlier times had quite definite experiences regarding the continuation of human development. This was that the entire human race, if it would be left to itself, would continuously degenerate, continuously be gripped by harm, continuously steer towards a kind of death, be continuously diseased. People have the idea that if they intervene in human evolution, then they become, by relying on what enlightens them out of the nature of the unconscious, the healer of illnesses, of what damages. During the times of unconscious development, humankind experienced all of knowledge and wisdom as a healing power, because mankind didn't want to stop in a corner and not participate in the outer cultural processes – on the contrary, mankind wanted to participate as healers in this cultural process.

The word which resounds to us from Greek wisdom, characterising one of the deepest artistic creations, called the tragedy, is the word "catharsis" which resounds out of the Greek culture and wants to say what actually is involved in the process of a tragedy. This process depends on the following effect: to create images of passions in people so that these passions seen in the tragic acting of the tragedy can be healed – emotionally, in the soul. Through the expression "catharsis" being sounded out as what rules tragedy, we are made aware of how the artistic aspect of life stood so close to Greek culture; that it is to be considered as a healing process in life. "Catharsis" is a word – we can merely translate it with the abstract word "purification" – which is also needed in a crisis appearing as a result of an illness; and when this crisis leads to the deliverance from what is harmful, then it leads to healing. The Greeks took the individual healing process as a task of the tragedy. They didn't think artistic form as being separated from the rest of culture, but that it existed within it.

In the same way, right inside living will and action, this spiritual science we have long been talked about here, wants to stand, and today in the face of perplexity – which has arisen from other areas in the glorious science of recent times – must stand as the most serious spiritual demand in the coming days. However, for it to be considered and recognised, many a harsh prejudice needs to be cleared away. As long as the belief persists, that serious science is only to be described through what is observed through a microscope or a telescope, what is stated in the physical cabinet, what happens in clinics, so long will this spiritual science be met with prejudices. If a person perceives that through everything that can be researched in this outer manner – if also in other relationships which are so valuable for humanity - it says nothing about the inner being of the human being itself, then the human being becomes, out of an inner drive - because he can't in any other way, if he wants to find enlightenment about himself – he is driven to knowledge about the spirit.

Just as one today listens to what is stated in the physical cabinet, in the clinics, you come – especially about acknowledging the essence of man – to listen to what the spiritual researcher undertakes in his soul by strengthening his thinking in such a way that this self- strengthened thinking no longer, like ordinary thinking, depends on physicality, but makes itself independent of physicality.

What today is jeered at the most, regarded as phantasmagoria, will in future be regarded as the strict, exact method which takes its course within the soul. People will admit that through the so-called meditative life – not however through the old, mystical meditative life which only alienates man from the world, but through an inner active meditative life – that thinking can become so strong, particularly when the strong willingness is added to it, as I describe in my book "Knowledge of Higher Worlds and its attainment". One is any case involved with a kind of thinking about which one knows: You think, but this now has become a purely soul-spiritual process, no longer with the help of a brain.- Then one rises up to supersensible knowledge through this inner strengthened thinking. Just like one has from a certain moment realised what one has seen magnified through the microscope, so one will come to realise, through the strengthened thinking, what is given as the results of supersensible research, through our intellectual soul content, which can't be fully grasped intellectually.

This is something which sounds like a paradox today but which, however, through the earnest demands of the coming days will be realised, as no longer sounding like a paradox. It will become clear that nature within itself is far richer in its processes than what can be grasped as laws of nature which only the human mind can grasp, what can be humanly extracted from an experiment. Much can be said about the inner human tendency which says: only what the human mind with an intellectually observed judgement can grasp, can be seen as an inner experience. – If however one stops at this point, considering natural laws to only be valid through intellectual kinds of experiments - then one must renounce the real knowledge of nature. What is the use of forever claiming: The only clarity that can be reached is through intellectual judgement – when everything that is the essence of nature can't be grasped by nature's laws. Nature is so that it doesn't reveal its laws but only images, images which we can recognise imaginatively, when our thoughts are so strengthened that they are independent of the body and we make them the content of our soul.

In any case, what is presented in this way as the actual motivation and nucleus of spiritual scientific research is not enough to be theoretically accepted. It isn't enough that a person's interests are for selfish results of his own inner soul and for the imagination of thoughts in this kind of world view, but it is necessary that an inner mood and human soul disposition, born from such observation, can follow from such a vision, penetrating into our own social life, infiltrated little by little – but preparatory to the horrors of the last four to five years – of this mere scientific, intellectual way of thinking.

Training people will have to start. This training must finally break away from what is today still considered the main issue of all school systems: that the school system is dependent on supervision by state authorities. The state authorities will out of themselves, since they have the task of organizing the state, always want to shape the goals of the school system in such a way that the individual becomes an instrument in the state organization. In the future, it will not be a question of preparing people for this or that, but it's going to come down to the fact that one has a sense for education, by observing the soul-spiritual in the human being, which has, from the earliest childhood, wanted to develop as spirit in the bodily nature. It will involve the school, from the lowest level to the highest level, having its foundation only and alone in the requirements of spiritual life itself.

Today in our public relationships we are in a position of only being able to make isolated attempts to establish such an educational system as is being done for example here under the aegis of Mr Molt with the Waldorf School. In the Waldorf School the foundation from the outset is that people work out of the deeply mysterious nature of childhood, which can with spiritual sight, week after week, year by year, be observed as it unfolds. The method of education is directed in such a way that a person becomes a full human being, that the pupils from the earliest childhood develop forces which will last a lifetime, making it possible that people in their latest years can retrieve what had been

56

developed within them. It must proceed in quite a different way than the way the educational goal has been from the scientific and materialistic point of view, with its prejudices in our more modern times.

Above all, it must come from the awareness: If I can assess all that is in the human being and bring it out, as to how he will be situated later in his social life, so that he chooses the arrangement and not let the institutions violate him, as is the case today where he is made into a machine in his profession, an imprint of the essence of his profession. Future human beings who are to be aspired through this school, must put the seal on external life, but not allow external life to put a seal on them. If this is expressed then one first of all recognises the Phrase which is so often needed for educational purposes. However, this remains a phrase, as many a phrase does in life today, when it is not connected to a real spiritual observation. This will first come through strengthened thinking delving into the depths of the human soul, driven by self-discipline of the will to the method required for spiritual observation.

It is the earnest demand of the coming days that among external research done in laboratories, in clinics, there will also be recognition for revelations resulting from strict soul methods of the individual, true, real being of the human being, which at the same time is the supersensible, eternal, within human beings. It's a misjudgement of all the signs of the times to dismiss such endeavours with prejudice and reduce that which man wants to make, out of his very own strength of will. It is a bad thing that some religious confessions tell people again and again that it is a mistake or dangerous if a person wants to develop himself inwardly in such a way that supersensible observation arrives; that the supersensible should be accepted out of what instinctively arises out of the faith of the simplest minds.

This sounds, because of human egotistic comforts, very nice to many. It sounds decidedly objectionable when spiritual science appears and speaks about the simple facts of the supersensible worlds, just like outer science speaks about outer sensory facts of life. It is objectionable when a claim is made about knowledge of the spiritual world for the individual who as a human being is connected to it and to describe it in the same way as when describing something in the sensory world. People would like to grasp everything possible as "the divine" from a completely indeterminate feeling as if in the twinkling of an eye; he doesn't want to get involved in conquering this divine within himself through laborious inner paths. People will however, because they don't want to get involved with a laborious inner path to conquer the soul, but rather cling to abstractions of feeling, they will ever more distance themselves from real life. What they will say about nature will be powerless to entering it into social life, intervene in political life, in ritual, even in moral life. Finally it will be powerless in maintaining religion itself, because people in the present age are used to strive for what is concrete, because people are accustomed to recognise science and not merely believe. The education they have acquired will also apply its powers in this area. If people are not presented with spiritual science, if spiritual sight is not spoken about, then they fight it and they lose the old, traditional religious confessions that stem from the age of unconsciousness. Their souls become atrophied.

Religious confessions, which oppose a living grasp of the spiritual world, are the ones which work against true religiosity for mankind. This knowledge itself is a serious spiritual demand of the days ahead of us. When people say today that religion must emerge out of the darkest urge, then it certainly supports the oldest facts, which say religion is to remain in the unconscious realm, it may not rise up into full consciousness.

What I have presented to you in this are as characteristic of today's actual spiritual striving, will reveal how to direct humanity towards a conscious experience of the spiritual world. To acquire a conscious experience of the spiritual world will only be possible if in public life, through the independent sharing of all spiritual striving and through the principle of all education of human spiritual powers, they remain independent from state-legal powers, independent from all economic powers – you may read about this in my book "Key points of the Social Question". A spiritual life which exists on its own, purely working from what the spirit says out of the innermost soul, independent of all authority, only such a spiritual life will also awaken in humanity, a consciousness of the spirit. This consciousness is needed in order to awaken to the connection of one's own spirit with the spirit encompassing the entire world. So, in the area of knowledge, humanity has acquired the necessity of finding the transition from the old unconscious demands to the newer, more and more conscious and aware demands which will have to appear stronger and stronger. In other areas of life, earnest demands are appearing in the coming days.

When we look at a second area in human life, the public life – this area which presents community life between one person and another, of mature persons, having come of age, how at the same time they develop support for aspiring childhood and youth which would mature in the following age – if this life is glanced at in earlier epochs of evolution, we return to the unconsciousness; yet this life also demands a transition to consciousness.

Out of what has law developed? From where did the origins come about which eventually crystallized into state legislations and legal regulations? I can indicate that here briefly. In olden times law developed out of an unconscious human evolution of habits which people had in relations to one another. Unconsciously a person developed a way of looking at another person; out of this, relationships developed. Unconsciously one person developed a feeling for the way another person behaved to them, in a certain way. This gave rise to legal customs. Customs, the law, developed out of the unconscious. Also in these areas, in the age of consciousness, something has been retained which only had authority in unconscious times. Into the age of consciousness, an adherence to remnants of the old habits has been preserved. Up to today little has been shown to have changed from one transition to another in the view of the legal- and state systems in particular, in a transition towards the observation, in full awareness, which grasps what the relationship between one person to another is in outer, social life. Just as a pure knowledge of the transition must be gained from unconsciousness to consciousness, so also in the sphere of legal- or state life, must the transition be found from unconsciousness to consciousness. This must be reborn out of what a person experiences through what he has learnt from his spiritual vision within the spirit. It must be reborn out of the knowledge of the supersensible in the way one person, in his legal-state, stands to another, in the social order. It must be reborn out of a human awareness from the supersensible into the conscious awareness: By you standing there as a human being facing another human being, we are not only one physical body facing another physical body; we are both carriers of the soul-spirit. Our communication is from one soul-spirit to another soul-spirit. – This soul content can't be gained through theoretical observation. It can only come about when soul content is experienced from the earliest childhood through an education which naturally links everything to the spiritual, that everything natural is also permeated with the spirit.

When a person stands right in truth within his innermost experience, then in his exchange from one person to another, he would develop feelings that he stands as such, as a spiritual being, in front of another spiritual being. Then, in the state-legal order he sees it initially as a result of the behaviour of people, but in a deeper sense he acknowledges that the whole of humanity is permeated with spirit. Because still for this sphere, the remnants of the unconscious from old times protrude into our time, for this reason that which had earlier come unconsciously in feelings for law, for the state, is transformed into mere convention. Convention must once again take up something which is alive, which can work in an elementary way between people. This again can only come about when people really find a foundation – independent of the rest of other human life – which develops from one human soul to another, as law. The old unconsciousness, which had an authority in a certain relation for past ages, has kept itself pure into our age, but has lost its meaning. The law has been preserved according to the outer wording, according to outer custom; the inner meaning has been lost. It could therefore not be practiced out of an inner life of the soul; it could only be practiced out of a physical power.

And so we see how today, initially still half unconscious, rose the appeal out of humanity – but an appeal which is today too strongly lifted out of the phrase, the phrase which needs to be clothed in reality – an appeal is raised up which exists only under the influence of outer commandments of power and which is to be replaced with a real law, transformed into a real law. What lives as power in our outer institutions on the basis of law or the state, simply originated as a result of what had appeared out of the unconscious beforehand, adhered to without meaning so that now it is not adhered to by the human soul but held by an outside power. It must be transformed – in a way which can only be sought in the transition from unconscious feelings between one person and another, to conscious feelings of an individual for the real soul-spiritual being of others.

Just as in the age of unconsciousness, cognition developed, and how custom and law developed out of the most elementary from that which is not included in the known, manageable customs, the rules of conduct - so likewise also customs and behavioural rules, of the outer life, developed. They developed out of the adaptation of people to their dealings, through their associations with outer things, through trying, through scraping, scratching and grinding at outer life, in other words. So the skills of the business world developed. In the age where unconscious old residues have remained, not filled with the new inner soul experiences which had before been filled with the unconscious soul elements in association with the outer world in relation to people, it has become empty, has become mere routine. The spirit must be understood, grasped. The supersensible need to grow in consciousness, then people will again penetrate the outer economic life with the fire of their enthusiasm. Then the outer world will again attain meaning. Then his profession will not shape a person but he will shape his profession. Then it will also become necessary that a person is not simply placed in some or other profession to which he must become accustomed, but it will be necessary that he is raised out of the requirements and forces of human nature. He will be able to fit into the structure of economic life, in which manageable associations will come about, associations between people of the same or similar professions, or adjacent professions in which associations would exist between those who produce and those who consume.

Such associations would only reach a size in which the entire scope of relationships between people will be manageable, that these manageable associations will have a free circulation of economic exchange with others. As a result economic life made of intuition will develop, gained through experience. It would be impossible – when people are locked in manageable associations – it will be impossible for one to offer another something, of which the other doesn't know its origin, where it comes from. Here one could build on the power of the organisation, which has created the associations. Then one will know with whom one is involved because it will be obvious how individuals enter into the association through economic and social associations. There will truly, in economic life, instead of the spirit-void, the spirit, rule. So, one can say that through associations - by people getting to know one another through commerce and business – consciousness will draw into economic life. Simply by being in the associations, a conscious economic life will be developed.

The transition from the unconscious to the conscious is something which people must understand in individual, narrow circles of public, external life, and that needs to be done on a large scale. We can see today how the unconsciousness works in great areas of the world. One could ask: How few are able to see this?

We have seen how, under the influence of events of the last four to five years, a world coalition has arisen against Central Europe, as the sad events of these years have highlighted the predominance of the English speaking population all over the world. In relation to this, humanity still has a great deal to experience. For those who can observe these issues with unbiased judgement, a very harsh future lies ahead. If one wants to look into the great world events, one also has to pose the question from the following viewpoint: What characteristic does the power in the public political life have, known as the English speaking power which strives for world domination today? What fundamental characteristic do the English-American politics have? It is hardly ever spoken about; nearly the whole world is subjected to these politics today and its foundations are hardly ever mentioned. One can see how certain phenomena in politics reappear repeatedly but one can't characterise these phenomena in the right way. One could have listened to what, in the last third of the 19th Century, people who were familiar in England with what they were actually striving for, could basically be predicted, for instance the destiny of today's European East, which predicted for instance that a big world war had to come. This policy acted under the influence of these drives.

This is what is so seldom understood. This is what must be understood if one wants to have progress in the practical shaping of life, if one wants to reach a practical position in today's public life. Then you have to say, however: Does English politics not actually appear to make forward steps, only to withdraw them again, and so on? We can research English politics in comparison to those of Egypt and Russia right up to today, and will see how in Lloyd George's behaviour a few months ago, how he took a few steps forward and how he took them back again. What is involved in all of this? A very certain goal is involved, which is related to the English speaking earth population. This goal is as much within, as in earlier ages human evolution came out of the unconsciousness, when people created goals. Then it moved into the outer expression, for instance in economic life, in probing and adapting to the environment.

If you look from the one side at what came out of the unconscious birthing of the English political ideal for world domination and observe these forward and backward steps, see what is tried and done by individuals, then you discover the one real indication of politics: It has created its great goals out of the unconscious, and in relation to single actions is experimental politics. It is so strongly experimental politics, tentative politics determined from unconscious goal policies that one should not be discouraged when one or the other does not succeed.

One merely then searches for another way. One always has the unconscious base, and experiments on the basis of consciousness, and when this doesn't take you far enough, so one tries to find another way which goes far enough. Here we have in the sphere of great world being, the world actions of main players of the unconscious, which merely tries and makes experiments, here you have also what has to be conquered for the demands of the coming days.

If this is understood, you will agree, my dear friends, what today mainly happens in the world, I would like to say, thank God, it is not for the coming days, but the twilight. The real coming day however would come out of the requirements which can only happen through an inner development of the human soul itself. This development has its goal to take what has quite rightly developed in humanity as unconscious, and lift it into consciousness. Admittedly this development must penetrate into the most intimate, inner forces of the human soul.

You have been told today that after my last lecture, pamphlets would have been distributed. In these pamphlets all kinds of things are written. Among other things, old fairy tales have been warmed up, that this spiritual science involves a mocking view of Christianity, mainly the mockery of Christ himself.

Now, my dear friends, that which has entered into human evolution on earth through Jesus Christ is a fact – a fact which stands within the entire human evolution. This fact must be understood in its own new way in each epoch in which mankind progresses. Depressing it must be, for those who believe one can be on a Christian basis only if old images remain valid and one must reject what appears out of new evolutionary stages of human soul life as an understanding of Christianity.

People who condemn what spiritual science has to say about Christ and the Mystery of Golgotha, are hardly inclined towards Paul's beautiful words: 'Not I, but Christ in me'.

Spiritual science very clearly shows that Christ descended from supersensible heights into this world evolution and that He is so connected to earth evolution that people today can't live with a passive hope into the coming days, but that they must develop their own inner power as human beings, that will bring about this coming day. Because the power of Christ through the Mystery of Golgotha has entered in such a way into human evolution that those, who unite themselves with the power of Christ, no longer just see Christ as the "Saviour of sinful man" and passively wait for their Saviour, but they become helpers in bringing about the coming days. In truth it must be said: 'Not I but Christ in me' – but not with Christ as only a saviour but Christ as the instigator and enlivener of all the powers that will then be able, in the following time, to emerge as powers of human progress.

Those who believe that they must push against such knowledge, who perhaps misunderstand the most elementary requirements for the coming days, do not understand anything about the true meaning of Paul's words. 'Christ in me' is no mere passive belief but an active power which is brought forwards within us. 'Not I but Christ in me' – this is said by spiritual science.

The others however, who fight against spiritual science do not say: 'Not I but Christ in me' but say: 'Not I but my old habitual opinions in me, my old habitual imaginings of Christ in me.' – The true understanding of Paul's words is such that an earnest requirement also for Christian progress, is being fulfilled.

With this I have today tried to characterise some of the requirements of the coming days, and I believe I want to close with just these first considerations: When human power is to be gained from the spirit, then there must also be a new grasp of the true, the real Christian nature coming from a spiritual source. And that is really not the last, not even the most modest request of the coming days.

Peoples of the earth in the light of spiritual science
Stuttgart on 10 March 1920

My dear honourable friends! Recent years have revealed how great the sum total of feelings of hatred and antipathy has been able to go through the souls of the peoples on earth. No one can close themselves off, in their feelings, from the knowledge of what is actually the truth: on the path of hate and antipathy, earthly life can make no flourishing progress. So, among the many observations I have had the pleasure of making before you, I may well be allowed, according to spiritual scientific knowledge to speak about all which, according to the knowledge of mankind, can unite the whole civilized mankind at least.

Of course, knowledge is not feeling. However, spiritual knowledge — also this has been spoken of here — spiritual knowledge is more closely linked to all of humanity, to the innermost part of humanity itself, than outer, abstract truths coming from outer sensory facts. For this reason spiritual scientific truths are probably also suitable to release sensations, feelings and will impulses from people so that out of this strong inner power, which out of scientific spiritual knowledge the unity of peoples can reveal itself, feelings of sympathy can also be strengthened; feelings of mutual love among different peoples of the earth. Since during the course of human evolution, humanity has progressed more and more from the instinctive, unconscious life to conscious life, to the full, random grasp of the human task, it is already so that for the future, not the indefinite, emotional loving will alone will suffice to unite the peoples of the earth, but it must be the conscious, mutual knowledge of how the nature of one people has to differ from the nature of another people and what they can expect from the other.

It is relatively easy to see in one area how necessary the unification of humanity is on the earth; we only need to look at today's terrible destruction of economic life. When we search for the ultimate reason why this economic life has suffered such damage, why it follows such a destructive path, we must first of all tell ourselves that out of an indeterminate urge from all of humanity, the striving tendency at present is to create a <u>single</u> economic area for the whole world. On the other hand, peoples of the earth don't go as far as the point of ennobling their national egotisms in such a way that really, what these individual nations can produce can become the overall economic life of the earth, but that one nation will snatch something away from the other. As a result, and out of old instincts, peoples develop impertinent points of view while new instincts are creating a worldwide economy required for the whole of humanity. This is knowledge which today, I could say, needs to be grasped with both hands, which is repeatedly stressed by ruling minds of the present: that this striving is available for a unified earth economy, but it was opposed until into the 20th century when the national economies, with their opposition to an overall earth economy, caused the process of decline of the economic life we face today.

This is to be hinted at only. This is not our essential concern today, something else is. We need to occupy ourselves with people's spiritual and soul discouragement as a result of the frightening revelation of hate, the frightening manifestation of antipathy we have experienced over the last five or six years. Certainly these were around for a long time, but only revealed in such a terrible way as in the course of the last five to six years. Where it deals with the knowledge of one people to another, it is concerned with absorbing the soul-spiritual being of another earthly people, then, my dear friends, we can't just go among these other people or be steered through our destiny, to, in this way — certainly through the communications which happen between one person and another daily — get to know the other people. To gain knowledge of a people, travel or living among other people has as little meaning as when, in trying to understand an individual, I merely observe his gestures and movements. If I have a sense for such things, his gestures and movements may let me guess something, only in order to get to know him directly, I will be in a better position if I allow his language to work on me, when I'm in the position to take from him what through his inner strength, he wants to convey.

Is there a similar communication of inner strength from within the being of one people to another? Purely the language and what can be observed on a daily basis from one people to another, can't be it, for it is only valid in the exchange of one person to another. Something must come to the fore which goes beyond the mere individual-human, beyond the recognition coming out of the understanding of the other person. We're basically at a quandary if we even want to talk about uniform folklore in an understandable way. Is there actually something of uniform folklore which is as sensually real as external things or external beings, that allows us to speak of a unified folklore?

We can talk about single people, about individual beings, even if we only want to allow sensory observation. Sensory observation only takes us as far as the sum of so and so many individuals. If we want to recognise folklore as something real, we can't do anything other than rise up to something supersensible.

In fact, for those who undergo the spiritual training we have more often spoken about here during the last weeks, who have in their human soul developed the otherwise slumbering powers of cognition, for them, what is called folklore, can indicate an actual being, certainly a real being of a supersensible kind. Then, however, for someone who is receptive for the spiritual world at all, for them what appears in the strange folklore is a spirit being, supersensible, which permeates the sensual being of people like a kind of cloud, which belongs to this folklore and envelops it. Only when one wants to try searching for such characteristics from one people to another people, which grows out of the supersensible, can one penetrate the being of a folk, like one never can penetrate in daily exchanges between single people. This is what I would like to try and sketch in a few lines for you today: how spiritual science wants to begin to recognise the togetherness of peoples of the earth across the globe in a truly profound way. This is important to me, that the single human being is really recognised out of the sources of spiritual science.

During my lecture in Stuttgart I have already pointed out that some years ago, in my written book, "Riddles of the Soul" I mentioned that this human being, as he stands before us in daily life, is no single being but that in fact the human organisation — I mean the direct, natural human organisation — is such that it appears in three clearly differentiable members.

First of all, we have in the human organisation that which relates to the head organisation as the central point of what one can call in the individual, the nerve-sense organisation. The human being experiences his sensory organs and his imaginations, his thoughts, ideas, through the tool of this nerve-sense organisation; a thinking person is a person of the earth through his nerve-sense organisation. Now, one gets an image from current science that the entire human soul spiritual organisation depends on the nerve-sense system which is to a certain extent set up like a parasite on the rest of the organism. This is not the case.

I ask for your forgiveness if I make a personal remark here, but I must say the following. A thirty-year-old follower in pursuit of human nature and being, a pursuit for the harmony of spiritual scientific knowledge with scientific knowledge, has made me want to reinforce this threefold division of the natural human being. It is the common judgement of today's science that the entire soul-spiritual life runs parallel with the nerve-sense existence. In truth this is different. In truth only the life of thought is linked to the nerve-sense system, while the feeling life, emotional life, is linked to all that happens in the human rhythmic system. Not merely indirectly but directly, the emotional and feeling life are linked to the rhythm of breathing and blood circulation, just as the thinking and perceptive life is linked to the nerve-sense organism. Just as the feeling and emotional life is connected to everything in the human being which has its origin in rhythm, so the life of will is connected to everything related to metabolism. The seemingly most humble in the human being, metabolism, is the carrier of the life of will — as a process, not as matter.

So, the human being is a soul spiritual threefold being. The spiritual will, the soul's frame of mind and the outer material expressions of organised thinking, imagination and observation; these are the three members of the soul-spiritual human being.

These three members of the soul-spiritual human being correspond to the three members of the human physical organism: firstly the nerve-sense apparatus, the nerve-sense mechanism, secondly, the organisation involved with the rhythmic life of blood circulation, which is given by breathing, and the third, metabolism, which creates all kinds of processes through both of them, within the human organism.

If we now look at people in a certain area of the earth, then they do not show in their threefold organisation that somehow, with all people in this threefold organisation all over the whole earth, they have to be essentially the same. This is again a big mistake in current thinking, that it is believed one can create something which can be commonly applied all over the world, for example with a social program, and that people must comply with such a common program, because people all over the world are individualised and specialized. For someone who wants to really understand the human earth wisdom, who really wants to learn to understand his gender on earth, he must be able to develop love, not only towards general humanity — which would only be the idea of humanity, the dead, empty idea of humanity — but love must be developed for individual configurations of human nature all over the various areas of the earth.

Obviously, we can't in the short time allotted to us, enter into all the singular, individual peoples and characterise them, but we could look into the main types in the human earth organisation. If we want to look at the oldest kind of human characteristics, we would firstly be directed to the oriental human type in the ancient people of the Indians and also other oriental people where it would be revealed in the most varied ways. It shows, namely in the characteristics of the Indian people, how the oriental human being has grown up alongside earthly nature, which he's grown up with. Now, as far as it appears to

71

us, this human soul has taken up, into his mind, the intense commitment to spiritual devotion, but as much as we are impressed by mysticism — we are studying the oriental person in hindsight of his folk characteristics — so we find that what is so admirable as the highest spirituality revealed within him is precisely dependent on the experience of the flowing will, which in turn is linked to the metabolism to which man is bound. As paradoxical as this may seem, precisely the elevated spirituality of oriental folk, also namely the Indian, is something which — if I could use this rough expression — "boiling up" out of the metabolism, the metabolism which stands in relation to his own being in the processes, the earthly nature surrounding these people.

Out there in the Indian countryside, out there are the trees, fruits, all that is the delightful, admirable nature for people — and particularly those of olden times — which came out of itself, and united in such a way with metabolism that what happens as the metabolic process is to a certain extent the continuation of what was happening outside, how the trees "cooked" their fruits, how the roots weaved under the earth and so on. I would like to say that these oriental people have completely grown through their metabolism with the earthly growth and its prosperity. That is how it is made up: while metabolism is the carrier of the will, will forces develop within people. However, what develops particularly in human beings, what is stuck in him completely and connects him to the environment, that doesn't enter so much into his consciousness. Something quite different streams into consciousness. Here it is just that which in the feeling life and in the life of thinking, the Oriental — particularly characteristic in the Oriental, the Indians — stream what apparently is experienced in human metabolism but experienced in such a way that in its spiritual reflection it presents itself exactly as spiritual life.

So, it seems to us that what comes out of the mind, out of the thinking of the oriental peoples, what they produce spiritually, is like a spiritual product coming out of the earth itself. When we immerse ourselves intensively, let the spiritually permeated Vedas speak to our souls, when we immerse ourselves into the instinctive Vedanta philosophy, into the yoga philosophy, when we immerse ourselves in the works of those like Lao Tzu, Confucius, when we have a sense at all for oriental poetry, oriental wisdom, then nowhere in this wisdom do we experience a feeling that it flows from a particular individual human, formed out of a personality. Just like the Oriental through his metabolism has developed alongside the natural environment, like the surrounding nature continues to web and weave, boil and simmer, that's how it is when we let its poetry, its poetic wisdom and its wise poetry work on us. It is as if the earth itself is speaking, as if the secrets of earthly growth would speak through the mouth of the Oriental to the whole of humanity on earth. One gets the feeling that the Oriental translates the inner spiritual secrets of the earth itself, in other words no other members of other peoples — no western people or people from the European centre — can translate or interpret what the secrets of the earth itself are.

Yes, if one wants to characterise the best members of the oriental folk it is as if they, when walking over the earth and wanting to express inner experiences of what is revealed as actually living under the surface of the earth, growing up from beneath this surface of the earth, blossoming and making fruit; it is revealed that what lives soul-spiritually in oriental humanity, is expressed at the same time in the inner earth. Through this we can understand why the Orientals, with all their being, for what is offered on the earth's surface as physical appearances, what is revealed as outer sensory facts, have little meaning. Within them they simultaneously carry subterranean earth forces in their own nature, towards the phenomena and facts. For this reason, they have little interest for what happens on the surface of the earth. They are metabolic people. Yet we see that this metabolism is revealed in them in a soul-spiritual manner.

What happens when an ideal rises in these people? Or, when these people feel an ideal which the oriental teachers of wisdom want to present to their pupils as a particular goal for the soul, they will express it somewhat like this: 'You must breathe in such and such a way, you must feel yourself in this or that way into the rhythm of human life.' — Instructions for the particular breathing rhythms, for a particular blood circulating rhythm, are what they give their pupils. It is extraordinary what the oriental teachers of wisdom give their pupils in order to rise to a higher level of consciousness and principles of feeling. The Oriental, as he stands in ordinary life, namely in as far as he belongs to the southern Asiatic peoples — is constituted according to metabolism. When a concrete ideal rises before him, as to how he can become a higher being, then he develops his rhythmic system, he looks for what he voluntarily trains as something higher which does not have to be acknowledged in natural phenomena.

Now it is extraordinary, when we, the more we go over from the Asiatic peoples into those in Europe, namely Central Europe, that in everyday life one finds particularly that member of human development revealed in what we call the rhythmic system. Particularly those peoples who live in Central Europe, not in the east nor in the west but in the centre of Europe — and as a blossoming within this race, it particularly emerges among German people — these peoples have in their everyday characteristics that which the Indian strives for as his ideal of higher man. There's a big difference between something first acquired through self-discipline, through freedom, or whether one has acquired it naturally, instinctively. The Central European person has in a natural way what the Oriental first must develop out of his metabolism which is closely linked with the earth. What is every-day and natural for the European is the ideal for the Asiatic, and so something else must become an ideal. The ideal for European people would be that which lie on a higher level: thinking life, as it is bound with the life of the nerves-senses.

These Central European people — how do they strive to express this externally in what seems to be bound to the spiritual scientific view as the tool of rhythmic life? The Oriental has something like unbridled imagination in his artistic creations; it really is something that rises like a haze from the inner earth process like mists from water. The rhythmic, inwardly united nature which is the essential thing in the life of Central

74

Europeans, already appeared in the old Greek peoples, from whom so much came forth into the whole of modern civilization, specifically in what we regard as the art of Europe. What appears to us as the expression of inner harmony of earthly human beings, where neither the material on the one side nor the etheric-spiritual on the other side is particularly developed, where the central part of the human being comes into expression, is what the Greek strived for. Look at the creation of oriental imagination: it flows to the one or to the other side. In Greece first the human form, artistically conceptualised, take on its harmonious curve, its inner unity. That is so because the Central European person captures the central part of his being in the rhythmic system. If he now imagines an ideal, then it takes place through his striving in an inner soul search, through his dialectic logic, through his scientific education; it is through the use of his organs of thought, just as with the Indian it is through the use of the rhythm linked organs in his being.

Like the Indian yogi sits and tries to organise his soul-spirit through breathing, so that it will make him go beyond the ordinary person, so the Central European — whose rhythmic system of the blood circulation and breathing develops instinctively and make him into a person — so the Central European is educated out of the thinking life. These ideas take on a form in the best individuals of Central Europe and translate, interpret, what the human being as such, is. That is what we notice when we hear about the deepening in artistic creations of the oriental peoples going over into those of European humanity.

With oriental artistic creations it is so that we, even in the highest of spiritual creations, see something like a blossoming of earthly evolution; the human mouth is similarly only there to allow the earth to express itself. This is not the case with Central European peoples, already since the time of the Greeks. With today's Central European people — if they follow their own nature and do not become untrue to themselves — it is so that when they want to echo their highest, express everything that they are as human beings, they would want to submit to acknowledging the fact that self-knowledge is the noblest fruit of human endeavour. The representation of the human being in the surrounding of people, in nature and history, that is the noblest human creation, which is finally what is essential when the Central European surrender to their own nature and essence.

Out of this we see how central Europe could actually allow such wonderful thoughts to develop as those we see in Goethe's book about Winckelmann — I would like to say it is like the sun of modern cultural life. In his book about Winckelmann, Goethe expresses all that lives in the higher feelings, deep thoughts and strong will of these prodigies, and compiles it all into his world view, by saying: "Now artistry enters, because by making man appear as the highest accomplishment of nature, he sees himself once again in all of nature, and nature itself must produce a pinnacle. To do this, he is enhanced by permeating himself with all the perfections and virtues, calling up choice, order and meaning and finally rises up to the production of the work of art, which, in addition to other deeds and works, occupies a brilliant position."

The human being gradually brings about a new nature out of his own spirituality. This directing of all human powers towards the comprehension of man himself, is what — according to folklore — is the most prominent in the Central European people when they are true to themselves; only in recent times this has withdrawn. There's every reason in the people of Central Europe to reflect, as they do when they follow their own nature and appreciate and understand it and penetrate the truly human as it is and should become.

If we now look from a more spiritual side, with a spiritual point of view towards the East with its ethnic groups, then we find that these oriental peoples have a spirituality which makes them aware of the connection the human soul created with the divine, precisely developed through them being metabolic peoples, while within them, to be completely natural, they must oppose that which hasn't come from the elementary world, because they must oppose what is the opposite in their consciousness; what is in their own nature. Through his heart the Oriental grasps and speaks about man's connection with the divine as something obvious, that no other member of any other people on earth can speak about in the same way. As a result, members of other peoples of earth, when they subjugated and conquered the Oriental peoples, even taking away their idiosyncrasies and imposing their own laws and orders on them, they were absorbing what the Orientals in connection with the divine had said, and took it up as something defining for themselves as well. We see lately how western peoples who have sunk into materialism, take on such oriental philosophies like those of old Lao Tzu, seeking refuge in Chinese points of view, in Indian world views — not so much as to discover ideas but to find that fervour, that in man can be sensed in connection with the divine, simply and strongly. It is more to enkindle feelings in such a way as the Orientals do in their speaking about the divine, to deepen themselves in oriental literature, and less to experience their philosophic content. However, the abstract nature of Europeans sometimes makes the concept of the Oriental inapplicable to the Europeans.

I have repeatedly had to encounter people who have read the sayings of Buddha with its endless repetitions and they have told me this should be shortened and republished; each repetition of a sentence should be omitted so one would not need to read repetitions. — I could only respond, repeatedly, by saying: You will learn nothing essential of what is great for the Oriental peoples because it is precisely contained in what you now want to omit. — Because, by the oriental reader endlessly repeating the sayings of Buddha, he reaches his ideal: the rhythmic recurrence of the motif. He returns ever and again to *that* sentence. What is an everyday occurrence to him is what is going on in himself as 'metabolic-man'; what is happening in him in the reoccurrence of Buddha's sayings is the most free striving in his soul-spiritual as a counter image of breathing: the blood circulation system.

If one really wants to become one with what is holy and great for the Oriental, one learns to recognise that as a member of another people it is something which one can't easily learn to recognise. The European has of course the need to eliminate repetition; because he lives in the rhythm of breathing, his ideal is to rise above it into thinking. Once a thought is grasped, he doesn't want repetitions; the European strives to go beyond repetitions.

You need to have another kind of understanding, not an outer thought-applied understanding, if you want to allow yourself to enter into such oriental repetitions. You need to develop an inner love for the various differences expressed individually and stand in front of these so that you can feel: What is regarded great for the one, the other does not have. — This you will only discover when you can love the other peoples, when you accept what is great for the other peoples.

Only when we enter deeply into the inner nature and being of peoples of the earth, do we find individual beings as so different, that we must say: the comprehensive human element actually doesn't appear through a single person, nor is it revealed by a member of a single nation, but it appears throughout all of mankind. If you, a single person, can recognise what you are as a total human being, so do peculiarities stroll in individual peoples all over the earth. Take in everything you can't have yourself, and only then are you a whole human being. You have that person in you; you only have to take notice of what is within you. What is revealed to the other, you don't have; you must seek it with him. You feel you need it. You feel it and now, when you find what is important for another person, what his peculiarity is, let it simply work into you. It becomes a need that you can't be without, what you receive from him, because it corresponds to your inner soul-spiritual desire.

The disposition to become a whole person is already within everyone, but we must find fulfilment by understanding the peculiarities of the being of the different peoples as they are spread over the earth. When we come to this spiritually, we can say to ourselves that in the Orient this spirituality is man's ability to express the divine as something natural in greatness.

However, today we find covered up as if by a layer that has to go away again, a layer of misunderstanding, something highly peculiar among the people of Central Europe, within the Central European people. If we look at all our great philosophers, among them those who thought about nature and god, I would like to say I have equally thought about it like this: There is nearly no great German philosopher, who has not in all intensity deepened the question: What is the law that prevails between one person and another? — The search for justice, however hidden and misunderstood, is a peculiarity of the Central European people. Whoever doesn't recognise this, doesn't understand these Central European people, and doesn't find the enthusiasm, from present materialism, which comes from something quite different, to find his way back to what actually in truth characterises these Central European peoples, this true German nature, this true German idiosyncrasy and being.

Just as the Oriental, himself being like a flower or fruit of the earth bringing its spiritual life into expression, he becomes the interpreter, the translator of the earth; likewise, the German becomes the interpreter of himself. He asks the same questions to himself. By his doing so, he stands in front of every other person as an equal and thus the burning question for him becomes the question of rights. Not the acquisition of the Roman laws but the research into legal nature — you find this in Fichte, in Hegel, with Schelling — everywhere where German thinking goes into the depths of the world. Finally we find as the abstract pursuit opposes the legal question, with Fichte, Hegel, Schelling and Humboldt, basically the same in concrete terms as when Goethe, in the course of all his searches, finds the expressions and statements of the true, closed in on all sides, harmonious human nature.

In this regard Goethe is the representative, I would like to say, of the essence of Central Europeans, the representative of the Central European, of the German people. Just as the Oriental relates to the earth, so the Central European relates to self-knowledge. Should we now go to the west of Europe, and further, we find the same characteristic expressed, over to America, of the true Occidental; we find that their essential nature is given to abstract thinking in particular. Westerners are predominant head people; the Orientals are the heart people who experience their heart in the process of metabolism; the Central European man is the human being of breathing who relates through this rhythm with the outer world. If I may use an image — as I believe — the extraordinary spiritually imbued Rabindranath Tagore used, the spiritual Oriental, then I could say: The Western person, The Occidental, the head person is used by Tagore who compares it with a spiritual giraffe — he loved them, one should not attach any kind of antipathy to using such a characteristic. He compared them with a spiritual giraffe, so one gets the feeling — essentially-spiritually it is shown — the head is distanced from the rest of the bodily nature, a long neck separates the head from the rest of the body, a head, which then only grasps abstract concepts, such abstraction which could result in the four abstract points of Woodrow Wilson. It has a long way to go until these abstract terms, these husks of words and empty ideas find their way to the heart, the lungs, the respiratory system, until they find the way to those places where they can become feelings, then be passed over into the will.

Here we have people whose characteristics are, what I would call, a thinking system. What the Central European aspires to as an ideal, what he yearns to achieve in freedom, the Westerner, namely the American, does not strive for in freedom; this he has been given as an instinct. He is an instinctual abstractionist. There's quite a difference whether a person is instinctive or whether this has been acquired. If it has been acquired, then it is quite differently connected to human nature — a person experiences it quite differently when he has freely acquired it than when his instincts have been granted through nature.

Here lies a great danger. You see, while the Indian can strive through his yoga philosophy through the rhythmic system, the Central European can aspire to the thinking system, but in the case of Western mankind, if it is not to lose its humanity, it should lose the "spiritual giraffe" of a head. Westerners are incumbent indeed upon what I have openly said where there is a gathering of Westerners: they are incumbent upon what must be characterised as the great responsibility of what present day Western humanity has. Western specification, Western folklore will be lost, obliterated, if it aspires through a system of thinking; if it reaches into the void or into empty spiritism, and where one finds a spiritual void, the spiritual is sought. Here lies the big danger but also the responsibility: the danger to reach the soul-void through aspiring beyond what has been given to human beings through natural causes, and the responsibility to reach up to real spiritual science — if you don't let it, through its world dominance, contribute to the demise of humanity.

By contrast, Central Europeans will have a healthy aspiration for freedom, which will lead them into spirituality, bring them to spiritual science. I might say: The peoples of Central Europe have a holy duty — because it's in their system — to ascend the spiritual ladder to spiritual cognition. They acquire, by their moving from their rhythmic- and breathing system to the thinking system, always still in something which lies in the human condition. For the Westerners there is the danger that they forsake the purely human, especially if they have adopted an ideal form — hence all those who are now regarded as general human beings, sectarian aberrations and similar endeavours of the West. This is certainly not clearly seen at present.

As with the case of the Oriental whose metabolic system is turned to the earth, a spiritual process along natural paths appear, so with the Westerners who have primarily developed their thinking system, the regard to the world of the senses is revealed. With the Oriental it is like something which works beneath the earth's surface; with the Westerner it is as if he only sees what is on the earth's surface, what he can see as facts appearing through the sun, moon and stars, through air and water. What happens in the environment could not be explained by thinking. I have mentioned in previous lectures here, how that which is spiritual within people, can't be explained by the outer world.

The Oriental knew himself, through what flowed as spiritual-earthly-blood through his own human condition, revealed what lived in him spiritually, as someone belonging to the entire cosmos, a member not only of the earth, but a member of the whole cosmos. What the Westerner developed particularly as a system of thinking — through modern science — was that nothing more of this cosmos remained for him except what he could calculate through formulae of mathematics and mechanics. Therefore the area in which the Westerner must see himself, from where his soul originated, if he must admit that as a thinking human being he couldn't have come from cosmic origins, then, in this sphere, he must say to himself: I have no other science than dry, sober mathematics. —

The Oriental has grown out of what flooded from the earth itself, into his individual human condition. What he reveals in his poetic wisdom is the blossoming of the earthly. What the Central European recognises as human is the same as what another person reveals through himself: here the human being confronts himself.

In the Westerner the most valuable thing is just that which is not derived from the earthly, but what he has from the cosmos. However, he has no other means to acknowledge the super-earthly, other than through calculation or spectral analysis which is probably as dry as calculating and the like, or even by similar hypotheses. This way the Westerner searches for what the Oriental in his inner nature seeks as an expression of his relationship with the divine, what the Central European seeks as an expression of the human in the Goethean wholeness of being, or in the lawmakers who see equality for all, the Westerner seeks by devoting himself preferably to the economic life. What the Westerner means when he speaks about rights, through which he characterises the spirit, flowers in him only through economic life. For this reason it is quite natural that Karl Marx came out of Germany where he could have, if he was blessed with the ability, to, in a humanistic, in a Goethean sense, come to know what the human being is, that he had to go towards the west, towards England to be shown the way to the human being, to see over into actual human nature and come to the belief that what the human being can acknowledge is no more than an ideology, as something that rises out of economic life.

This is no absolute truth but it forms a foundation in a certain way in the nature of Western people, just as it is the foundation in the nature of Orientals, to regard nature as a minor planet in relation to human beings, and that they can speak of the connection of the human soul to divinity as if it is something self-evident. As a result of this so many Westerners who feel a need to look at the divine, develop a longing — then, if they extend their conquest beyond the Oriental peoples — they take what these people have to say regarding the relationship which human nature has with divinity, because in human beings, as I've already said, there's a need to be full human beings.

So we see — and we could also extend this to smaller groups of peoples, to individual peoples, we can only refer to what is typical — we see, that actually a full human being is not expressed in the members of a people. We see that this full human being lies in us as a need and out of this need, only love to all other human beings must grow, particularly for these human qualities which we do not have, which we can only acquire by devotionally seeking the knowledge for that essence that lives in other peoples on earth, and to connect it with our own people.

This has been the kind of internationalism that prevailed in the time of Goethe. This has been the kind of internationalism which saturated Wilhelm von Humboldt's "The limits of Effectiveness of the State." This quest for cosmopolitanism is achieved by taking up, through love for all other peoples, the essence of one's own people, ennobling and elevating what comes from one's own people to find in other people what they find as great and good. So, even in Germany's intellectual heyday, there emerged out of the rhythmic life what at that time, in the noblest cosmopolitanism, was found by Germans searching among all other peoples. See how Herder went on his quest to all nations, how he sought to unravel the deepest essence of all peoples of the earth! See how he permeated with what basically lives in us all — ensouling the single, individual flesh person that we each carry around — into a greater, more powerful, different ensouled human being who lives though us, but who can only be found when we pour ourselves out like this over all peoples.

One needs to note what happened at the turn of the 18th and 19th Century as the system applied to the largest part in Central Europe, to confront what is today known as internationalism, you can't say it pulsed through the world but was preached through the world, seducing mankind, as Marxism — Marxism, which only believes in human thinking and *that* in a more or less weakened form, which didn't have a clue of how all of humanity was differentiated all over the world, which believes that humanity, as human beings, can be forced into an abstract form. Marxism isn't the first in the rise, it is the last in the decline, one of the last in the decline because it is devoid of all striving for true internationalism because precisely though taking up what can be gained through love of all peoples, it elevates one's own folklore. This internationalism which appears in Marxism and all its derivatives, means getting immobilised in one-sided systems of thinking, in impractical thought systems, which are merely pinned to the sensual world and does not penetrate folklore.

By contrast, true internationalism corresponds to kindling the love which touch all peoples, the light which all peoples may receive in order for deeds, experiences, creations of individual people to become a great choir of all peoples on the earth, that this may contribute to the full understanding of peoples, an understanding which can only unite what comes out of true, essential, mutual knowledge of the peoples of the earth.

Now, my dear friends, today I wanted to speak of what kind of knowledge could unite peoples of the earth. I didn't want to talk about other things which could be more programmatic or details of spiritual science itself. I wanted to speak about what as a spiritual scientific knowledge, is inspired through other spiritual research about the possible course of love flowing into community life of peoples on the earth. One can quite certainly characterise the most varied points of view needed for the future of humanity. One can certainly speak about those impulses. However one has to admit that to everything in the social political, in the legal state area, what can be said in the area of education has to join in — illuminating all this — that comfort, that soul comfort, that spiritual comfort that can come from such insights as have been tried today, I would like to say, suggested in a rather cursory sketch rather than something more comprehensive. Consolation can come from insights which are based on rhythm, the possible, I say explicitly possible, rhythm related to human factual life, which we want to get to know the day after tomorrow in all its peculiarities though spiritual science: that that, which has lived through history, shows how it directly stuck inside our immediate present.

Today's considerations will show you that it is possible from the waves on which hate and antipathy have flooded over humanity, also healing from the knowledge of unity has emerged from a wave of international human love and a love of nations, just like new wave crests appear from out of the troughs. It is possible. However, we live in an epoch where what is possible in people must be consciously and wilfully aspired to. People must look at which conditions of unity among peoples of the earth exist so that each single one can contribute his knowledge to it, so that after the wave of hate, the wave of human love may follow. Only out of his human love can that be healed, that hate has destroyed. If love is not willed, then destruction will remain. That is the terrible alternative which confronts people's souls, people of discernment. Whoever really experiences this dreadfulness would say to themselves: Souls dare not sleep otherwise it could happen that through spiritual powerlessness of the sleep of nations, they will be unable to rise from the wave of hatred up to the wave of love.

Whoever can see this through, will take in the knowledge which comes to him from a spiritual view of the relationships of peoples. He will take up this knowledge in his feelings and develop human love out of it. He will take this up in his will and develop human deeds out of it. He would say to himself: The development of time itself, everything that appears so frighteningly, so paralysing in the present, I will place before my soul as a duty: In the face of all that has in the most modern time right up to the present caused fragmentation in humanity, I will gather it all to be united through what is love in humanity. — This unity through love, to seek for this unifying through love, is not only a feeling which somehow or other develops in us, but it appears in those who look through relationships in the present, as the biggest duty of humanity in our present time.

Mankind's history in the light of Spiritual Science
Stuttgart on 12 March 1920

My dear honourable friends! Thoughts and spiritual struggles which recently separated the affairs of individual peoples due to their specific education, must by necessity become a general matter in the entire development of humanity at present. Such a generalization, which recently had been more or less a concern in the thoughts of individuals, regarding acquiring relationships for the peculiarities of individual peoples living on the earth, was what I mentioned the day before yesterday. Today I want to speak about another matter; I want to speak about what is regarded as history, the evolution of humanity in the broadest sense of the word, under the influence of the latest striving in humanity.

Quite recently the question arose: How should we actually relate to human history? – This was more or less a matter of scholarship. The excellent artistic writer, artistic thinker and observer of art, Herman Grimm, made a remark, which I have allowed myself to mention several times here in these lectures, a remark of extraordinary importance regarding the evaluation of our view of history. Herman Grimm said, by wanting to characterise what is mostly regarded as history and historic writing, that people today felt with this kind of history they have to drag too much ballast along with them.

While we certainly admire what has been revealed in recent years from all kinds of excavations and discoveries of external documents of humanity, we still need to admit that this gathered material, the noteworthy accumulated material of history, today lacks the great points of view in the historical consideration of mankind. These important viewpoints are the one and only things which give history a value in life. When does history have a value in life for mankind? It only has value when that, which can be thought through, which can be seen through in past human destinies and human expression, provide results for our own souls, something which warms our own being, which can enkindle the mind and develop forces which can be made our own and position us correctly in life. In this regard we can already say that we have to drag ballast along in present historical considerations while great points of view, which we need today regarding burning needs in present day humanity, are missing.

Not as if historical consideration of earlier times in their way had such great viewpoints. Not as if we value what it could mean for a young man, for a young girl, to get to know the great figures in ancient history and emulate them and retain a saying the poet used: "Everyone has to choose his hero, whose path he copies up the hill to find Olympus". The way such individual role models were chosen and what was being tested by them, is to be absorbed into one's own will, which depended on you living in a time when a lively admiration could sprout forth for personalities, and for legal, state or church figures, who were flourishing at that time, from where we originate after all. Expressing it rather radically one could say: Today we could, in the same way as earlier, warm young people toward Alexander the Great, since they have become more or less indifferent to what Alexander the Great himself regarded as his ideal. In earlier times masses of people looked towards single ones who attended to the affairs within encompassing kingdoms which they conquered so that history in its old form with its great viewpoints could have an effect on humanity, namely on the will of the people.

This is the most significant fact in modern history, that members of the broad masses of humanity take part in all public life and that everything that can have a human face to it, wants to join in and look at affairs as if these are their own affairs. This is the thing which finally considers how the democratic spirit floods into our present. People participate in the big public affairs of life while they have become more or less indifferent to what had inspired their relatives of earlier ages. Here, above all, is the point – because the spiritual interests of mankind have democratically spread to all people – here is the point, the necessity, for how to arrive at a new way of looking at history. For those who want to allow unbiased facts of present events to work on them without prejudice, especially for those who are well aware of the hardships of the present time, they are among many who have idealistic or ideal questions among the great spiritual questions, it is this: How do we bring the contemplation of our forefathers into the child and then into the young person in order to have such an effect, such an experience, that it toughens the will, that life's orientation can be clarified precisely through the influence of such a historic method of observation?

So, what interests we have after all, as human beings – that spirit is interwoven in the developmental history of our earthly lineage - we let it weave into the big questions of education, pedagogy, didactics, weaving it fundamentally into the big social question of the present. It is concerned with what we said yesterday and in lectures the previous week, to live in the intellectual epoch where the mind plays the leading role in ordering human affairs. This human mind in its sobriety, its dryness, has not been suitable to write history in such a way that it could really become what it should become in the sense of what has just been said, if it is to receive the right value for humanity. Just here is where spiritual science believes it is able to lead towards a new formation of a historical approach.

Spiritual science assumes that knowledge is gained through increasing the inner life of the human being. What is regarded as our knowledge and other human capabilities in ordinary life, should be developed through spiritual science towards a higher seeing and this higher seeing directed to an elevated soul life; it should be developed as a child's capabilities are developed from a lower stage to that higher stage of capabilities of a grown-up person; out of the inner human being's sleeping capabilities it should be allowed to spring forth. Strengthened thinking, a strict self discipline through the will, should lift out powers of vision and knowledge from the deepest inner human being which could reach into those spiritual depths of the world and of human existence, of which they would have no clue without these developed capabilities. That's the peculiarity of this spiritual knowledge which is meant here, that it takes hold of the whole person.

When we can admit to ourselves that with our striving for clarity, intellectual knowledge, which has grown so big in the last three to four centuries, not only rules our life of knowledge but also our practical life, when we admit that it's preferable in addressing our intellectual nature as humans, then we must say that spiritual science does not strive any less for full clarity, for inner logic, for clear concepts, but that these concepts, while before, they had been derived from previously practiced thinking and previously practiced will, they do draw on the powers of the whole person.

It would be a great mistake to believe that spiritual science, as it is meant here, wants to be created out of dark feelings, that this spiritual science wants to have something in common with all the nebulous, mystical streams with which one can so easily become confused. No, its path will be such that it will gain spiritually clear ideas and insights in the same way as science is striving for clear, precise and exact knowledge. However these ideas should spring up out of such a development of human soul life - despite its clarity, despite its exactness – that its power would fulfil the whole human being, taking the whole person into consideration. We are as a rule not engaged with our temper and feelings when we discern today's scientific formulations, because these scientific formulations of laws call out little incentive for the will. One can say that what is recognised in the sphere of spiritual science regarding world coherences, so readily pulses through a human being and changes him, that it pours into his will and he orientates and positions himself in practical life, in order to accomplish single deeds in accordance with the great mission of humanity on earth.

If one wants to understand in a correct way what it is about – I have often characterised in lectures details how such knowledge may be arrived at – then one will easily have insight into what follows.

When one, first of all, looks at the human body, one really only does it through an observation made in the present moment. If one looks at the human limbs, as a lay person or scientist, in the way the body is presented, then we are actually considering what is before us in the present even though this human body contains traces of its past within it. We hardly consider, while we look at the human body, what this body preserves from the past, no matter how scientific. If we move forward to ordinary spiritual life, things will be different, we don't just see the human being in the present but we see ourselves as human beings in our own past, right up to just before birth. In a thoughtful way we grasp everything we have experienced, in essential points. Then we know we would be mentally ill if we could not properly expand the memory of our experiences. There we stretch out the interest from the present moment to our immediate past. Yes, we stretch it in a different way by wanting to gain from impulses and forces of the past, what we can work into our future. We connect the present with the past and the future.

So a certain elevation in methods of observation is already apparent in ordinary life when we rise from a bodily to a soul experience. If we now proceed from soul experiences and develop them in us in such a way that they strengthens our thinking, letting thinking become seeing, then from will move to inner spiritual experience, something quite different turns out. When we look over our own few decades which we have lived as earthlings, where we have come from our individual childhood to grown adults – look over our existence as our ordinary soul life – then a new element of our entire being steps in from our inner life, our own past steps into our memories. If we extend our human being further through spiritual cognition, when we develop beyond earthly cognition to see the spiritual, then the connection of evolution of the whole of mankind enters into our vision. As paradoxical as it may appear to many members of present day humanity, it should still be said: Much will depend on a healthy, prosperous soul-spiritual development in the future, for you to see how the human being – through grasping inwardly his own human power, his power of cognition – becomes one with all of humanity. What we research in outer documents about history can be supplemented by what we, through our inner knowledge, can recognise: our connection to all of humanity and feeling ourselves as a real member of humanity.

Here is the way which I can only indicate as a sketch today: spiritual scientifically it firstly rises to a comprehensive historical point of view to then continue further as a common theme in the evolutionary history of humanity.

Science which, with a certain authority in modern time, includes the physical bodily nature of mankind, speaks about a so-called biogenetic basic law. It has become famous in connection with the examination of ancestry in more recent times. I need to characterize it here only in a few words. It is said that the human being, before being born and still in the mother's body as an embryo, repeats all the stages of development, represented as individual animal forms. Development begins when the embryo resembles a lower animal by its fish-like form. It then develops through to higher animal forms, gradually taking on a human form, which then sees the light of day. Added to this it is said: Human evolution is a repetition of those physical, animal-like forms which the embryo goes through before it has taken on its human form. The development which the human being undergoes from conception to birth is a brief repetition of what human beings, it is said, has gone through in the development of his form. People are now trying with this outer mental examination – you can't call it anything else – to connect it to scientific results, whose greater or lesser authority I will not dwell upon here. People have also tried to see the soul-spiritual historical aspect of humanity in a similar way. People want to take what developed into culture at present, what people of the present day regard as civilized people, people with a certain education, and consider it with connection to the past, like they look at the embryonic development in relation to the past. People have come as far as wanting to research how ancient cultures somehow are repeated in childhood and how, when a person grows up, he repeats later cultures and so on, until he – after he had from birth to childhood repeated earlier epochs – he develops out of this what we actually have as a living human being.

Spiritual science enables certain self knowledge precisely through its spiritual exercises, so that through the strengthening of soul forces it provides an intimate judgement of people which in this way gains a more precise observation of one's own - or the course of life of others - than what is possible with the superficial possibilities or through the search of today's soul sciences or the like. That's when it turns out that man, if he can be made aware through spiritual science of the possibility of a true self-knowledge, is advancing, and actually through this self-knowledge gains something different than is usually assumed today. This self-knowledge through spiritual science provides much about childhood; not exactly according to scientific methods, but this spiritual science has extraordinary things to say about the periods of childhood. This alone is important for the renewal of pedagogy; it only requires a precise and honest application of ordinary human abilities in order to understand the developing child and become a proper teacher and educator of this child when you are directed by spiritual scientific principles, also when you haven't seen it yourselves. One can be a capable teacher in the sense of spiritual science, if one only has the honest will to respond intimately to the development of the human in the child, even without sight.

With reference to the older stages of development in the lives of individuals it is not so. What is important here only comes to one's awareness when one's own cognitive abilities have been thus strengthened as they can be within spiritual science. Then one notices that from about the thirtieth year of human life onwards there are already inner abilities which are hardly indicated; one notices that these to a certain extent intimately appear in the soul life out of mysterious depths, that they firstly announce themselves so weakly in ordinary life that they can't be handled property – they are so weak that they become drowned out by the storms of external affairs of the world upon the individual. One needs intimate observation in order to see what is taking place in people's mature years that want to rise up continuously in their soul life, which doesn't resemble its original form but as if it were the echo of something completely different than it is now. If one looks more closely, then through spiritual observation one discovers something quite extraordinary: if one wants to observe the natural foundation of people in relation to what people have gone through in their prehistoric forms, then one has to go back to embryonic development, to the period of development preceding childhood; one must go back to the beginning of life.

If one wants to look at the historical evolution of humanity, one has to look at the final years of an individual's development. Look at the intimate skills which scurry through the inner soul, which do not really surface. These are only rudiments, indications of something that has gone before, the historical past, as today the suggestive forms of embryonic development in the womb are suggestive forms of what had happened historically. For the natural development in human beings one has to go back to the beginning of life; for the historical development one has to, through the sharpening of powers of cognition from spiritual science, acquire a view of the end of human life. If one wants to penetrate what I could call a faint sunset approaching mankind today, if one has passed the thirties then one has learnt to recognise in these shadows that flutter up in the soul life, what makes us understand another person, echoing from long gone times of human development. One is then looking at what one calls prehistoric cultures, yes, one even sharpens one's eye for the prehistoric, which only left an echo in history; one allows one's gaze to drift back from the Vedanta philosophy of the Indian, the Vedas, back to where they came from, from where they must have originated, for they do not show themselves as original products, but as final results. From this one can learn to recognise what this strange element of power is based on, that flowed through the ancient Indian culture, this first dawn of an earth culture. One finds a kinship with the shadowy part of human old age compared with what was provided for in primeval times as a youthful freshness in the culture. Gradually one learns to recognise the spiritual reversal of the biogenetic fundamental law in nature. One learns to recognise that in these ancient times to which one has to return in order to understand the evolutionary history of mankind, the human being needs to be connected, through keeping up to his latest age of physical development, with the soul spiritual capacity of development.

During our childhood today we make an important jump for our soul life around the seventh year, when the change of teeth starts; here a very important developmental period in the child's life comes to an end. The body goes through a metamorphosis guided by a soul-spiritual development. Then again, at the start of puberty, the body undergoes metamorphosis and also here the soul-spiritual constitution of the human being accompanies this bodily metamorphosis. What develops at these stages of life includes a soul-spiritual development simply because the body also experiences these developments. Then for us human beings the possibility disappears of seeing such transformations, or even admitting to such transformation. Admittedly it is very clear that we still go through a transformation at the beginning of our twenties; it is just more intimate yet it is clearly there. What appears at the end of our twenties and even what appears later, are actually only present in a shadowy way. Only those who have sharpened their gaze through spiritual science will notice how these shadows of transformations rise up, these transformations having been clearly present in earlier human evolutionary stages. Just as today the child's transition through the change of teeth and through puberty experiences it simultaneously in the body and spirit, how through this we are natural human beings, simultaneously going through a soul-spiritual development and as it were feel ourselves as whole human beings in our development – while later our soul-spiritual becomes separate and goes its own way – so in earlier evolutionary epochs man and earth, together, clearly went through a bodily metamorphosis at the same time.

Once we have grasped how the human being during the first historic period which we can research, lived on the earth in his body, how he felt by living in his body up to a ripe old age, then we understand that quite a different language was uttered in the oldest documents which speak about the historic development of humanity. Then we also understand the freshness with which these wisdom-filled documents meet us. Then we understand what had at that time been poured out as poetic and which we today produce as only abstract philosophy, we understand how a Confucius brings forth the higher

95

wisdom when we know that this which we only experience in childhood, has been experienced in those ages when hair had already started turning grey. Even then man still experienced his physical being. He wasn't speaking in a more abstract soul-spiritual way, he spoke out in full lifeblood regarding the most abstract affairs of mankind. This is the stream we encounter not only from writings, but also from what has been handed down and overheard in public affairs of these prehistoric people.

When we look back we feel we are members of this entire human development, this development of humanity, we feel what it must mean that in these times the human being, despite becoming aged, remained child-like and experienced everything as children do, but what today is experienced as sober and dry in old age. People believed, because their inner soul life had a different colouring, people believed that the way people lived together was such that the childlike, the youthful person looked up differently to the older person than is possible today. The younger person could say to himself: When I become old myself, something will rise up within me which is only possible when I have become old; one can be happy about becoming old because aging gives one a kind of joy which you can only experience once you have aged. One could also look up at old age in other ways than if one believes the aged only have a sober and abstract outer countenance – like people are made to believe today. The entire positioning of man in relation to the world therefore becomes something different.

We can understand the entire character of ancient times in a different, inner way, not merely as outwardly dry, if we allow ourselves to feel into the primal times of human development. We learn to understand how there was a first period of human development in which the human being lived in such a way in his body, that he experienced his bodily stages of development simultaneously as soul-spiritual fact in the same way we feel today when we experience something soul-spiritual as such. At that time people felt themselves in full harmony with nature. The person of this olden time hadn't had the possibility to despise any material thing, to underestimate or even overestimate something because for him all spirituality revealed itself in material things. He ate and he drank but what he absorbed from food and drink was revealed to him as spiritual. He wasn't aware of matter only. He could, after taking fruit from trees and taking joy in the fruit, say to himself: Through the blood, in all that grows, in the power of the trees, the divine works, it gives me fruit as a gift; I experience the divine directly in myself in this respect because I go with a spiritual-bodily relationship into the world.

In this way the human being experienced in the first earthly epochs that he was spiritually linked to how he ran his economic affairs, ran legal matters and spiritually interacted with nature and other people. He experienced God as present on earth, he experienced God in all that was also revealed physically – of a spiritual life separated from materiality he did not yet know. Everything presented to him as earthly-sensually, he also experienced spiritually; he orientated himself in his organizations according to what was revealed to him as divine.

The organizations that people of that time were making, one can only call them theophany (a visible but not necessarily material manifestation of the Diety - translator). One can only describe it by saying: Through everything that people experienced inwardly, what was within them and around them in the environment was spiritual; what happened in economic life was only a reflection of the spiritual, like a shadow of the spiritual.

It is quite erroneous for spiritual scientific observations to regard ancient humanity as something animal-like living out of animal instincts, like superior apes. It is clear through spiritual science that the human being started from a physical experience but that his experience of matter was spiritually-divine; everything about his affairs was a mirror-image, a reflection of the soul-spiritual established on earth. Man started his historical evolution from matter albeit out of a spiritual experience. He only progressed further when he stopped being able to discern in a more advanced age, in the forties or even in the early fifties, the inner soul-spiritual metamorphoses in harmony with his aging body. The human being was reduced, already in younger years, to be locked out of a sense of unity of the soul-spiritual and the physical. During the earlier cultural age the human beings could sense a harmony between the physical and soul-spiritual right up into his thirties but no further. In the middle of life he could experience coming into his thirtieth year, in what is called, the physical-spiritual, but then it stopped, just like today the ordinary earthly life ends earlier, how we already feel older earlier, without us really experiencing aging inwardly with the body.

During the second period of human development – it began about 8th century BC – the wonderful folklore which still falls into our life in modern times, gained such a great, gigantic influence on the whole civilized world, came into the development of the Greek people. Whoever is unable to feel how basically this great Grecian folklore differs from ours, doesn't really understand the developmental history of humanity.

Oh, this Greek folklore! You really enrich your life when you put yourself in the shoes of the Greek, no longer remaining young like the ancient human being up to a ripe old age, but who could feel up to the middle of life as a unified human being, and still in the thirties sense a soul-spiritual connection with the body, a bit like we sense it up to the time of adolescence. That which lived and weaved there as a unit in Greek nature is what created the foundation of this harmonious art and for this spiritual creation of Greek culture. This possibility that people could in the midlife of existence still sense life as a whole, as inner harmony, made it possible that from old forms of artistic creation, drama and musical feeling could develop to what we know as Greek culture. We only really get to know the true human part of Greek culture when we link our gaze to the individual Greek.

Oh, this Greek! He should be our representative of this second epoch of the evolution of humanity. He still saw nature around him in a different way to us. Because the growing forces of his soul-spiritual nature was still being taken into account up to the thirtieth year of his life, growing forces streamed right into his sense observations.

Whoever can sense what bodily-physical powers work into the being of a person so that he expresses himself soul-spiritually right up to his thirties, must say to himself: Into the very senses themselves another force pushes in and because of this, another kind of concept of sensory reality is the result. In this way one can learn to sense into the entire development of humanity, one learns to sense into individualities of prehistoric times. One learns to feel how he looked at his surroundings in such a way that nature with all its flowers, with all its other expressions, yes, with stars, sun and moon, with clouds and so on, in all nuances of impressions, worked differently on him, than it works on us. When you pursue with your feelings as to what was different for the ancient Greek, one can say to oneself inwardly in recognition: The Greek vividly felt the very light in his natural environment, everything that stood out, that was lit up and glowed - while he had no sense for anything that didn't shine or glow.

Whoever believes that the Greeks saw their surroundings in the same way we do, has no sense for the historical development of humanity; he looks at it like a forty-year old who believes that the child sees its environment in just the same way he sees it. However, the Greek, who lived in the second epoch of human development, saw nature around him as alive in greater vividness. He saw what shone and glowed around him, what spoke directly to people, he saw also in other people, what was more active between one person and another, what was shining more from one person to another person. Right into the skin colours of the face of another person, the Greek saw them differently as to how we see our contemporaries. This is what spiritual science can reveal, from its discerning compassion for the evolutionary history of mankind. This is not disproved through outer observation, but fully confirmed, in whatever way one might argue about these things.

Whoever examines Greek literature without prejudice, will notice that the Greek actually does not have a word for *blue*. They have the word γλαύκος (glaukos) with which to indicate dark hair and also the dark-coloured eyebrows of certain people, and with the same expression they also refer to the blue stone lapis lazuli. They use the same word for everything which is blue and black or even dark. It is quite interesting also that they have a word for green Χλωροσ (chloros) but with this word they also simultaneously pointed to yellow resin, to honey and hair – like blue-blind people today can't distinguish between green and yellow. Hence we can say: external history also confirms that the Greek saw the light colours as those which were important to him, and he did not yet have a strong enough feeling for blue, for the dark colours, that he could even describe this feeling in particular. Here we are looking at quite a different bodily-soul constitution of the Greek person. This gives us a historical observation which inwardly recognises the course of progress over the whole earth. This directs us to the inner being of humankind.

When we now continue in this way and have once followed such a point of view, then other issues can be considered in a similar way. Then one can understand why Roman writers tell us Greek painters had painted with only four colours, with black, white, red and yellow and didn't mention they also painted with blue. Perhaps they also had what we see as blue, and covered the surface with it, but they didn't call it blue. Everything they experienced was only in as far as it was bright or lit and shone. That means they lived in a life empowered by nature and didn't know about the element of contemplation. One learns to recognise that this contemplative element in the developmental history of mankind can only appear, even if the thirties no longer affect man in such a way that he is able to perceive the soul-spiritual still in harmony with the bodily-physical, when a sense of unity, so to speak, where one experiences the simultaneous metamorphosis of the bodily physical with the soul-spiritual, stops in the twenties. From then on, there develops what the human body is most readily regarded for, the aging body, developing what in earlier epochs had in full clarity only been as traces, in shadows. If you research these things without prejudice, then you can say that in our present epoch normally the dependence of the soul-spiritual on the bodily-physical ends around the age of 26 or 27 for normal people, if the human being himself doesn't get a hold on his inner development, for then the only things that arise within him are what had settled in him from his education while still a child.

Now something extremely meaningful appears when we consider human evolution in this way. Let's look back at earlier times in human evolution. We can understand that people were more satisfied with an education where the human being grew up with his surroundings by imitating natural conditions. We only see the deep human importance of education and teaching in essence appear in the third, "contemplative" epoch. We learn to realize how we are situated in the evolutionary history of the whole of humanity; we no longer feel our relationship to all of humanity as something abstract. We sense our mission in this particular time epoch; by belonging to it we realize in particular, for example, the educational tasks approaching mankind – one of the most important being the social question belonging to it.

During the first epoch of humanity and as an echo in the second epoch, in his youth man could say to himself – according to what he learnt from moods and communications of the older people – by you growing up and turning older, you will experience this and that, which you simply through your bodily transformation will experience in an older age. – In our time the thing that makes a person fulfilled in old age must be germinated by his education and training in his youth. More and more the time is coming – it is already here to a large extent – where we have to feel the strong commitment to educate the youth in such a way that at quite a later age he will be reminded about what he had learnt during his years of schooling. While life in its most elementary events no longer gives one what had been given in earlier epochs of mankind, now, what is experienced during years of schooling would have to work - I would like to call it – in an elastic way, in order for it to be joyful and uplifting and inspiring and invigorating for the whole of life right up to turning grey, colouring and illuminating life. In a way such as this, history can acquire points of view; in such a way history can give us insights which in turn can strengthen the will and give orientation in life.

To this spiritual science repeatedly call our attention - that we endeavour to penetrate more deeply into our life and existence, into those regions where this life and this existence are uncovered as spiritual, which can directly render service to practical life.

The kind of history that just indicates the outer surface will not be able to offer a person such vastness in his consideration of historical development which can offer life forces at the same time. It also doesn't give him ideas towards the solution of what happened in human evolution.

It is extraordinary when one hears, for example, that one of the great historians of the epoch just past, Ranke, was always doubtful of how the figure of Christ Jesus should be placed into human history. His conviction was to position the figure of Christ Jesus as purely religious, which means to regard it on a different page to the one we usually view history. He wasn't in the position to allow the Christ life into history as a creative power. Herman Grimm tried to improve on this deficiency of Ranke's view, but he did not succeed because with this viewpoint, under today's restrictions of the present day and age, something can only succeed if done through a spiritual scientific approach.

What has the human being basically become through his development as "more contemplative", that he has developed towards contemplation since the middle of the 15th Century in this intellectualized period? What has he become through developing all those things in the area of technology, in the field of external life and external insights out of intellectualism, which is, even so, something big?

In the first epoch and for the most part still in the second one in which the Greek can be our representative, there the person felt himself as a member of the entire world, simply through his body being a member of the whole world. He saw lightening and instinctively knew that the power inherent in lightening was connected with the power living in his own feelings. He sensed himself within the world's existence. His inner life was rich because he felt himself to be a member of the whole world while what lived and weaved in him as a human being, was the same as what lived and weaved in the whole world. He regarded his destiny in the movement of the stars. He could follow not only nature's laws into the most distant heights of heaven, but also what was morally in him, this he could follow into the cosmic widths.

Today we have other experiences. Since the beginning of a renewed spiritual life in the third evolutionary period of humanity, we have experienced, as thoughtful humanity, how well we can calculate with Galilean magnificence and Bruno's insight, when looking up into the starry worlds. However, we don't derive anything from them but mathematical, mechanical formulae regarding planets and the sun's course, and at most all that spectral analysis has to say about it today. Here on earth we have become lonely. We know we are standing on this earth, but we no longer feel we have a relationship to the world of the stars.

If we are honest, living within the contemporary mechanistic point of view, we no longer feel like a vital member of the world. Lonely, we stand on our earth in space, and about that which is not our earth, we only calculate. Could we actually, if we are honest, still develop a biblical belief that out of this world which we calculate so well, from out of these heavenly heights the Christ could descend, to fulfil the important event which would make sense of the whole of earthly evolution?

What humanity has conquered through calculation, through mechanistic knowledge, are things brought down through spiritual understanding of the evolutionary history of human beings themselves. Spiritual science will only connect meaning to it again, if that, which lived in Jesus, having come down from spiritual heights, concludes the great marriage of the spiritual world with the earthly human beings for the salvation of humanity. That the Mystery of Golgotha is spiritual is something which can reach human souls with full clarity only through spiritual science. Only when the Mystery of

Golgotha is thus experienced through a spiritually scientifically renewed viewpoint, can one say, spiritual science pushes itself further, apparently only as an incidental fact in human evolutionary history but which has a shattering effect on those who can feel it in all its depths.

Then one discovers that by characterising the inverted biogenetic basic laws, a fact which says: That which the human being experiences today during different age periods in his individual development are shadowy indications of what clearly had been experienced soul-bodily in his forefathers and is, still today, being experienced in external human metamorphoses from earlier developmental epochs. How, in a natural way, the physical human being is in embryonic steps of development a repetition of what had been experienced in his human ancestry over millions of years, today appears during the age periods of human beings as a shadowy repetition of what was clearly, inwardly, present in pre-humanity. In this way we connect the relationship of our present life to that of prehistoric times.

When you research through spiritual science, according to what I have often characterised here and what you can read in my books "Knowledge of the Higher Worlds", "Occult Science" and "Riddles of the Soul" you will find facts which enable you to say that it is possible through inner sight to discover how, in the pre-Christian times, the human being remained able during his development, to inwardly experience his soul-spiritual and also his bodily-physical nature right up to his thirties, right into the last year of his thirties. Then this went further down, right into our time where the third epoch in the developmental history of mankind, the human beings experience the soul-spiritual together with the physical-bodily only up to his twenties. In between lies an important transition in human life.

The human being, in that he has shaped his developmental history over the earth, has, so to speak, descended from the youthful and childlike experience of aging in those times and only experienced this unity into his thirties. From the depths of the world the form was revealed to him which lived as a model for him into his thirties as to how he should live, so that he could absorb the strength in his youth

104

and carry this strength, absorbed during his youth, into old age. In the time following the Mystery of Golgotha, the human being can no longer carry the strength resulting from natural development into old age which he needs for that age. That is why the life of Christ Jesus, which only reaches into the middle of earthly life, has been presented to him on earth, which is a divine-human example for man up to the 33rd year. By grasping the strong forces in this example, one can inwardly understand: "Not I, but Christ in me"; so that we direct all education, all schooling to be Christ-imbued throughout, that in its youth we let the child absorb these forces, who then, as I've indicated, can with time-linked elasticity stretch into the oldest age, so we can allow all people to become Christ-imbued – then we work for the progress of humanity in this area, out of the knowledge of human evolutionary history.

Like I have been able to indicate in certain areas how a really inner, lively understanding of human evolutionary history repeatedly presents points of view from spiritual science, how it can show us what we need to do in our present epoch, so we can likewise point to other areas. We can point out how people were able to recognise the divine in matter. What we have inherited from relationships which human beings had to the divine continues to work in us; we have to do it on our own because today it wants to be independent. It wants to become an independent member of our social life.

In the second epoch of human development, where the human being still experienced agreement of the bodily-physical with the soul spiritual somewhat up to his thirties, which went into the middle of the earthly course of life, in this second epoch particularly instinctive forces in the human soul life awakened fully, those instinctive forces which for instance are expressed in rights, in state formative factors of public life. With this we notice in the second epoch of human evolution the germinal structure for what we can call Law, not through reasoning but through instinct. Because of this there is always something controversial in all legal terms because they were instinctively created during the second epoch.

In the third epoch, starting in the middle of the 15th Century – one can easily follow this historically – this third epoch in which we are now living, is particularly one of reasoning, contemplation. Human beings have withdrawn from the cosmos. The human being has withdrawn from what the human being of the first epoch thought he was connected. The human being has become lonely on the earth, and this loneliness of spirit on the earth turns everything upside down. In the first human epoch the soul-spiritual was experienced as obviously flooding the world, where the economic activity was regarded only as a mirror image of the soul-spiritual experience. In our epoch where man is separated soul-spiritually from the external in later epochs of individual lives, where he, only in his twenties, feels like a complete person in harmony with his physical-bodily development, during this time economic life becomes decisive. Economic life extends into the state configuration, the economic sphere becomes state economy, becomes empire. It becomes what we can see appearing now, in the one-sided method turning into Marxism; what becomes theory and acts that way, appears as if economic life is everything and spiritual life, which once had been everything, is replaced by economic life which had only been its mirror image; now spiritual life would only be regarded as an ideology.

Because of our natural development through evolution, humanity has separated from the outer physical because it is the normal development of human nature. The human being now needs to find harmony between those things that separated him, through his culture, through his civilisation: for the spiritual, which he must cultivate independently for himself, because it is no longer connected with physicality, and the economic life, which he must nurture so that he can battle properly with it, so that he can re-introduce the spirit which earlier had obviously been incorporated within it. In the middle of this he must nurture the state-legal aspect as an independent member.

To rightly understand history, looked at inwardly, gives us a true social insight for the present. It lives in what we want to include into the social organism. Humanity has gone through these epochs by

106

more or less developing the three members of the social organism separately. Now the time has come for us, out of our human consciousness, to develop the three members independently, so that we become strong through our inner humanity and we connect with one another through these three members: an independent spiritual life, an independent legal- or state life and an independent economic life.

The Greeks who still experienced harmony in their middle age between the soul-spiritual and bodily-physical, these Greeks were still condemned to divide the people outwardly into classes: into teaching (doctrine), defending (military service),and feeding (nutrition). We are striving towards a social formation, where, not the people are divided into such groups, but that life has its members in a threefold way, and that each single person can live into these members and single people can work together in the three members.

That however, my dear friends, which in the strongest sense allows consideration of the three-foldness in this way, needs to be the historical consideration of mankind which will offer new points of view. I want to say that in the witty scholarship that Herman Grimm found, historical facts which are so numerous today are dragged along like ballast - but great points of view are missing. Yes, like history learnt during the last few years, we need such great points of view because what has up to now germinated from human thoughts and feelings, could only have been experienced by a few. This kind of history, as Herman Grim presents it, will not be edifying to numerous people who come out of the great masses to participate in public affairs.

If out of spiritual science we can establish human history, through which one can see how people through the millennia have felt this way or that way, when one learns through historic evolution what these people experienced within, what they had to experience in order to simultaneously experience what all other people were experiencing, then we will have a history which we need in our time, regarding how the coming epoch can be used: an historic examination not merely through the intellect but an historic examination which as it were is created out of clear, objective concepts, which penetrates into human life so that it warms the knowledge of the mind and that knowledge thus warmed, build the will forces. When a person experiences that finally everything necessary for the furtherance of social progress is not dependant on establishments – because these themselves depend on people – but must depend on people, then one craves for a powerful will in people to become the strong disposition for strong deeds so that the identified establishments deemed necessary are also liable to be met. However, the people we need, the creative, the insightful, who orientate themselves correctly in the public world will only be those whose will and deeds glow and are illuminated, not with dead intellectualism, no, but with lively, spirit filled knowledge. They will be when they feel they can recognise themselves as members of the entire evolutionary history of humanity if they can point to their past history by discovering light within it, a light illuminating them to work, to be active, to be productive into the future.

LECTURE 5
Healthier thinking for contemporary life
Stuttgart on 8 June 1920

My dear honourable friends! Today it is impossible to form an opinion about the great affairs of the day without before all else looking at the deeper forces regarding the work and aspirations of the whole of humanity, which has been continuing for decades and has reached quite a special culmination today. Under the current conditions it is not possible to create an opinion of important things going on in humanity, without at least looking at the deeper foundations of all human striving as it is expressed in the present time. Therefore, please allow me, in this first of my next two lectures, the continuation of which will be given the day after tomorrow, to give some sketched observations of the deeper seated longings in contemporary humanity.

It was in July 1909 when a momentous speech was held in America by Charles Eliot, who had been from 1868 and up to the time of delivering the speech, the chancellor of the Harvard University. At that time Charles Eliot spoke, as one can see from his speech, out of the consciousness of looking at the soul and spiritual concerns of all civilized humanity according to his point of view. He called his speech "The Religion of the Future" and wanted to give the impression what this religion of the future would not be, and what it would be. If I look back on this speech however, the content Eliot spoke about seems to me far less meaningful than the actual attitude of his words. Above all, the most important for me seemed to be that a representative of the people of the current civilization would look for a healthy way of thinking about great world views and questions about life.

Now, my dear friends, when one points out something like this one may never forget that between that which was pronounced by even the most outstanding people at that time, and that which today lies in that terrible world war catastrophe which teaches more than all such words can teach – what all these people called big questions about the world and about life, instantly lights up in a completely different way than they could have been dreamt of back then. Towards a healthy thinking about the world and life, Eliot wanted to guide mankind. He looked back at the manner and way religions were in those times when science did not illuminate the souls of the greater masses of mankind. What he found most disturbing in all old religions was that they relegated man to a God who in a certain sense lived outside the enormous insights provided by natural science which was so great in the modern age. The human being felt himself to completely be a person of his epoch. To him old imaginations of the spiritual world appeared as those which had been created in a childlike humanity. It was particularly important to him that this scientific age could no longer see daemonic, spiritual beings in mountains and rivers, in trees and clouds, that a scientific age no longer could maintain the old pictorial concepts of God. It was also important to him to show that the concept of life, the concept of the social world had often suffered damage because of the fact that religious confessions, which were the leaders of thought for the vast majority of the people, the depressed people, miserable people, unable to cope with life, were relegated from the physical-sensory existence to a supernatural existence in the beyond, so that instead of processing life, instead of courageous intervention in life, for many people it meant looking beyond their immediate physical social existence. Everything the various confessions had to say about the reasons why one person was struck by some or other fate, also everything the various old confessions had to say about the world wielding divine laws, appeared out of date for Charles Eliot, the modern man, the man positioned in a time which started with Darwin, a time which for him meant particularly great accomplishments in medical progress which physically called upon for the relief of sick humanity's pain.

In a certain way he wanted old priests, who always pointed towards the indefinite super-sensory, to be replaced by a physical doctor able to alleviate even those pains a mother has to endure at the delivery of a baby into the physical world; he wanted to replace old priests with those able to help with the physical work because for him it was a matter of shaping the physical conditions of this earth in such a way that as many people as possible could experience joy and satisfaction from life. All of this - so it appeared to Charles Eliot – has in some way to take up healthy thinking and he hoped that from the views given by recent scientific developments humanity was provided with insight to bring them the goal they longed for.

I mention this especially because in this short speech about the religion of the future, everything is drawn together, so to speak, in a representative person what the so-called educated, namely learned educated, imagined as a path to modern healthy thinking.

Now this speech about the religion of the future, which I have just characterised, had a highly peculiar content. Because I had already said something similar before the war catastrophe as I'm saying now, I shall become – because I say this frankly – not one of those who can be accused for what many can be accused of today: that now, after the war has raged for so long, they are in a strange way right to reflect on what was before the war. Charles Eliot spoke like a man with a certain concept, like a man can have who stands within the modern scientific knowledge and who out of an honest heart wants to give humanity a view of life that leads to their happiness and satisfaction derived from these scientific notions. But how does he speak? If you choose to read between the lines, what can we say about the way he speaks? Observe his thoughts: they are born out of the spirit of the times but they can only be spoken when one is surrounded by a world in which first of all, in the social and in the direct living conditions, these thoughts don't become reality. These thoughts can only be uttered when one is surrounded by a world whose view of life is based in a much older time, when one was surrounded by a world when in the souls of people there lived certain concepts which certainly hadn't been created as is sought by such a scientifically educated religious person but which have a deep influence on the organisation of social life.

In other words, my dear friends, one can say that such a man can talk, but you can sense in his thoughts that the moment the full consequence, unflattering forms which he says, are to be realized – then, when the old traditions no longer work in the surroundings –

these ideas will actually turn out to be powerless. For those who can understand something of the horrific events in recent years, would say: These events since 1914 have significantly positioned themselves between what could have been spoken about at that time, and that which today appear to us as the great, overwhelming questions of the time. To a certain extent Charles Eliot pointed out at the end of his speech that he could not know how this, what he regarded as healthy thinking, could directly be realised in practical life, for that, only experience would have to show.

Now, my dear friends present here today, as strange, as paradoxical as it may sound to you, there is a part of the world today where these experiences can be submitted. What this educated, learned man could allow to be spoken about in the middle of an environment which no longer needed it, to show the final consequences of these thoughts, this is out of another kind of mind, out of another soul mood, being implemented in the east of Europe and already tried in a large part of Asia – as paradoxical as it might sound. While the thoughts of Eliot, meaning the last social consequences of a scientific world view could peacefully be expressed and with it still be valid for a good, brave citizen in the midst of an environment where people don't even think about drawing on the latest consequences of reality, the existence of human beings are destroyed, destroyed the moment where tabula rasa is made of old relationships, where the environment is no longer created by old governmental traditions, where people don't allow that to continue living in their environment based on old traditions, even originating through a particular tyranny.

When you reveal the consequences of these final thoughts to outer reality, you become a Leninist, or become a Trotskyist; then you begin to actualize what should originate purely out of what Eliot was looking for as healthy thinking from what wants to be born out of the purely scientific world view point. However, when you try to turn it into a reality then you don't build anything up, but only allow the destructive process to continue, which started in 1914, which will continue to make bitter, bitter experiences for humanity. That, my dear friends, is what a review teaches after a relatively short period of time, of what has become a sincere conviction of a man imbued with the entire education of the present day bringing his ideas into the open in 1909.

When we now ask ourselves what kind of connection exists between what a person, I could call him one with a certain materialistic Sunday sermon manner, could say in an otherwise quite different world, to another person about what has developed in Eastern Europe and over a large part of Asia? Then one has to, in order to examine the social connections at present and in the all of the conditions of life of modern man, one has to go even into deeper foundations. One learns by looking at the question: How has this materialistic world view which is so important to mankind, which should actually bring happiness and satisfaction, come about in the course of modern times?

If I want to designate what characterizes the most modern kind of thinking, the thinking that is now about to become a social reality, I must say: This thinking is characterized by its inability to build a bridge between what is knowledge of the natural side of the world and what is the moral world, what are ethical ideas, what are moral forces. On the one side is what consists of the natural side of the world, fixed in ideas that are immensely plausible for every person who has just heard of contemporary sentiments as they have developed over the last centuries and especially in the 19th Century.

The other side, spoken out of the corresponding human focus, asks what moral demands are and what should uplift people's perception to a view that these moral claims are rooted in the world order - a world order, where the moral and the immoral can have a consequence in shaping the world, where the moral and the immoral can intervene in the events of the world, just as a lightning bolt intervenes in the events of the world.

Here we have two worlds drifting apart for decades. Here lives the newer way of thinking which, according to healthy thinking, certainly strives to establish a natural religion with it. It is able to envisage what knowledge exists in the facts of nature. It is able, when a human being is conscientious, to also consider the other: from within the human breast speaks the voice of morality which should point the way to religious awareness.

However today there is no bridge between the two worlds. There is the one world, the world of knowledge of natural facts. They believed a basic law was to be found which became the unshakable law as a result of the 19th century, that of the unshakable law of the indestructibility of matter and substance – the law that is supposed to tell us that everything that is happening in space is the result of the sum of its forces, which may well be transformed but which will never increase or decrease, can't be created or destroyed. With these forces cooperating, the form of the world is brought forth and world events which outwardly take place, seen by the senses, come about and from which we ourselves as physical people grow out of. Now if these forces can neither be created nor destroyed, if one can speak in the absolute sense of the preservation of matter and energy, then all the beliefs that appear in the wake of this view can't be dismissed. From this we must accept – according to the same thinking habits in which humanity is forced to adhere to this law of the transformation of matter and energy – what would come about is that the earthly-cosmic, within which we find ourselves, is created out of the famous Kant-Laplace primal fog out of which the entire solar system originated through an agglomeration, and that in the course of this natural process man has also developed, after he has passed through the various animal forms. So we come to suppose that in the human soul the flashes, like inner life illusions, which appear in this human soul like the forces which alone can guarantee man his dignity are moral ideas and that which leads to a religious consciousness.

However, whoever clings with all its consequences to this world created out of the primeval fog of Kant-Laplace, has to also think about the end of the world along these lines. He has to think that this world is changing in which everything that humanity offers, including everything that has ever been offered in human souls and human spirits, disappears; he must think that within a grand cosmic scheme the whole human delusion of morality, of divinity is merely something that is born out of natural law - just as lightning and thunder, the alternation of day and night, and so on, is born out of natural law. As we look at a non-spiritual, non-soul like world creation; so we will look at a non-spiritual, non-soul world end. For someone who clings on to this world, with all the consequences, the best thing for him is that mankind thinks, dreams, is spun into the processes that take place between these two ends – the beginning and the end of the world; the best for him is for this mankind to think it's just an episode, eventually vanishing into the pure natural universe.

My dear friends gathered here, with the best of will there is nothing to say about all the quackery that people still want to put forward for the validity of a moral and religious world when they argue for the one, with all the consequences, that is based on this scientific attitude. I know how much is preached in this direction today, that yes, despite this scientific attitude an ideal world view is still possible. It is only possible for those who don't really want to go into all the consequences of their thinking. Man is quite motivated today to ask: why don't people make this clear to themselves today, what has been hinted at here? Why this in particular, actually? About that you might get information if you remember, I could call it the springtime of that which has today become a general opinion, but which one does not admit to as a general opinion among the so-called enlightened when you refer back to this springtime of theoretical materialism, which flooded over the civilized world in the middle of the 19th century. Today it has admittedly become modern to regard those who boldly pulled out the last consequences of the scientific attitude in those days, such as Moleschott, Büchner and so on, to be flat – which they undoubtedly are. But then even more is needed than what can be brought forward from the learned or unlearned side to characterize the whole relationship, which determines our stand towards them.

You only need to visualise a few facts to be able to appreciate all the seriousness and significance related to the social situation of contemporary man. I would like to mention one thing, for example what in the seventies (1870's) a renowned cultural historian said: It is one of the most important results of modern times that scientific knowledge shatters everything that was born out of the old religions as an ethical ideal. – Yes, this cultural historian wrote it down drily, characterising it from the side of truth or untruth as only a scientific result could be, like the falling of rain, considered from this point of view.

But, of particular interest is a letter written from a very bold, inwardly daring personality to a former nature researcher. In the letter the following is stated: The modern worldview teaches us that everything which people live through is based on underlying natural causal laws which we see with our senses in the outer world. Everything coming from people out of their inner and so-called good deeds and good thoughts, what they bring forth as religious ideas, all this is nothing other than results of pure natural processes happening in people just like the gathering of clouds outside happen in nature. What holds true for me, this personality said, is that everything people have imagined as moral imperative is an illusion. I'm of the opinion that whoever is equipped to be a robber, a murderer, is entitled to live out his killing and robbing abilities to the full, just as another might be who is born to the contrary. I'm convinced, so this personality wrote, for the full worth of it, for its full moral integrity, people predisposed to impairment are therefore immoral, if they don't live up to their abilities.

Obviously people are going to say today: This is a paradoxical truth. – But why would they do this? They say this on the basis of, on the one hand, having an unbelievable respect and complete faith in authority of above all what they've learnt from what's cooking in the kitchen of science and on the other hand, they don't have such equal courage as this personality who has written this letter, also handling its consequences. They remain standing half way, because they won't admit to themselves that if they once draw such conclusions, others must follow along the same path.

Now I would like to say: Just as Charles Eliot in 1909, in an environment that did not think of translating his thoughts into a social reality, could speak as he did, so also a personality in those days could rave about the full expression of criminal instincts because the complete acting out of the criminal instincts belong to the moral worth of the personality. In those days the time had not yet come for the creation of social facilities and social institutions which the people intended in this direction. However, now another question was asked: How should these institutions be created, which are now seen as a construction shaping our declining order of life that goes with it?

My dear friends present here today, when one really looks at the living situation of people in the present time, and then really looks at what actually lives within them – what is created out of what lives within are finally all that is expressed outwardly in economic, industrial and practical life – when one considers all of this, then one admittedly arrives at a bitter judgement of contemporary man's life's situation. What would it look like if a large enough number of people has the courage to awaken the soul, wake up the sleeping soul and say to themselves: If we take the totality of what has flowed from thinking during the last three to four centuries from scientific knowledge then everything that flows into social life will have to be shaped according to laws, empty and barren of everything that springs up in man as moral impulses or a religious world order because such laws can only be derived from the scientific point of view.

The real beginning of such a social order of life which divides the social society only as it appears in natural phenomena in outer life – we see this made in Eastern Europe and spreading over Asia; we see it theoretically learnt from Marxism, since decades. Marxism could also talk, as long as it didn't involve the environment responding to its talk regarding the shaping of reality. Now the face of the world has turned more serious. Now it is important to raise the question in a comprehensive sense.

Could this way proposed to healthy thinking also be a way of life for mankind on earth? – For this reason, because the issue is so serous, it has to be really examined in the whole way people are, particularly because of those who believe in the achievements which are only good from a branch of knowledge of nature, to be able to construct social life. What have these achievement brought us?

I have often and for many years here in Stuttgart pointed out the greatness and importance of the scientific worldview, and those who have heard me more often will certainly not regard me as a despiser of this scientific world view – within the limits in which it is justified. But what this is about, is something else. Now there's the question: Is a scientific worldview possible when it involves bringing in laws of human knowledge into shaping social life?

In order to answer this question one must go into the intended path to healthy thinking which this worldview has taken. Then one sees that this scientific worldview has based all its facts of nature on what it can encapsulate in the application of technology and industrial life. There one sees that, what has been achieved through the laws of nature in technical and industrial life, and in transport, has been expanded on a large scale. All of this achieved a pinnacle when the catastrophe of 1914 broke through which indicated how little social consideration had taken place in those who built machines based on the knowledge of science which created the world with means of transport clutter and so on. Indeed, what we see in technology is equal whether it leads to constructiveness or destruction, this is related in a certain direction to scientific thinking. This direction of scientific thinking wanted to become universal, wanted to be generally accepted, wanted to mean something for the whole human life.

There we see, however, isolated spirits I could call them, stand like eccentrics in the general development which had nevertheless proceeded from the conviction "how delightfully far we've come". We see how they look at what is coming up and with tremendous concern look at the future. One only has to point out Soloviev, the Russian philosopher, who unfortunately only first became known in central Europe during the war years, and who had died already at the beginning of the century. He made profound observations of human life but he was also enlightened enough to consider practical life with his extraordinary good willing, mild soul and observe practical life as such. This philosopher Soloviev was overcome with bitter concern when he said to himself: Also over my Russia the inwardly rotten domination of all that the modern world view has derived from a scientific basis is spreading. Here Russia is flooded with all the delights – he's not saying it ironically – all the delights of modern technology, modern transport and what is disappearing as if stolen from this world is what served as the basis for healthy Russian thinking. What disappears with each railway line set down, with every industrial plant, is where healthy Russian thoughts should be growing: on the earth and land. –

So one listens to how Soloviev speaks, how he has an understanding for human thinking being connected to the land, in a different way than the kind of thinking which has torn itself free from the earth and land, on an abstract level, as it were, even if it exists as a physical reality and is based on scientific foundations appearing as modern culture. Certainly, one can call it one-sided; it was after all one-sided in a certain way. How can anything after all be regarded from all sides when one lives in a world, where at the same time external forces strive to surrender everything in the world on to the basis of a scientific attitude? What is needed to achieve a healthy peaceful judgement against the materialistic dream of the whole of humanity, how can this one-sidedness be thrown out when he expresses his concern, which must have seemed in a certain way insane at a time when this modern culture was not yet so much in decline as now, after Soloviev has been dead for twenty years?

Also, this Charles Eliot, of whom I've spoken, roughly indicated what kind of futuristic religion he was thinking about when people would no longer believe in an super-worldly God or if in wider circles, they would no longer believe in daemonology. He said: The view of a unified God will be the rule, being inwardly in all things, also within the human soul and working in all of what is in laws of nature. –

One can see clearly stated in this speech, that there is also for such a well-meaning person like Charles Elliot, this God, connected with all he knows about the proliferation of matter, which is eternally changing, yet is an indestructible force. Basically the unified God was nothing other than a unity of matter and energy, for him. Out of such theoretical confessions he preached about the world which is to serve as the practical basis of life. He stressed: Eternally the saying must light up: "Serve your fellow human being". Serve your fellow man – this is repeated again and again in his speech. However, with such a sentence, such a demand, it is certainly not only about the fact that words are expressed, but it is also about the question whether what is demanded from the people, can also be fulfilled by these people – fulfilled by allowing soul forces to be released from the depth of their souls which finally will find results in social human service, in social work according to the sentence: "Serve your fellow human being". In other words one must ask: Is a worldview capable of providing a foundation to create true human love?

Is a worldview capable of being the root of a plant which, as it grows out of the earth will blossom and bear the fruit of human love? This question does not leave itself open to be answered in a logical, one sided and theoretic way. This question can only be allowed to be answered on the basis of what is happening historically. Had Eliot only waited for the experience which is now being shaped by European East and Asia, then he would have had his doubts. Because the historical result is that this socialistic teaching which only wants to build on the same scientific prerequisites, on which Eliot wants the world of the future and life in general, to be built on, that this socialistic direction is not capable of creating social life on what freely rises within people and turn into the fruits of love in the world. Out of this social doctrine and social tyranny nothing resounds which would awaken human love. Nothing resounds in us from the saying: "Serve your fellow man" because you love them – but what sounds in us is the encounter of dry, empty, man-killing words of duty to work which is driven into us like the military drills it into people.

I would like to mention that if one listens on the one hand to Charles Eliot of 1909 where the experience of the present was not yet available, where from the chair of the Harvard University he had held his pragmatic speech, it is like an echo against a later speech which the Russian socialist War Minister recently made, who said: Those people who are honest about the social order, will not fail to recognize what we owe to this war. It returned our sons as soldiers. They have become diligent soldiers. They have learnt to obey and comply with authority. Let us not fail to recognise what war has given us, that it has trained us as officers who can command, who by coercion can force people to know how to move up a position. Let us not forget war leaders who are capable of organising so that authority is added to this organisation. –

This speech sounds like an echo of transposing militarism on to social life contrary to what we – only as world view, because no one in this sphere thinks of making it a reality – derive as countered by Eliot's speech. People don't know that they have searched for healthy thinking on the way which the final consequences gave them, which is so clearly seen today. People don't readily admit to the connection between what has for centuries, particularly in the last decades, presented to them in the world and life, what now appears as the will to form the social world - but which is completely powerless to shape this world in such a way that in it a worthy humane existence is actually possible. Out of this will-not-to-understand lies the very basis of searching for a path towards healthy thinking of life's situation in contemporary man.

In my book "Key points of the Social Question at present and in the future" everything emerges from the efforts brought into being for the federation of threefoldness of the social organism. Here the way is sought for calling to life healthy social thinking without submitting to illusions, by keeping in mind what is involved in this question: Which thoughts underlie that which wants to be realised today as life-destroying? Which thoughts underlie the events that led to the absurdity of events that began in 1914? Whoever doesn't want to create a clear, healthy judgement, can, in whatever position he might be standing, not participate with what is working today in every person according to the measure of his forces and his position in life. What is important today is clear, consequent thinking. This clear, consequential thinking only leads towards asking the question: Where does this so-called healthy thinking based on science, come from?

Anyone who knows about historical connections knows that in relation to airing our ideas, in relation to producing concepts in public life we have not brought them further than the Middle Ages. Much talk is raised about the darkness of the Middle Ages yet we still think in the thought forms of the Middle Ages. Where we have progressed, is in achievements of the knowledge of nature which has its counterpart in technology, in the achievements of knowledge regarding inanimate nature, actually only a part of lifeless nature which has its counterpart in technology. What we have achieved, what can be mastered by means of calculation, by means of geometry, *that* has become our worldview. This has gradually conquered such a position in the imaginative life of human beings, that it appears as the self-evident foundation of all of life's views.

Besides this, has humanity concerned itself about further developing its inner power of thought, inner power of the soul in any way? No, that can't be said. Thought forms, the art of thinking, the entire configuration of thinking with which science apparently works in the most exact and strictest way, are the same as what had been applied by scholastics in the Middle Ages. With the scholastics of the Middle Ages these thoughts were great, these thoughts were astute. Why so? Because these thoughts set the task of looking over into a spiritual world. One may think about a content as I've just indicated as one likes, but what training and formation of scholastic thinking has brought about, this can't be indicated in a different way than in the way I will try to do now, through a calm, objective observation of the course of more modern culture.

For someone who knows what astuteness, what control of thinking techniques require such observation for thoughts of the Trinity, how the Sacraments and Consecration of Man to Christ can be followed – which at that time was observed in social life within all of humankind – will know with what kind of acumen these views can be pursued, which have no corresponding image in the sense world, where thoughts must depend solely on thought, they would say: One may think about the Trinity as one wants – but what at that time had developed as thinking techniques and logic with an inner responsibility towards the forms of thinking, was grandiose. It lives on as an inheritance. We don't think in any other way today than the scholastic catholic scholars thought and now we have transferred this way of thinking to scientific fields. We think within the medieval thought forms locked into materially developed fields of recent times. We just don't think with the same sharpness, because we don't develop this sharpness of thinking.

We renounce, if we're enlightened people, training this thinking for ideas like the incarnation of Christ, the Trinity and so on, we don't train this thinking for looking at the super sensory world. If we would ask on what basis we should train this scholastic thinking and inwardly sharpen the contours, then we have to admit: because – what positive religions may say, often hiding the true facts of the case – because this thinking developed itself out of that looking at the soul which in antiquity still existed up to Plato, yes, valid up to the New Platonists, because this thinking develops from the observation, the spirit-soul observation of a spiritual, supersensible world. If someone wants to reach this thinking, he must look into the spiritual world, he must develop his thoughts in such a way, that they don't only vanquish what is before the eyes in a course sensual way, but also that which must be grasped with the same delicacy and sharpness like things of the supersensible world.

In an instinctive way, not in a conscious way, presented as a world view I have been lecturing about here for years – in an instinctive way, but still in a spiritual way, the thinking of those ancient times was founded in the ranks of Augustine, the university scholastics of Albert Magnus, of Thomas Aquinas - on a thinking that was trained in seeing the supernatural world, because this thinking was a germinal shoot for a kind of looking into the supernatural world, even if this is denied by the positive theologians.

This thinking was already weakened in the Middle Ages. In ancient times, this way of thinking sought to penetrate into a spiritual world through the inner strength of man. In the Middle Ages people regarded the spiritual world as something which was not to be researched but interpreted by the soul itself. Now we are, in relation to the schooling of thinking, heirs of scholastic thinking. We certainly stand within the same stream of thought, only we can't bring it to perfection. No longer are we able to develop really sharp logical contours in thinking because we don't train our thinking through spiritual problems where thinking is left over to its own forces; we can only pursue what is visible in experiment rooms.

Where, today, do we find the last shoot of Catholic scholastic thinking of the Middle Ages? Where has the last shoot come out of what was considered a social view from the God state of Augustine and his successors, from this constricted organization, this militaristic arrangement of human community living? Where is the last shoot of medieval Catholic theology in relation to forms of thought? – That is Marxism. It is what prepared the great masses for socialistic doctrines today. All forms of thought of what modern socialism is, is nothing more than the last, decrepit shoot of thinking, which in higher scholasticism still only reaches half its height, which was born out of super-sensible vision, but which is no longer suitable for a scientific age. We have come to the point of describing the wide world in its natural existence, we've geometricized and mechanised it - people like Charles Eliot do speak about this point of arrival, but we haven't been able to find a way into this world via a thinking route. For this reason we had to speak as Du Bois-Reymond spoke about the limits of knowledge of nature and the seven world mysteries. At the time, what question did Du Bois-Reymond answer in his sensational speeches "Recognising the limits of Nature" and "The Seven World Riddles"? – It answered the question that inherited scholastic thinking cannot penetrate natural science. That is no wonder. Thomas Aquinas had the doctrine of revelation in front of him; he had the doctrine of supersensible worlds before him as it was then common practice. Modern science didn't exist at that time, he couldn't use the argument of a newer science.

If one were to continue working in spirit – not in the sense of warming up Catholic scholasticism, of neo-Thomism (developed by Thomas Aquinas – trans.) - then one would have to say: This has become obsolete, something that in Lenin's and Trotsky's theoretical socialism consists of scholastic, over-scholastic thought forms out in the east of Europe and in Asia, which wanted to become realized. All this thinking, which has become decrepit, must again be transformed into a thinking rooted in perceiving inside the supersensible worlds. Just as at that time there was scholastic thinking which now has turned decrepit, has become weak, to really manage social relationships, which can't form the roots in which love can blossom and bear fruit, this thinking has to be replaced with such a thinking whose roots are within the realization of supersensible worlds.

As Charles Eliot complained that what he imagined healthy thinking to be, was not quite popular in the widest circles because most people only want to deal outwardly through hypocrisy, he said: On the one hand there are those people who are serious about science and would seek such a natural religion for the future and expand it later, yet we still see how a part of these people, who also count as part of the educated ones, in all possible secret societies seek substitutes for old traditions, like in the Masonic Lodges, in the Odd-Fellows-Lodges. We see – Charles Eliot says – how a large portion of people are honestly looking for the supernatural, in spiritism, where Christian Science is looking for a way to reach the spirit. We see how the broad masses out of old habits cling to traditional confession – this Charles Eliot complained about. This is what he regarded as opposing the pursuit of this path to healthy thinking. He doesn't realise that what he is developing is outside the reality of science. He doesn't even think of telling himself that what has been raised must be grasped with a different thinking than the thinking which is only the legacy of medieval scholastic thinking, which is a thinking newly born from the spiritual world.

Truly, what has been raised today as socialism - is anything but what has lived through the centuries during the Middle Ages, which has not been overcome in the minds of the masses until today, by the newer culture. Even if these people appear as opponents of the confessions - their thought forms are quite in keeping with these confessions. With the same thought forms which the medieval human

125

being wanted to penetrate God, with the same thought forms they now turn to today's researcher of nature, who popularises today's worldview layman, the theoretical socialist regarding the unity of matter and energy.

What must be achieved as a new seeing – will be represented for many years from this position and certainly in Stuttgart. It is important to perceive how that which is nurtured through the Threefold Social Organism is a necessary result of this new seeing – being necessary for the renewal of thinking, a rebirth of thinking coming out of the spiritual world. Only this rebirth of thinking can direct us towards building this bridge which could not have been built in the last century until into our time: this bridge built between the world, which stands there as the world of natural facts which one can observe as natural causalities, and that world which springs forth within, the moral world, the religious uprising, the religious world plan. Only by man having the courage to try hard to express thoughts in relation to this world view, through this alone man will reach clarity about what is important, both in terms of the view of life and also the social direction for the present.

My very dear friends, so inwardly - while based on knowledge - so inwardly permeated by the existence of a spiritual-divine world is this spiritual-scientifically oriented world view that is meant here. It is completely clear that in all knowledge living within man, what man inwardly experiences as his thoughts about the world, also what rises in him as human will in individual or social relations, that in all this the divine also lives as it lives in the outer existence of nature. This is what my "Philosophy of Freedom" already at the beginning of the nineties wanted to express and which has again been expressed in the publication of the new edition of this book. This is something which really wants to create a bridge between the observation of nature and the observation of those impulses in humankind, which need to come out of human freedom and absolutely only out of freedom must a justified structure of social coexistence be created. One thing is necessary: it is necessary to summon up a little more inner thinking courage than what the sleeping souls of the present have in common.

For this reason it is necessary to seriously work with the question: What is at the root of what we expect as the future of mankind?

Outer observation of nature says: What we expect for the future of the earth, for the future of the entire solar system, must result from the transformation of matter and energy of what we see around us, what is here already, today. It is calculated, by applying mechanics, applying mechanics to atoms, about which so much is being said, formerly in absolutes, now in the hypothetical sense or in the sense of fictions. Now one reaches the conclusion: what we see as the end of the world happens through the transformation of matter and energy but without what happens in humanity because this is only one episode in these world facts. This is the inevitable consequence of a purely naturalistic view of the world.

This naturalistic world view appears to be the kind of world view I have for decades represented, so, as if someone were to look at a plant root and say: everything that is there must originate out of the plant root. That means, he would assume: there is the root which shoots into stem, leaf, stem, leaf and so on. He will only look at what can develop out of this root and he would not see that this root in front of him, is rotting away, decomposing, and from the plant grown out of the root, a new seed is created in which the plant is already invested.

If you read what is available in the literature of the anthroposophically oriented spiritual science, you would see: In this way this spiritual science evaluates the great world view relationships as it is created from supersensible vision, as it is portrayed in my book "Knowledge of the Higher Worlds and its Attainment". You say to yourself: on the basis of us now having the physical sensory world in front of us, there arises, as if sprouting within it, what is developing within our souls as moral impulses, as ideal observation, as ideal thought forms, as religious courage for the truth – one must only see this in the right light. There it develops like a small shoot developing in a plant. When once this entire world which surrounds us as a world of matter and energy, would decay, become corpses, turn to dust in the world realm, what will the end be then?

The end, when everything around us is atomised in the world, will be what now is emerging as a germ of the spirit in the human soul. This atomising, this destruction of matter, destruction of energy, is what we look at but just as from the human corpse in death the human soul lifts, so what lifts out of this atomising is what lives as the germ in the human soul, in what lives as the moral impulse, what is ethical idea, what is elevated to the Divine; this forms the future, this is the new world. Not by the transformation of apparently transformed matter and the apparently transformed energy does the future world come into being, but through what lives in our soul as soul knowledge, as spirit knowledge.

There in the human breast, there lies the future, also as a germ. When one now looks at the future of the cosmos, which lives in us as an inner germ, one must have the courage to combat this Law of the Conservation of matter and energy. One must have the courage to redirect what in the 19th century spread as a view of the world and of life from a scientific view, back to its true foundation. One has to build a bridge between what is external and sensory, to what is internal and spiritually real. One can't build this bridge as long as the illusion of the conservation of matter and energy prevents it. One can only build it through a new looking spiritual world which opens up a new way of thinking which has also grown out of social life.

This social life, it makes man, if he is able to look into his inner being, so that he can see with all inner conscientiousness, with all his inner strength and emotion, say to himself: when everything disappears, which my eyes see, what my ears hear, what I feel in the outer world – that is, everything which science only talks about – then as a metamorphosis everything that I now have kindled in my inner being will live on, then that which is of moral value, which gives man his dignity from within, will live. – This is how spiritual science establishes the reality of the ethical, the reality of the moral, the reality of the religious, because it does not indulge in the illusion of the eternity of matter and energy.

If you look at the metamorphosis of matter and energy as Charles Eliot presented it in 1909, you would see that such a spiritual world view which we represent here, has within it the power to say Yes to life as a germ of the future. Let us imagine such a humanity, living with such souls. Let's imagine that the people with this responsibility – don't come with illusions of causality in social life – step into social life, then we dare hope that such inner conscientiousness, out of the sense of a cosmic responsibility what comes about would be able to bring the social organism back to health. What comes from the newer spiritual science is the way to healthy thinking. It is also what can create the right relationship with life's situation for present day humanity, if it is present in a sufficiently large number of people.

For those who can't create this bridge, for whom the moral world order only appears as one episode, that will – in order to have validity on its own, while it pushes back everything else that wants to oppose it with a spiritual scientific world view – that will still ad absurdum continue, how all that we have progressed with so extensively, have been brought ad absurdum by the terrible catastrophes of recent years. Anyone who cannot learn from the lessons of recent years, cannot have insight into the social forces that lie within thought that comes from looking at a new way of thinking – a thinking which equips a sufficiently large number of people which can begin to cope with what we know today as the great questions of the world view.

My dear honourable friends here today! With this I have basically, even if only as a sketch, brought an impression of what I wanted to present as an introduction today to what I want to express more concretely the day after tomorrow. After that, so that my task is done, perhaps I may come back to say a few words about some of the things I said here last time, otherwise the wrong conclusions will always be drawn if one keeps quiet about certain things.

Education and teaching in the face of the present world situation

Stuttgart on 10 June 1920

My dear honourable friends! After a lengthy absence I managed the day before yesterday, for only a short hour, to once again visit your Waldorf School where I could also take part in lessons in the local eighth elementary school class in which World History was being treated. If I now may speak bluntly, I would say I have the impression, if we really succeed in continuing this way in terms of education and teaching shown here — at least essentially — we may hope to get individuals out of our school who are able to cope with the increasingly difficult questions of life in the near future and who would take their stand in life. Undoubtedly some of what was aimed for was being achieved, it seemed to me to a certain degree, what I would like to call: History as an expression of human development. For the children here, who are in their 13th, 14th, 15th year of life, history has already become so vivid that this history will accompany them; what they receive will work as empowering thoughts, also making it possible as a strength for their entire next life, not merely as a historical understanding but as an understanding for the circumstances of life, for life's relationships.

If I now ask myself: How could I — after I had dealt with it almost a year ago — pedagogically and didactically let the ideas for the Waldorf School of which our friend Molt has just spoken here, lead the way — how could the interest which I now had to take from the way which the impulses were given in reality at that time, how could this interest be satisfied in such a way as I have just indicated? From this I could see that, what entered as vivid in history was due to the teacher, Dr Stein, who found the inner courage to add to his view of history that which is the power of this spiritual science which I have taken the liberty to allow myself to present for many years, here and also in Stuttgart. This spiritual science certainly should not be merely as an inner comfort to

131

souls who have turned away from the world, but it is meant to be something that actually recognises everything human and penetrates and fertilizes all human actions and human creations. It should be something that is not merely acknowledged but should instil such ideas, I could say, which ensoul heart-blood pouring into the human limbs, into the spiritual and physical limbs, making man more dexterous, more handy, more able in life in any relationship.

However, one must, in order to oppose the many prejudices that still penetrate branches of education, teaching and life which carry impulses of spiritual science, one must, in order to overcome these prejudices in the widest circles, have the inner courage — courage which can only flow from a soul inwardly connected with the persuasive power originating from knowledge of reality derived from the view of spiritual science as I have often suggested here. From what I've taken the liberty of speaking about so directly from that day, thoughts can easily link to a phenomenon which, in today's general world situation, is all too often the case, well founded and only too understandable. We live — and I have already in my lectures the day before yesterday indicated it form a different point of view — we live in a time today when the social question can no longer be one depending on institutions and organisations, but one where it is a great question of human worth, human dignity; an issue of humanity in general. It is no longer important today to think which institution is best where we could find this or that kind of thinking about the social life, but it involves this: how can we win the broad masses of people who have appeared on the scene of life with those who in a certain way, through their intelligence, by the intellectual direction they have acquired, must nevertheless, in a certain way, be leaders in all that is incorporated into the social life of the present?

It becomes extraordinarily difficult to speak out about certain truths which may now sound not quite as paradoxical today, yet still somewhat cruel. Again, and yet again the truth must be pointed out which is all too clearly learnt from events of the recent years. It must be pointed out that in the last century, in particular in the last decade, the bearers of the present education, the bearers of actual civilized life — apart from the survival of traditions — have fallen into a certain materialistic view of life and that they have not found their way out of it towards what meanwhile has developed in the broad masses as theories, as views of life. What developed as religion, as science, as art among the ruling classes did not have the inner strength to seize the broad masses of humanity. In particular it didn't have the strength to support the broad masses of humanity which had as a result of the upswing of our industrial life been placed before machines in industries and so on, who had to be asked to be brought up to what the content of education, religion, science, and art were of the leading classes. One left the broad masses of the proletariat to themselves. One left the members of the proletariat to what they could see was merely mechanical equipment, merely lifeless, heartless, soulless machines and machinery. From gazing at such a mechanical environment, connected to a life with machines, life could be viewed by the broad masses in such a way that it came to be expressed more or less as radical Marxism and now, unfortunately, already wants to shape reality as I hinted at the day before yesterday.

A bridge between that which was once old traditions recognised by the educated classes as their civilisation, and that which has entered into the sphere of the newer life in the broad masses of people, such a bridge doesn't exist today. Quite unsurely do we face the great questions of life today: how can a bridge be built between those who from knowledge of the being of man create conceptions, how should our social life go on, and those who understandably only progress in life out of a sphere which is actually only based on the lifeless, and thus the belief that all life, all religion, all science, all art could equally develop from it like a superstructure of production conditions which is distant from all spiritual life?

This, my dear friends here today, this is the most horrific riddle of the present time: When will we ever succeed in bringing together these two parts of humanity — who, despite all that is said, must come together — when are we ever going to meet that demand? This weighs more or less unconsciously, on many, obviously. Out of this burden various well-meaning efforts have originated in the present. This is when it becomes difficult again to find anything to say, what I must say to them now, as I certainly want to acknowledge the well-meaning endeavours.

My dear friends, it is no use today to somehow not hurt or offend people, to hold back what is based on deeper insight in the developmental laws of humanity which must be spoken about, so that we can move forward with the rebuilding of our social life. Many people feel the neglect of something with spiritual content for mankind and letting this flow as spiritual content into science, religion and art, which could be the persuasive force of the great masses — these masses which up to now only want to accept what they, out of their own life history, about living together with the machine and with mechanism and so on, say. As a result many have concluded: It is necessary that we bring a certain education to the broad masses, because after all our social question is essentially a question of education. It is the well-intended aspiration of many that this education would be in the position to develop ideas about the dissemination of information about possibilities of human coexistence, possibilities of social reciprocity. So people think in many circles out of the most earnest intention about adult education centres and any other similar educational institutions.

You see, this is the hard part, that one must speak about such well-meaning things, as I have to do now. It involves taking for granted those who out of an honest will wish to spread education, the propagation of science so that science, as it presents itself today, how it is taught and learnt in our educational institutions and colleges, is now given in an appropriate way in adult education centres and similar institutions. Many find this quite understandable. Why is that? Because many do not want to ask the question of today's life situation in a sufficiently consequential way. Today people see how many disturbing powers there are in their public life. People see the dimensions of the declining effects but have become accustomed to them over the last three to four centuries, to what has appeared as generally accepted science and common art, establishing an absolute sense of authority. So people say: Yes, when you take what can be absolutely right, absolutely appropriate and now carry it over into the broad masses, it must be a blessing. Surely it is basically obvious for such a view to come about when people's questions are not yet consistent enough at present? However, can the other question not also be raised, my dear friends, namely: Yes, were there not also up to now ruling classes of humanity, were they not the owners of this science and art of the spirit, which people now want to throw into universities and similar institutions — were they not those who had mankind's leadership in hand who brought present humanity into today's situations? Had this science which is to be given to the broad masses today previously been saved by the leading classes from letting humanity plunge into the absurdities of life? No, it did not!

Can one now hope that something else will come out of the signs of decline when the ruling classes, despite being soaked in this science, in this art and so on, have been sheltered in the current absurdities of life and are not shielded from this science rushing in? Does one want to popularise what apparently played a part in the decline? Does one want to drag the broad masses into it so that these broad masses are in an energetic way led to such absurdities, to which the leading circles have been drawn by this science? This question is a cruel one at present, but it is the kind of question which has to be raised even if one suffers from its utterance because one knows from the outset how little one can be understood by raising such a question. For this reason *so* little would be understood because most people today still believe: Surely, something solid like the science of the last centuries does exist after all, we can build on it, it has just not yet entered into the masses enough; if it enters into the masses then it will give them a firmer ground. — One can understand that people want something which would mean a firm ground under their feet. However, today the seriousness of our present world situation is so great that it is impossible to recognize certain things you think you know from the course of development of mankind, and simply continue to be silent because in a certain sense, they radically contradict prejudices of the widest circles. What is basically an answer to the fateful question just posed, stares one in the face, as this spiritual science of which I have been speaking about in Stuttgart for years, while this spiritual science wants to be something quite different than what is desired in the widest circles through prejudices; spiritual science always wants not only what it believes could broaden ordinary scientific education but it always wants a thorough enrichment of the whole life of civilised life with a new spiritual insight. It can only promise some enrichment of all of life's civilizations through a new spiritual vision.

So, we aren't thinking of directing our intentions towards making common science as broadly based as possible, but we are thinking of a renewal of the entire scientific and world view spirit of the present day and going into the near future.

You see, from such a basic attitude, what is known as pedagogy and didactics, as education and the basic principles of teaching, has flooded the Waldorf School here. Out of such a basic attitude, what has come about is what was spoken about in the time between my previous and present Stuttgart sojourn, over in Switzerland, in Dornach, to a number of doctors and medical students. There we examined the present day form of medicine, particularly with a therapeutic relevance in order to show how everything which can form the basis for this medicine and what can develop further, in fact could be illuminated through spiritual science. Here one wouldn't proceed from what is called science, and apply it to adult education centres, but one would endeavour to gain a new foundation of knowledge and to fertilize science with it and then only to introduce these into institutions first because the old science may not take away from it, what is to be for the common good. A science of the people, from the healthy ones to the sick ones, must be given through this spiritual science. It is still in its beginnings. Obviously one thinks humbly about everything related to these great problems of the present while in the middle of it. This knowledge of the healthy and sick was because of a belief that only a spiritually illumined science will be capable to work in the widest circles of people, to work with such vital strength that it can rise above what the broad masses through their view of the mechanical have gained. This can never be achieved by the science that has so misled the leading classes; it will only be possible to produce a world view that penetrates sources of knowledge quite different from those to which the intellectual and artistic worldview was inclined to penetrate human conscience during the last centuries, but especially over the last few decades.

I must firstly allow myself, my honourable friends, despite this being such a large gathering today, to speak in an apparently unpopular manner by referring to something about which most people say today: Oh, we really don't want to speak about the new form of life's situation of present day humanity. This lies far too much in certain spiritual heights which the broad masses surely can't understand. — Yes, my dear friends, I am speaking of such points of views as I was implying earlier. When it is often said to me that that, which comes from here, is incomprehensible to the majority of people, then I am always reminded again of what I often heard from theatre directors, whose entire efforts have always been directed towards performing as shoddy pieces as possible to the audience; they've always reasoned that it was what the public wanted because they didn't understand better things. To me it was always obvious that the relevant theatre directors who make such judgements didn't understand the better pieces. So I make nothing of it when someone or other complain about incomprehensibility but I believe that we, perhaps in part, involved through the plight of the times, are mature enough to take up some of the things that the decades of swimming in philistinism have conveniently called incomprehensible.

Many things have happened to me which I can cite as proof of this incomprehensibility. For example, about twenty years ago I was once

137

invited to give talks to a circle of educated people in a German town, about Goethe's "Faust". There were certainly a number of people to whom it didn't occur to mention that what I said was incomprehensible. Yet an enthusiastic representative of the muse of Oskar Blumenthal appeared who said: Yes, "Faust" is indeed no piece of theatre, it is a science. — It has gradually come about from certain foundations which I will not characterize here, to have an educational ideal handy which says: People should speak in a more popular and more generally understandable way. Precisely because of this comfort, we are in the position we are in now. We won't come out of it any earlier, my dear friends, until a large enough number of people decides to listen to their conscience in order to understand that it can't be communicated as clear as water where you can also be unconscious.

When one speaks about the meaning of education and teaching in relation to today's world situation, then it concerns mainly something than needs insight: The teacher, the educator of today, can only be what he is supposed to be in a fruitful way through a real knowledge of the developing human being, out of a real gift, by looking into what is revealed as human riddles from the first day the child is born, right into the days when it has grown up. However, we don't have a general world view which can direct us really in an intimate way into people, namely the becoming of a person. Our world view during the last years, during the last decades and centuries, has not actually steered us towards people but away from people. It has indicated in a very shrewd way to identify man as at the top of the animal line, how he has evolved from lower animal forms and today we believe we can recognise what kind of relationship man actually has to the nonhuman. By us raising the big issues of humanity in the common sense, we don't actually ask: What is a human being? What is the inner being of man? — no, we ask: What is the animal, what is the inner being of an animal? — We study the development of the animal kingdom, and when we have studied how the animal kingdom develops up to its highest peak we remain stuck at this level in order to reach an understanding of people only through the evolution of the animal kingdom.

From a certain point of view it was certainly a great and meaningful route to take, but it is characteristic of the basic principles of the view of development in recent times. As a result the human being is through this not regarded as an individual within his own being but he is only standing in front of himself insofar as he is at the pinnacle of the animal kingdom, insofar as he is something other than an actual human being.

In what way is man an animal? This is a question we ask today and in all kinds of ways. That brings us to the question that got lost: To what extent is man in the true sense of the word, man? And so it becomes almost a fact that people, I would say, grit their teeth on logic at the question: What is the relationship between what we call soul, what we call spirit in human beings, and what we call body in human beings? — In all kinds of forms this is raised in current philosophy, but people only bite with logical teeth. How remarkable it is when sometimes such a white raven is put into the number of viewers who today are so correct in their world view while dealing with such questions, to then speak from a certain healthy common sense. For this I have an example which illustrates much.

For a long time a spirited philologist, Rudolf Hildebrand, worked at the Leipzig University as a student of Jacob Grimm's linguistic research, also editing to a large extent the famous dictionary concerning the parts that Jacob and Wilhelm Grimm left to be edited. This Rudolf Hildebrand also wrote a number of newspaper diary pages which were published by Diederichs in 1910. In these he expresses himself as the kind of person whose life is within teaching and education of the present time and contained in the attitude, I could say, which suddenly stopped and him wanting to use common sense in all that was going on around him, especially in those people who, in today's scholastic and doctrinal manner, is talking about questions of a world view. An interesting sentence sequence can be found in the chapter where Rudolf Hildebrand writes about his education, upbringing and teaching in his daily column "Thoughts about God, the world and the self" which only appeared after his death. Here he says: When I bring to mind how my university colleagues actually spoke

139

about the world view question, then I often want to, while the lecturer spoke above and the listeners sat below with their sense of duty or even listening to something other than him, I would like — so says Hildebrand, and not me — that a man of the people would come and give a lecturer an earlobe tugging, not too weakly, but enough to hurt, and say to him: You! Look me in the face, or look into the faces of the students, as a person to another person, and try accept this empirical fact, and then ask yourself if everything you say is only talk, because you are obstinate in yourself and don't have the awareness that in the social life you are standing in front of another human being. –

Rudolf Hildebrand said it would be particularly interesting, if once the wife of the lecturer would accompany him and remark, by tugging his earlobe, not too gently but strong enough to cause pain, and say: You! Would you really dare to say what you say under the influence of your authority to me at home in private, and do you think I would attach any value to it? — Now, my dear friends, I have expressed this to you not to merely hand down a verdict of my own, but the judgement of a man who, for decades worked at a representative university throughout his career, saw that the observed issue at stake here has become a real matter of conscience. What the issue here is that we need, today, with the present world situation and wanting to work in teaching, in education, is a real human knowledge — a knowledge of human nature which we must demand so that at the same time it stimulates us to work with people, and that is a human treatment, flooded through and through with human love. Only such human knowledge, permeated with skill for human treatment, permeated with human love, may direct teaching and education in such a way that the coming generations are positioned in the right way in life's relationships.

However, my dear friends, this is precisely the difficulty that our present science is lurching around in abstract heights, it believes, with its atoms and atom groupings, that it grasps a reality, while it only drifts around in abstract heights of thinking, in abstract terms. So, if one first

140

creates a concept of the soul and then creates a concept of the body, without thoroughly penetrating the actual human body's configuration, the actual being of the human soul through direct spiritual looking, then one can't arrive at anything but a logical grudge against these big riddles of life, which must underlie all human knowledge.

There is a point where what is meant here as spiritual science, applies in such a way that it is possible to determine the relationship between the body and soul, not according to abstract philosophical formulas which are almost exclusively sought today, but that a search will be undertaken towards really looking at the soul activities of people as a way to self-education and self-discipline in the sense of spiritual research which I have often described here, and an attempt is also being made to look at the physical, the corporeal, in the sense of spiritual research. For this one has terms, a few of which I will characterise today. Through these few terms I will be able to show how such a living human knowledge springs up from such a renewal, from such a refreshment of a human life's view of the world.

We see how a child grows up from birth, where it enters into the physical world out of the spiritual world. We see something appearing out of the deepest inner being of a person as it expands, week by week, month by month, year by year, ever more full of riddles yet ever more magnificent and meaningful in the outer structure, in the outer corporeal-bodily form of the human being. We see how this person grows up, how significant life events strike at its human existence. These life events are usually only described by what is now popular science, and underestimated. I will name two of these life events first; from other points of view I have characterized it often already for you.

I want to mention that at about the seventh year of a child something occurs which replaces the original milk teeth with permanent teeth, I already called your attention yesterday to the complete change in a person's soul constitution at this age. It is at the same time the age where the child comes out of his parents' house and enters the primary school. This is the age we need to look at if we want to gain a methodological, didactic pedagogical starting point for the primary and elementary school education. I have drawn you attention to how, in the years up to the change of teeth, a person is predominantly an imitator, how in his soul he is formed in such a way that he lives from his instincts outward, into all that goes on around him in his immediate surroundings and to a certain extent doesn't seem to be able to detach himself from his surroundings. Hand gestures of the mother and father, the tone of voice uttered by father and mother are imitated by the child, while it is to a certain extent, if not so visibly, connected to the father and mother and the immediate surroundings; just like the father's arm and mother's arm are connected to their bodies, only to a higher degree. However, what I have pointed out already I don't want to refer to today but to something else, which is in relation to it.

What appears as a change of teeth is in a way the conclusion of an entire organic process; which culminates, so to speak, in the emergence of the second teeth, which are the results of forces that have been generated in the preceding age, forces which now flood through the whole human organism. Here we don't need to differentiate between what is soul-spiritual and what is bodily-physical. When we look at the facial expressions of the child, as its face changes from one year to the next, we see how the spiritual is working on the physical. To a certain extent we only see deeper into this soul-spiritual working when we see how the soul-spiritual works organically in the child, how it penetrates outward into the outside world by finally finding a conclusion in the insertion of the second teeth. What is actually working here?

Now, I can only sketch it, but what I sketch, however, can be determined with scientific precision into its smallest details — so what is this really, that happens in human beings? One first observes what happens soul-spiritually with a child while he has to undergo the change of teeth. At the same time those human ideas that are so fluctuating in earlier life are not remembered in later life in sharply defined terms. Just think how far you need to go back if you want to remember the first sharply defined concepts you had in your childhood; during this age up to the change of teeth concepts are still unclear, fluctuating, not sharply outlined, not firm yet, that they are woven into the soul-spiritual life that can be kept in such a way that all these memories outline the whole of life. The relationships of the soul-spiritual with sharply outlined concepts and imagination, which can be assimilated in thoughts and memories, are established at the same age as the change of teeth takes place. If one now investigates what is actually present there, it turns out that the same forces which then appear in our memory, in what we carry as the power of thought in us, the power or memory in thinking, that these forces are so to speak emancipated from the physical-bodily, had been working in the physical-corporeal right up to the change of teeth: these are the same forces that drove the teeth outwards. So we have up to the change of teeth the same forces intimately connected with the physicality of the human being which then become powers of thought; they work in every bone formation and find their conclusion in the change of teeth.

My dear friends, here we are looking at quite an actual, a very real, relationship between the soul and the body. Later in life we have our sharply contoured memory concepts, we know what the power of thought and imagination is, we gaze into ourselves and observe these powers of thought and say to ourselves: There powers of though work as a free power of thought in us only from the seventh year. Before that it was submerged in our organism and had orchestrated those powers which pushed out the second teeth. We have an intimate relationship between the soul and body, we are looking concretely at this relationship. We are not speculating about it: What is the relationship of the body to the soul? — We look at the soul and we see where we can observe, so to speak, where the free ideas occur in our memories. We see how these forces, before they became free for memories, worked in the organism, how they were organically formative.

You see, this is the progress in the world view of spiritual science from the abstract to the concrete, from merely moderated thoughts that imagine themselves to penetrate to reality, to the actual, truly realistic. This is the advance to the true being of man, because now one knows how to answer the question: What works in the body of the human being before his seventh year? — This can't be described abstractly, you have to somehow refer to facts, pointing out a few things that are active there in human beings. What is working there is the same as what works in our powers of recollection. This is one example which will characterise what a radical shift in our scientific approach is taking place in the direction of our thought, and must come into our world view. As you can imagine, my dear friends, something like this lies quite beyond the minds of the so-called educated people because no-one — science in the least — wants to know about it, what concretely exists in the soul-spiritual and bodily-physical of the human being, for this reason man is a stranger and why you can't see inside people. How can you create the foundation for education and teaching if you can't see into people?

A second life event I want to draw your attention to is puberty. Just as much as what happens in the years from birth to the change of teeth, proceeds from the change of teeth to sexual maturity. When you now look again from the same spiritual scientific standpoint to that which works into puberty and in puberty reaches its culmination, then you can ask, what is this actually? Just as the power of thinking work within the body and — if I may express myself in a trivial manner — push the teeth out, in the same way — this is shown in spiritual science, I can only sketch it here — in the same way it works up to the fifteenth year, in the will. The will has an organic forming effect. It works in such a way that it controls the growth conditions, the inner organic conditions. These inner organic processes of the will find a conclusion, just as the process of thinking at the appearance of the change of teeth. What is found as a conclusion here appears in the outer formation of a person in puberty. The will forces don't take root in the head but in the entire

144

being of the person. The will forces are what regulate human growth forces until sexual maturity.

Then they dam up. In a way they have the tendency to extend into the formation of the head. These will forces also dash forward before sexual maturity; they were inwardly organically active in the whole person; with puberty, they accumulate. They dam up in the human vocal organ which is at first the most intimate outflow of the human will, just as the other forces accumulate in tooth formation. They accumulate below the head — the head, the organ of the actual intellectual human being, is being excluded. The will forces accumulate and this accumulation in the male nature is the transformation of the voice finding expression through the larynx; in the nature of the female it is something different. In this lies the release of those will forces which now have to deal with the outside world in experiences and in life — those will forces which had until then been working internally in the human body in a soul-spiritual way. It is just the same as with the powers of thought which first came forward in the change of teeth and are then emancipated in their own form in the powers of thinking.

So, as spiritual scientists we look on the one hand at the thinking human being with powers of thought and on the other hand to human beings with will forces. We aren't talking abstractly of some or other soul, but we are talking about the soul we are observing. We follow the activity, as souls of thought, up to the change of teeth, then we follow their release, their becoming independent, independent of certain inwardness in the organic process. In the same way we follow the will. That means, we are not posing some or other theory of the soul and the spirit in relation to the body, to the physical body, but we observe and aim for reality. You see, here, a way is being taken quite differently, but, I believe, to be quite suitable, to flood general human education, in a way in which an honest mind once had the idea of giving the lecturer a tug on his earlobe, and not too gently either. Now it involves something else entirely. It involves not only attaching importance to results, to the knowledge gained in this way, but that one should bestow value to how one can be guided through spiritual-scientific methods as I have depicted in my "Occult Science", in "Knowledge of Higher worlds" or in "A way to self-knowledge", how through such ways of thinking one is enabled to truly recognise much, much more regarding healthy and unhealthy people, which to science, deemed so authoritative today, it's depths are simply closed. Here the mind has to be schooled in a certain way; the mind needs orientation in a certain way. Here the mind must take a different direction to what it is used to, today. Much depends on this. After all, results are just results; they can be more or less important or unimportant, interesting or uninteresting. However, what we apply by taking the path to such knowledge, what we make of ourselves by forming ourselves in our being, what we make of ourselves as people by taking the path prepared by such knowledge — that is essentially what matters.

It always comes down to what we make of ourselves as human beings through our particular soul constitution and in a very specific way look at the world from within ourselves. This enables us to have a life free of illusions and still look at it in its wonderful greatness. We watch for example, a child in its first years and later in life, engrossed in a game. The direction and control of the game belongs essentially to the tasks of a reasonable, humanely correct educational and teaching art. A child plays. For someone who has now sharpened his gaze for problems of the world and people's lives, notices a large difference between how one child, and another child, plays. For the superficial observer, nearly all children play in the same way. For someone who has sharpened his gaze, every child plays in a different way to other children. Each child has his own way of playing. How extraordinary it is at all, if one looks at what the game means for children at that age: an actuation of the individuals in the soul-spiritual, as it is present when the actual powers of thought are still within the organic form right up to the change of teeth. It is very strange how this childlike soul-spiritual, which has not yet absorbed thoughtfulness, moves in free play — in this game whose design lies separate from the benefit and purpose of life, this game where the child follows only what flows from his own soul. It could appear to be a breakthrough in the principle of imitation because of the way the child lives into it; it is surely something that comes from the freedom of the child's soul — however only apparently. For someone who observes more acutely it certainly appears as if the child's game comes out of what the child experiences in his environment and all that is happening around him. If one has sharpened one's gaze, then one sees this game not only as something interesting, which happens in individual children's lives at certain times, but you put this game with all its character into the whole of human life.

By observing this, you learn to compare what happens at different ages of a human being's life. Just as one can compare zinc and copper in the lifeless element, as one can compare a May bug with a sun beetle in the living element, so can one compare the different ages of man with one another. It shows something which is quite strange. If one does, with the sharpened gaze — characterized today — created a real idea about the child's play, then one has to search in the various ages of man, where this particular character of the child's play flows. One discovers through quite experiential searching that when the human being, between about the 20th to 28th, 29th year, is in the position to find his position in the world, to deal with what the world offers him as an experience and guideline for an independent life, and if one now look at how mankind intervenes in life, is touched by life, you actually find a certain level in the metamorphosis, a transformation of the special character of the child's game. Before the change of teeth, the child has to deal with what doesn't belong to life, with the doll, with other playthings, freely formed out of its soul activity; it is activated in a certain configuration, a certain structure. Learn to recognise this, look through these and observe the human being then in his twenties, how he is within the seriousness of life with what is purposeful in life, with what is found through experience, and you find that now he has been invested in the usefulness, the expediency of the world, in that which is demanded of life, positioning himself in such a way, with such characteristics as he had displayed freely in his childhood games.

Consider what this now means. You want to focus on education and you know: what you see as a particular character trait in the childhood game, what you then understand and how you guide the child's game must be done in such a way that it comes to fruition, when the person comes to terms with the world in his twenties, as being useful and appropriate to his life. Consider what feelings are worthy in the soul of the educator when he knows: What I achieve with the child is what I do for the adult in his twenties. This doesn't depend on basic educational laws one knows in abstract form and that can be applied from intellectual foundations and didactic-methodical rules, but it depends on such knowledge we enkindle in our hearts with a deep sense of responsibility. True human knowledge doesn't speak to our minds; it speaks to our feelings, it speaks to our experiences, to our entire view of life. It flows and weaves though us with a sense of responsibility in the posts we represent.

We aren't looking for a kind of art of education coming merely out of some spineless or other justified cleverness, saying that one should educate in this or that way, but we are looking for the kind of art of education in relation to the present situation of man, which — out of the knowledge of the human being — puts into the educator a sense of responsibility, social responsibility towards all of mankind. The art of education comes out of a sense of responsibility which can only develop in us out of the correct foundation of our world view.

I do not speak to you here of a renewal of science for the reason that I am particularly interested or excited to tell you that there will be other results of science and that these other results would create a different world view to the one which is common today. No, I'm speaking to you in this way because I believe that the whole procession, the whole characteristic style of the world view and scientific life will change. I say this because I believe that a science, a world view of life will come about which will penetrate the wholeness of the human being, penetrate the body, soul and spirit and which in quite a special way would relate to our present situation in life, important for all art of education, all art of teaching. Yet something else is connected to what is based on such a new view of man.

What are we striving for today when we speak about science, about a scientifically based foundation regarding a world view? We speak about what is presented largely in abstracts concepts and we are satisfied when we can say to ourselves: That is what we must insist upon, only what sharply outlined concepts can give us: we must challenge such concepts precisely because of our prejudice. — Yes, but when nature and the world is not as we would have them fit into the concepts we demand, when the world comes about according to completely different forms, when nature for instance isn't shaped according to our law of nature, when these laws of nature only to a small degree include actual reality and that the essentials of nature are not formed according to abstract laws of nature and ideas, but according to images — then we can still for a long time discuss the logical foundations of sharply outlines natural laws, but we are not penetrating nature because nature doesn't submit to such laws because it requires being captured in images. Human nature in particular requires to be captured in images. Then one is led through all I have sketched here today also by a figurative, by an imaginative mode of imagination.

I would like to mention: When one observes people in this way by looking at how the power of thought weaves in his organism up to the appearance of teeth, how the powers of the will weaves, how they draw up into the larynx and take care of the transformation of the voice, when one looks at all of this, one can't remain fixed on cultivating these abstract laws of nature which are so loved today, but one arrives at making the soul active, more pliant, in its effort to understand a human being. One is able not to remain with abstract concepts, with abstract precepts, but one arrives at images. In other words, one becomes able to take the abstract-logical scientific concepts and lead them into an artistic conception of the world, to an aesthetic grasp of the world.

One acquires understanding for the deep foundations Goethe spoke about in his world view: 'Art is based on the observation of deeper natural laws which will never reveal themselves to man without art.' — Goethe meant that they would never be revealed through abstract natural laws, but they would reveal themselves through the observation of nature in pictorial form. In this way, one takes the path from a logical-abstract view, from a mechanistic view of outer nature to an artistic understanding, this kind of artistic understanding gives our entire personality a different suppleness of soul than the abstract concepts do.

We can think of those people who have swung upwards from scientific human knowledge to an artistic grasp of the world and mankind, one can think how these people are flooded, permeated, with this artistic image-rich view of people and them practicing education and the art of teaching this way. Life flows from them directly over into the developing human being; there it is not a philistine, abstract educational science, here a living educational art is at work which in the most beautifully social interactive way can take place between one person and another. Here finally from a deeper foundation of knowledge, fulfilled out of a more humanistic sentiment, Schiller tried to present in his letters: 'The aesthetic education of man'. In fact it makes it clear that the human being, in true cognition holds the balance between mere abstract reasoning necessities and mere sensual natural instincts; it becomes clear that man is caught between these drives and that he acts out of an attitude that is as valid as an attitude in artistic creation or in artistic observation. It asserts itself in such a way that what we pursue as spirit is at the same time sensual; it makes what we pursue as sensual, spiritual at the same time. It is out of his attitude that we begin here at the Waldorf School to educate and teach. Here pupils are not given something prescribed, here we give ourselves as teachers, as educators, completely over to the developing human being; we educate the entire person who can capably position himself in life. I have only mentioned a few examples. Just as we give, through directing the children's games towards what is best for his or her integration into life in his or her twenties, we can observe other things in the nascent human being which we establish in our education in order to give him or her, the best for their life in the future. Here we have established the foundation for an education which accounts for the whole person and for the whole of human life. One can already say: the seriousness of the present world situation requires that one looks a little deeper than only into what can become better, out of which suffering and hardship can be overcome in the present. This can't be done with indifferent means or with superficial means but it can only happen through deeper means. Only in this way will we bring people to us who will have what they must have in the most eminent sense, because it is precisely this that is missing in the present world situation.

When we look at people, how they are today, when we look at what life wants to direct on the surface, what life wants to direct in what is lived out in public relations, the way they have been unfolding these past few days — we see everywhere there are two things missing in people today, which one would so like to wish for them in the most intensive degree: today people lack, to a high degree, what one could call self-confidence, but also what one would like to call trust in humanity. Examine, my dear friends, why people today do so little in themselves to engage actively in present social life, which needs the energy so urgently. We discover: Self-confidence [The German word "Selbstvertrauen" literally means trust-in-the-self, which translates as "self-confidence" — so wherever "Vertrauen" (to trust) appears it means both *trust* as well as *confidence* in this text. – trans.] is missing in people. However, self-confidence is only justified and can only exist when it is carried by trust/confidence in other people. Like the North Pole and the South Pole belong to one another, they can't exist without one another, so self-confidence can't exist without confidence in other people. Never will a teaching science, an educational science, supply people with self-confidence, with what it means to trust in humanity, if it is not born out of such a love for humanity that has its origins in the knowledge of human nature, as I have characterised today, because that is what you experience, my dear friends.

If one learns to characterise as I have, how to know people, if one learns to recognise how the soul-spiritual work in their organism, how the various ages in human beings work together — as I have for instance taken the children's games and their effect on the twenties of the individual — if one learns to intimately know the soul-spirit-bodily being of the human being, then one can do nothing other than at the same time draw this knowledge to actual human love, because the power of the soul is connected to another soul power, just as in the plant's blossom the stamens are connected to the pistil; if the stamens are perfect, they require a perfect pistil. So out of love for humanity a true knowledge comes out, not developing into those abstractions which people often despise today with good reason, but to something on the other hand, which also draws them near to true human love.

Teaching and education which come out of such human knowledge, out of such human love is what we have tried, in our pedagogy and didactic as a curriculum and timetable, out of such a recognition of the nature of man as far as possible today, we have tried here in our Waldorf School. This has the effect, my dear friends, that love dawns in the child for other people. Human confidence kindled within the child through the power which is born within us as true human knowledge, which becomes an artistic understanding out of the natural human being, creates out of us that power which in the child can enkindle the lasting, the unfading self-confidence. Two other qualities that mankind today lacks so much and that can only be passed on to the human spirit through such an art of education is what I would like to call prudence on the one hand and on the other hand joyfulness, willingness to take action and the ability to be active. Today these things are not clearly considered, really not clearly, because people don't think from reality, especially not from a social reality.

I have in the past offered very praiseworthy words to the gracious scholar Rudolf Hildebrand. For this reason you are not going to believe that I don't want to recognise this man. However, he too, was a human being — despite sometimes being driven out of instinct to such considerations as I have mentioned — he was a man exposed to all the prejudices that have brought us into our present misfortune. In his diary he wrote this strange sentence: 'Compare a gaffer standing in front of a target to be shot at, with a shooter beside him, who aims for the target. The gaffer can hit the target with his gaze; he hits it every time. The shooter must first learn to hit the target, only then does he hit it in reality. Likewise there is a difference' — this is what Hildebrand says — 'between one who is a mere gawper of life, that is, the one who is philosophic or scientific or mystical or theosophical or otherwise, to the one who is actively involved in life.' — There's a great deal that's the truth in such a sentence, yet despite that, a great deal of one-sidedness. Let's think for a moment not just about the example of Hildebrand, but about a "gaffer in life", about someone who has only looked at life, for example Leibniz, who discovered the differential- and integral calculus. Let's imagine how this "gaffer in life" who had discovered the differential- and integral calculus has now become the cause of all that which is made today in technology through the differential and integral calculus, to all that, what is done in life today by the "shooter", by him, who puts in a hand.

When one looks at people in an isolated unsocial way, the comparison of the life-gaffer and the shooter who aims at his target, is striking. When one looks at this however in a broad social sense then one has to admit: when the one who is the life-gaffer has a fruitful thought out of his life's gaffing that leads to innumerable deeds, then with respect to the interaction of people, with reference to the social life, perhaps the life-gaffer is far more active than the one who one compares with the shooter. It involves the fact that we have gradually come to observe life in its isolated circumstances in a one-sided way, that today we lack the opportunity to look at the big social connections. In order to point this out, we need prudence, contemplation.

153

Today it often happens that people avoid contemplation, this being-turned-inwards into oneself, this "gazing" at life, because they are too comfortable to let thoughts or ideas become deeds because they don't want to enter into actual relationships in life, because, when misery pushes one into the window, when it reaches right up to the mouth, when misery is so great, they turn into fatalists and say: 'From some or other corner it will getter better by tomorrow.' — Discretion, active life within effective thoughts is what we need. On the other hand we need a new readiness to act; it will follow from such thoughts in those people in whom we ignite human love, which we can draw from true spirit-, soul- and physically gained knowledge — as the basis of a future world view, as we have described it today. The best, the ultimate is that we can provide teaching and education in the face of the present world situation, that is, that we acquire an open and free sense for life, if the human being is given such an understanding of human nature as is meant here.

In our time we experience people misjudging life in a strange way. They imagine themselves as spirits of reality but when it comes to reality, this reality is truly quite, quite far away. I offer an example.

You see, in the course of the 19th century a certain judgement was made. Please read the parliamentary reports, read the best speeches of the best minds, read from newspaper reports, what the most respected practitioners have said. You can always find them in the parliamentary reports, in the speeches of the best national economists, the best practitioners, as they have arrived at a certain judgement, which has been of utmost importance for the development recently in political, governmental, and economic relationships. People started to introduce the gold currency in certain countries. One can read what was said about it. The best practitioners, the most conscientious national economists have predicted that this gold currency would bring a lifting of customs borders; in particular the gold currency will support free world trade. — If you now research what these life practitioners, these business people, these industrialists, these parliamentarians have said, which had arisen from a knowledge such as one had in the 19th century, one finds — I do not want to mock, I only want to speak the truth — one finds that they said something very clever; but in reality it happened quite differently. They said: Customs borders, protective tariffs and all that will be taken out of the world when the gold currency enters. — The opposite happened.

After the introduction of the gold currency, customs borders and protective tariffs have been erected everywhere. So, the opposite of what the cleverest people have said, happened. I say explicitly, the brightest people; I am far from saying that the people who so radically fumbled past reality were fools; they were the opposite of fools. Out of their education according to how current time shaped them, they said the cleverest things, but no one can come to the truth if the truth is not given by anything, when the conditions around us are such that one can't see through reality even with the sharpest intellect. That is why the cleverest people then talk nonsense in such an area. For this reason, because the economic conditions in their connection with the state-political conditions were so entangled, because the threads were so intertwined that they could not be overlooked, as clever as one was, one talked nonsense, of course, because one could learn nothing from reality. One could not create reality beforehand in such a way that one could have learned from it.

What we term the idea of the Threefold Social Order, intends for the economic life, just like the spiritual life and state life on the one side, to be placed on its own foundation; that these three areas of life should exist side by side as interactive members of the combined social organism. Here it is required that individual economic areas, be they areas of production or consumption or professions or something similar, develop in such a way that they are not influenced by government or other organisations which themselves had to be created according to an economic authority. It is demanded that they form themselves so independently from professional competence and expertise of the people working in them that one organization, which can only have a certain size, connects to another, and to a third, and a fourth in a certain way; depending on how such associations are formed, they will again be associated with one another. In this way a net of associations will come about. Whoever is then in one association will know: in the other association in which I am involved in traffic, in goods exchange, is someone I know; one overlooks the relations of the two associations. The mutual relationship is regulated by contract.

This is how we can concretely look into the economic area. Through the principle of association, overview ratios are created and life comes about in such a way that one can learn from it. The time situation itself demands that the unmanageable economic life, through the associative principle, is replaced by something transparent, the essence of which you can read about in my book "Key Points of the Social Question" and especially in our newspaper "The Threefold structure of the Social Organism", which has already been published in fifty issues. One can't learn from something which is not transparent. Life wants to be shaped in such a way that, if one positions oneself in the right way in life, one is able to learn from it.

People who are trained in a teaching based on genuine, true knowledge of man, from which, according to natural law, human love will follow — such people will feel how the economic life wants to shape its independence through associations. Such people would have learnt in their childhood that this learning was for them such a school that they now can constantly learn from life. This is the greatest empirical science of the school, that we may come out of it in such a way that life for us will always remain a continuation of a great school. In this way we are guaranteed through our entire life: We develop further, we don't remain standing in one place, we carry the world further. Right up to the end of our life, right up to passing through the portal of death into the spiritual world, we can learn here to expand our soul-spiritual nature, make our physical body more skilful, so that we consider our entire life as a school. The present life situation of mankind demands this. What it demands can best be expressed when we say: everything that comes from the renewal of such a view of the world, as it is meant here from the foundation of spiritual science, must lead to the development of an art of education, and art of teaching, which comes out of true, genuine knowledge of mankind, gives birth to that love of mankind, which educates such people who have come out of the childhood school to be released in the right way into the school of life, because only through this learning in the school of life the right process is possible to exist on a social basis.

Next week I will speak about this in my lecture regarding "Questions of the Soul and questions of Life". Today I only wanted to show that we need to say about education and teaching at present, out of all that is pressing and powerful in this time, that we need to keep the saying: Give education, give teaching from a deeper view of the world and more profound basis of education and teaching. Because through this you create the true, the genuine, the firm basis for a solution of those social and human questions which are now so pressing in the whole of human life.

LECTURE 7

Soul questions and life questions today
A lecture for present times
Stuttgart on 15 June 1920

My dear honourable friends present here today! When one observes today's conditions of hardship, misery and hopelessness, and if one looks at the causes from which all these things have emerged, then one is forced — I think — to cast an unbiased view of life on what appears as the first riddle of our present day, which stands there as the most insistent mystery: How can humanity unite and in a thriving way build our social and other future conditions in such a way that it unites the ways of the soul with the ways of life?

Since I intend to provide a supplement to some of the things I have said for years here in Stuttgart from the point of view of anthroposophically oriented spiritual science, you will forgive me if I connect it in an historical sense to something or other, and thus perhaps create the impression that these connections sometimes appear more personal than what I have presented here in the course of many years. Only, it will be merely apparent.

Right from the starting point of my lecture on the present situation, the fact is that I take the liberty of pointing out to this very question: How can contemporary humanity bring about harmony between the ways of the soul and the ways of life? — how this question hovered in my mind when in the end of the eighties and the beginning of the nineties of the last century I worked out my "Philosophy of Freedom," published in 1894, as the basis of the world view that has emerged in the course of many years. Basically the way in which it could be given to me in those days, this "Philosophy of Freedom" already answers the starting point of considerations involving destiny questions of humanity. I don't intend to discuss the content of this "Philosophy of Freedom" today, but I would like to touch upon the intensions underlying this writing with a few introductory words.

The intention was to answer the question: How a person, situated in the present, can face the great social demands of the present with the most essential feeling, the most crucial longing of the newer time, and manage with the feeling of freedom, the longing for freedom? The essential thing is that this consideration of the essence of freedom has broken away from the whole way in which one has always asked about the justification of the idea of freedom, the impulse of freedom. People ask: Is the human being a free being according to his natural disposition or is he not? — This kind of question appears to me to need revision due to the entire evolution mankind has gone through up to our time. Today we can, according to what humanity has gone through in the last three to four centuries, only really ask: Is man in the position to establish the basis of such a social order so that he, while he develops from childhood to a ripe old age, can find what he is entitled to call the freedom of his being? Not whether a person is born free, is asked in my "Philosophy of Freedom," but in this book it concerns the possibility of discovering something in the depth of their being that lift up from the subconscious, or the unconscious foundations into full, clear light of consciousness, and whether by this lifting it up, a free being can be drawn up within it. Directed through this consideration I was led towards the most essential thing that human development in our newer time can only be justified by two things: firstly what I called at that time intuitive thinking, and secondly what I then called social trust. Since I am not referring to something abstract and theoretical but to things with reality, things of life, it was so that my writing was quite, quite slowly understood, because we simply live in a time of abstractions, as I have often mentioned here.

We live in a time of theorizing. If someone claims that only that which comes from a sense of reality is then validated into ideas, then people are exchanging what is actually taken out of reality and clearly appears in the form of ideas, with what appears in them as abstract and lives as unrealistic ideas. You see what actually is working in people as a real impulse, as something utopian or the like — for most of these people who have only the utopian in their heads, see something like this as utopian.

What was in this intention for a universal human education in the sense of "Philosophy of Freedom"? It was the idea that the human being will never become free if he only takes those ideas into his consciousness that have come out of the scientific viewpoint of the last three to four centuries, and is only filled with what he can learn from nature. Now, my dear friends, I have often said already that the objection is made: Yes, but how many people are there who today absorb into their whole consciousness those concepts borrowed from the observation of nature? — It could appear so, some people think, that only single persons educated in natural science, and then perhaps also those who experience something from natural science who then recruit those with a monastic — or how it is usually called — world view, but that this still won't have an influence on the broad masses of mankind today.

It is not like this, my dear friends, it is different. It is so that we are slowly moving out during the course of the last three to four centuries into a spiritual life, have entered into a life which is essentially fed — already out into the outermost regions of the country, not only among the city dwellers or the so-called educated — through that which flows through our journal-, newspaper- and book literature: People, without realizing it, absorb into their imagination what comes from bookish, popular science, journalism and newspaper literature. This is what they fill their souls with. They can, when they go to church on Sundays, believe to be good Catholics or good Protestants, they could give themselves over to the idea that they quite honestly believe in everything that is preached to them. But in what they are, so to speak, in everyday life, the form of their thoughts, the whole configuration of her imaginative life is shaped by what is unconsciously flowing in from all the sources I have now mentioned. We can determine this through a kind of cross check.

I believe that actually a large number of you are of the opinion that a certain community which has ancient religious beliefs with very intensive powers, want to seep into the present — ancient religious ideas. Who actually doubts, for example, that what members of Jesuitism strive for in ancient religious beliefs, they want to trickle into present life? — It is the case certainly, when Jesuits write about what they believe, it is necessary to say that on the basis of confession, when they speak about what people should believe, when they speak about the relationship people express to the church and so on. When Jesuits however write about objects of nature today, about objects of human nature and believe that science is to be taken into account, what are these Jesuits then? They are just the most pronounced materialists. Whoever researches what a Jesuit presents as secular literature in addition to his theological and religious writers, finds that the entire aim of this secular literature attempts to establish materialism in the broadest sense.

One can have very clear ideas about why these are done. From this point of view one strives to withdraw everything that includes questions about the soul which are questions about the spiritual life, from human research, from direct human thinking. In relation to the questions about the soul and questions about life, people are not supposed to do research, but they should submit themselves to what is traditionally available. As a result everything regarding soul questions and questions of spiritual life, is to be removed from what research should cover. It should not be looked at from the view of the spirit, from the view of the soul in nature, at the real, true circle of life because such research, from their point of view, is unchristian, is not pious. When one is not allowed to research life from a spiritual viewpoint, then research becomes materialistic, and if the spirit is not brought into the research of matter, then the spirit remains outside the research into matter and one only has the most blatant materialism in hand. Therefore you will see the most blatant materialism next to the assertion of all traditional ideas on religious or theological grounds, if [besides theological literature also] secular literature comes out of this very circle. It is of no use today to indulge in any kind of delusion about these things, because only an unbiased look at these things can be useful.

So we can say: Even those who in a certain sense officially represent piousness — how could one not believe that Jesuitism obviously represent piousness officially — even they are crass materialists from what has happened in the course of modern times. So we can of course always see how people go to church on Sundays and adhere to what they do not understand, while during the week they only understand what comes to them from a materialistic world view. It is actually this situation — and I have often emphasized this here — that has led us into the distress in recent times. It is easy to see that such relationships will not lead a person to find his soul, which leads him to the ways of life. From what on the one hand is the misunderstood, only traditional and what's more, traditionally incorrectly handed down spirit, and on the other hand, what is only materialistic, the soul can never build itself a path which leads on to a strong, into a secure, mobility on the paths of life.

For this reason my "Philosophy of Freedom" tries to point out how people must again not only infuse their consciousness with what can be eavesdropped from nature, what the newer science passes down, but it points out that in man himself a source of inner life can develop. When man grasps this source of the inner soul life, then he grasps that within the soul which does not come from outside through the contemplation of the senses, but what comes out of the soul itself, then he educates himself by this grasping of the intuitive soul content towards free decision, towards free will and free action. I try to show in my "Philosophy of Freedom" that a person is always dependant if he follows only nature's impulses; I try to show that a person can only be free when he is in the position to develop what is revealed to him as his own intuitive thinking; intuitive, pure thinking in his human soul. This reference to what man in his soul through self-education must conquer, in order to really become part of freedom, this reference then led to the fact I necessarily sought to give in the continuation of the one indicated in "Philosophy of Freedom" and I have tried, in the course of the last decade, to give it through what I call Anthroposophically orientated spiritual science. If it is pointed out that the impulse of freedom, intuitive thinking, is to be lifted out from the depths of the human soul, then it must also be pointed out what comes from people who turn to this inner source within their soul life.

Basically, the sum of everything my "Philosophy of Freedom" points out, are statements of anthroposophical writings kept for the next few years. I have pointed out that in the soul are paths to be followed in spirit towards thinking, which do not just intellectually combine elements of the environment but out of inner vision lifts it to an experience of the spirit. In addition I was forced to show what one looks at there, when you look into the spiritual world.

Certainly, something may, indeed must, be emphasized today: This nebulous mysticism which people may refer to when they speak about this inner source of the soul, this unclear floating and rambling that gives itself over to inner reverie, is not meant here. However, this has resulted in a double situation. The one is that those people who do not want to apply themselves to what feels uncomfortable today by following the paths of clear thinking, feel so little attracted precisely by what lies in the direction of my "Philosophy of Freedom." This is the one thing that has happened.

The other result is that, however, a sufficiently large number of hoverers and wafflers, who rely on unclear, nebulous paths, want to search for anything possible and get attached to what should be striven for with clarity through anthroposophically orientated spiritual science. It has happened that through this adherence enough evil-willed spirits have come to fight against what people say, with whom I have nothing to do, and who, by fighting, have attached all this to me, that the hoverers and wafflers, the nebulous mystics extract, as their own making, from what was just meant as a most intense need for the culture of the present.

This is exactly what we particularly need on the one hand: Clarity of inner striving -which distinguishes the true natural scientist today in his outer striving, but also in the clarity of his *inner* striving. This is what we need on the one hand. Not darkness and twilight, not twilight mysticism, but bright, light clarity in all that involves thinking. That's the one thing. The other thing based on what I wanted to express through my "Philosophy of Freedom," is social trust.

We live in an age when every individual within his own consciousness need to strive towards his own thinking, feeling and willing. We no longer live in a time in which people tolerate being led only by authority; neither do we live in a time when people truly want to endure their entire life as being organised. Organising only arose as a kind of counter pole. I tried to point out the underlying facts in 1908 in the following way. I said: On the one hand, for three to four centuries a general human power existed where people want to focus increasingly on their own individuality; wanting to find within themselves all the impulses they actually strive for in life.

However, while this exists in many people as something deeply unconscious which they not only don't want to clarify because they basically fear their innermost being itself, now — I could call it, like a shadow beside a strong light — this striving for freedom, this striving for individual expression of the individual person towards what has been working against all that human nature has been forming over long periods of time, something emerged in the last three to four centuries that worked against all urges of human nature and is being done in the present to an ever greater degree.

I said: While it is actually natural for people to strive for individual expression, one sees how people, while they don't understand themselves in their most modern striving, actually outwardly set the polar opposite goal. I characterised 1908 somewhat grotesquely, but people will today still understand me as they did at that time. I said: It looks as if people are not at all striving for the shaping of their individuality, but for the kind of a state, a societal organisation which makes nothing else possible for human beings than for all paths and bridges of life to move in such a way that there is a doctor on the left and a policeman on the right — the doctor for his continuous health care, without any personal judgement required regarding his own health, and the policeman, who sees to it that a person finds direction in his life without himself giving the direction.

One only pursues, despite all enlightenment, despite all alleged sense of freedom, what is oriented — more or less unconsciously — towards this ideal in modern times. It must have been said already: if we keep going in this direction, we will come to a terrible decline. We will only be able to rise up again if we strive to draw people gradually into a social cohabitation which is completely filled with mutual trust. We must gain faith in human beings; we must gain faith that, through a corresponding education, held in a genuinely human sense, through a development of our humanity it is made possible that in the affairs of life, that require a bit more than just passing each other along the street, but that we get along with each other when we meet. When we come across people on the street, one goes to the left and the other to the right; they pass one another, they don't bump into one another. That is obvious. If that source is opened up in humanity of which I speak as the true intuition in my "Philosophy of Freedom," then in the higher matters of life a social community is built on trust, just as one must ultimately base everyday life on trust, because it is unacceptable that when two people meet on the street, a policeman joins in and tells you: You must go there so that you don't bump into the other person. — This matter of course in everyday life can be carried into the higher life, where seriousness of life exists, where seriousness concerning life is cultivated.

Admittedly two challenges regarding the path of the soul are then given in the "Philosophy of Freedom." The one requirement is that one should not be satisfied with a thinking which is so popular today, even popular in everyday life, popular in science, but that one must rise up to educate what newer times require: to a thinking which flows from its own original spring in the human soul, to a thinking that is full of light and clarity itself. Here I must point out something again — disregarding the fact that I can be accused of saying things that are difficult to understand — here I must point out where traditional

166

educations leads people to: it leads to the opposite of what I described in my last lecture here, as a necessary requirement for the future.

If a person is educated today from nothing other than what flows to him from traditional confessions and from the newer scientific world of ideas, if his everyday thought-forms are based on nothing other than what he has learned from representations of the scientific worldview, from popular literature and literature in general, journalism and the newspaper industry, then, my dear friends, then a person becomes a materialist. Why a materialist? He becomes a materialist on the basis that his thinking is not freed from his bodily nature, because he doesn't strive to find that source in his soul that separates the soul from corporeality; through this the human being decays into a life dependant on corporeality.

Why are we materialists today? Not from the basis of falsely interpreting life, but because we live life falsely. We live and educate our children in such a way that they don't think with the soul but with the brain because the brain can become an imprint of the thinking. We switch off the soul and think with the brain. No wonder that we then also talk about thinking this way, as if it is dependent on the brain, for the majority of people today, it depends on the brain. People are materialistic because they have become material in their whole life, because they don't strive to achieve freedom though thinking that is detached from the body, that becomes bodiless — if I may use this expression which I have often justified. If someone wants to develop themselves in today's demands, then he has to free his thinking from his bodily nature. He must transform thinking into unrestricted movement from out of his soul existing in itself. He must know that it means: to think within mere thoughts, not to think where the thought is only a result of the brain.

Today this question is absurd: Is thinking a result of the brain or not? — It comes out of the brain if we do not first free it from the brain. Here I point out a tangle of errors, in which today's humanity is ensnared because today we are by what humanity has achieved in the course of historical development, able to detach our thinking with full, light clarity from corporeality. How does one free it? Not — I have often emphasized — because one would inevitably become spiritual researchers oneself, although to a certain degree anyone can become one, when he takes note of what is written in my book "Knowledge of the Higher Worlds and its Attainment," in my "Occult Science" and what is given in other similar books, but you don't even need that. You only need to accept from the spiritual researcher what he has to say to the world — as one does from the astronomer, from the chemist, receive from the physicist what the astronomer, the physicist has to say. You only need to approach and receive this with a healthy common sense. However, then you will make a certain discovery.

A person will discover that: If, for a long time, you research with your materialistic thinking based on science and present-day thinking and you then pursue what the spiritual scientist says, then it appears to you as fantasy, as infatuation, as something you have to reject. You only first understand what the spiritual researcher says when you are conscious that thinking can be untangled from corporeality, that you can delve into that thinking which is drawn in from spiritual worlds at birth or conception, which will draw in, into spiritual worlds when you pass through the gate of death. Making thinking free from the body is the first great goal on this path which needs to be followed by the soul in life today.

Another great goal is necessary. When we develop willing, as it is methodically described in spiritual science — in the mentioned books it is presented — then this will goes in the opposite way as thinking. Thinking frees itself from the body, is loosened from the body. The will however, through schooling, as it is described in the books, seizes the body all the more. That's the peculiar thing about people today; they indulge in abstractions regarding the will, indulge in abstract ideals with the will and they hear abstract commandments preached from the pulpit, but these abstract commandments are not in their arms, do not enter into their bodies, not enter into their actions. That man becomes one in what he calls the impulses of the will, experienced in his body itself, leads to the second link of that education and human development which is meant here. The spiritualization of the body with the will, the introduction of the will into all sensual, into all physical and into all social things, that is the second thing this spiritual science conveys.

What becomes of the ideals injected into the body, as it were, according to the method of spiritual scientific thinking? These ideals, they are seized, from what is otherwise only directed by ordinary sense far from this body. That which awakens gradually in the body in childhood, love, sensual love, when a person grasps spiritual science, results in all ideals no longer remaining abstractions, that they don't remain mere thoughts, but that they are loved, loved by the entire human as a being; they become so that the spiritual at the basis of our moral, our ethics, our customs, our religious impulses are so loved, like one loves a loved one, that what otherwise remains abstract becomes completely real to one, like a being of flesh and blood.

With the help of my "Philosophy of Freedom" all of Kant's categorical imperatives must be overcome; these disturbed Schiller very much already because these categorical imperatives intruded into human life like something which one submits to. The kind of consciousness that has to be overcome for us to progress is what Kant says: "Duty! You sublime, great name, which doesn't grasp anything popular in you that ingratiates itself, but demands submission" that you "establish a law ... before which all inclinations fall silent, when they secretly counteract it" — this must be replaced by: Freedom, you wonderful spirit, that includes everything in itself, to which my humanity would like to surrender lovingly!

Schiller was upset by Kant's inhuman categorical imperative, and he said: "I gladly serve my friends but unfortunately I do so through inclination, and it often troubles me that I'm not virtuous." — "There is no other piece of advice; you must try despise them and then with disgust do as duty demands of you." Schiller sensitively saw all that was philistine and inhuman in this categorical imperative. He wasn't living in the time — like in the present — when one has to point out that beyond all natural foundations, in spiritual foundations, what must be searched for in spiritual science must unite with the being of man, is that which must live in us spiritually, made out of an impulse of love. If such an impulse of love among humans becomes a social impulse, then the social community is placed on trust. Then one person stands in front of another in such a way that what happens between them, what happens during an earthly life of individuals does not happen as if people live like a herd of animals in some kind of higher organisation to which they must obey all commands, that everything is ordered: what the direction, the path of their lives should be.

So one can say: At the beginning of the nineties with my "Philosophy of Freedom" I strongly wanted to raise the call for something which is the opposite today of the terrible, murderous opposite asserted in the east of Europe, and from there, further infecting others, right over to a large part of Asia.

We live in our newer time in social relationships in which — out of perverse human instincts — we are looking for the complete opposite of what man should aspire to for the realisation of the true, deeper goals of modern humanity — during this terrible tragedy of our recent time. It is also the unconditional necessity of the newest times in our striving in future that we recognize: This is the way the social order must be built as it can only be built on free thinking, on trust, on what Goethe meant when he wanted to define duty and said: Duty is when I love what I ask myself to do.

My dear honourable friends, when an education for the path of life and the path of the soul work so that people out of a stirring interest in their environment know how they should relate to others, through their whole existence being impregnated with human dignity, then alone can the ideal of the newer time be fulfilled. This can't be accomplished through an organisation, because it removes so much from what people, in freedom, need to strive for if they follow their nature, and that need not be in freedom but lead into bondage, lead into decline.

170

I've never made it a secret that my "Philosophy of Freedom" and its foundation as Anthroposophically orientated spiritual science, is what I represent; I have never made a secret that I don't care for this or that content, with regard to some or other detail. I have always spoken with a certain irony of those for whom it is the main thing to hear: Out of how many limbs does human nature consist of? What can one find in this or that district of the spiritual world? –

I've always spoken with a certain irony about such endeavours; on the other hand I have always been interested in answering the question: What will become of the whole man, of the human attitude, soul, physical and spiritual man when this man endeavours not to think in the way given by mere science today, not to think in the way organizations have inoculated him, but in such a way as is meant in "Philosophy of Freedom" and anthroposophically orientated spiritual science? — I always draw attention to the fact that thinking, simply through the absorption of this spiritual science, becomes mobile, that it opens up widely for interest in current affairs, that it gives a free and unprejudiced view for what is necessary and for that which restrains our forward progress in human development.

While there is much which holds us back from our progress in human development — I can say, it confronted me early on, more than forty years ago, when I became more closely acquainted with Gervinus through one of his pupils about such people who within German intellectual life thought like Gervinus — Gervinus, this remarkable German who, under the impressions received in the revolutionary years around 1848, wrote his history of the German literature and his history of the German people of the 19th century. Those who delve into the history of German literature of this Gervinus, even today, say: He actually indicated guidelines which later all literary historians followed. He gave broad outlines according to German antiquity, the German Middle Ages, Minnesang and Meistersang (traditional lyric- and love song writings — trans.), according to which the prehistoric times of the German classical period is to be assessed. He also indicated the guidelines for a healthy assessment of the Goethe-Schiller-time. One could find him somewhat pedantic today — those who followed him were even more pedantic. There are some who believe that they are standing on the heights of a particularly modern, expressionist era today; one can see how through this snobbery a pedantry appears that is much bigger than the old braids they had, but I do not want to protect their pedantry with this. However, something strange happened with Gervinus, with the Gervinus who became really bitter in his seventies, so that he — despite being owed so much — aroused offence among those who believed they were under the auspices of this seventy year old and sailing into the golden age of the German nation but anyhow did not suspect how the germs then already lay in what has now become actual.

This Gervinus, what has he pronounced as his own, well-intentioned result especially in his history of German literature? He said a strange thing: German poetry ends with Goethe's death. — Just think, my dear friends, he who first described this German literature with all his deep love, he concluded his description with a final statement, that the German people should not further listen to what is said by all kinds of poets, writers and the like, but should become aware of that which until 1832 had wrestled itself to the surface from the deepest essence of Germanity. Further along, Gervinus believes, German people should no longer devote themselves to poetry and drama, no longer to fiction but to politics and practical applications. The time for practical application had arrived. In a strange way I encountered the first germ of this: I felt at that time, a good forty years ago, I was handed down the whole of Gervinism in this way at the Technical College, in Karl Julius Schröer, my dear old friend Schröer. At that time I felt something which was a germ of another, which I would say, you encounter today, in full formation.

There was quite a number of such people who, like Gervinus, out of a largely justified realization said: The time of inner meditation, the time when one closes off from outer practicalities and aspired to spiritual heights, is over. It is now a matter of devoting oneself to practical life. — However, one could, by taking note of this germ,

172

already get a feeling for something: that now all these people who speak in this way, point to quite an abstract, a more unrealistic practical life, that they, to a certain extent regard old ideals as successful, so to speak, and point to a new, practical life but have no impulsive ideas, no impulsive forces for this practical life.

If you asked something of Gervinus like: What is the spiritual content you described already by 1832? You get an enormous, great tableau in the representation. If you ask: What should live in the hearts, live in the souls of those who are to move out into practical life, who are supposed to lead this practical life, who now are to find ways of life through the ways of the soul? — Nothing came, there were no new ideals! In the soul the thoughts must rise: First of all the spiritual world has to be found, and out of this, new ideals for practical life would be found: first this spiritual life must be explored scientifically, like the natural world has been scientifically explored for three to four centuries.

Basically, time has shown that the world, without drawing from these spiritual sources, wanted to establish practice, but practice without spirituality — and this need to establish practice without spirituality has led us into this time of decline, a time of distress, misery and hopelessness. Many things have been said again and again, about where we are actually heading. Yes, many passed through my lectures which I have been giving here in Stuttgart for two decades, and some of what seemed necessary for me, from the anthroposophically orientated spiritual science brought to human consciousness when things should go upwards — moving up should not be done by cannons and guns but by a practice of life carried by spirituality, but a kind of spirituality which must first be newly created. So I may point out something today which I have said from various points of view as belonging to our spiritual science.

I said: If someone applies the same observation method which has emerged from science, filling thought-forms with scientific delineation, .if someone applies this method to history, then what is observed only leads to decline, because in history there are always forces that cause effects of decline. If one follows history only with the methods that are common in science, as for example as the English cultural historian Buckle did and his followers, then one only sees in history what leads to the downfall, then one only sees the afterglow of history. In order to see in history what caused advancement, one has to look into the spiritual world. What works in history as an ascent, are impulses which come out of the spiritual world.

I have already pointed out here that, for example, Gibbon gave an excellent history, written from the scientific age, about the decadence of the Roman Empire. However, what we still lack today is a historic presentation of the impulse of Christianity as it fell into the perishing Roman world. One can describe the fall of the Roman world in scientific thoughts; but one cannot describe what ascended in Christendom with scientific ways of thinking. I have pointed this out. What comes out of what I have indicated — apparently perhaps only idealistically, apparently only in thought, but in reality with regard to the paths of life? What follows from this?

The following happens: If someone would step forward in our age in which science has taken over all circles, all minds, even the circles of the Jesuits as I have indicated, if someone would come forward from this scientific mindset to give his view on historical life, what would he have to say? He could only show signs of decline because he is looking at our western culture out of scientific thinking. What should such a person write, if out of this scientific way of thinking, he would write about our present? He would write: "The Fall of the Western World." And, don't we have — in contrast to all healthy thinking through spiritual science — now also received this terrible literary product: "The Fall of the Western World" — a morphological view of history by Oswald Spengler?

My dear friends, that this is possible, can only be understood from the fact that those who are saturated today with only scientific thinking can only see signs of decline, so that they must prophetically predict: all of culture must perish. — That is the content of Spengler's book: the prediction of the fall of our culture. Must it perhaps not perish when everyone thinks the way Spengler thinks? Likewise one must become a materialist if one does not detach thinking from corporeality, that's how one must think about Western culture if one thinks the way Oswald Spengler thinks, if one only looks according to scientific specifications at western culture. If everyone looks at it that way, if everyone believes that we must perish, then we will perish as well. That's why I call this a terrible book. For those who become infected by these ideas, by these impulses, and absorb them in an honest way, they must become carriers of decline from the deepest depths of their soul, they must move along soul paths which, on the path of their life, lead them down into the abyss. From time to time one has to look at such phenomena because it is an indication of what depths of human life phenomena of decline are present, right into which depths the ways of the soul are prepared for the rush down into the abyss.

Such things oppose anthroposophically orientated spiritual science. It keeps a gaze focussed on what is rooted in man in the spiritual world. This is precisely what is most attacked about it, that it asserts that man could come to seeing the spiritual world if only he develops the soul forces available in him. Today it is roughly regarded from all sides as effusiveness, yet you can easily follow those paths to the spiritual world which I have tried to reveal in my book "Knowledge of the Higher Worlds and its Attainment" and in my efforts toward meditations regarding self-knowledge and so on — that these ways are just as safe as those that lead through absolutely, clear, sharply defined thinking in the fields of mathematics. This spiritual research is not only thought about but other, actual, soul forces also come into consideration in this research, than they do in mathematics.

Spiritual research certainly must speak about the spiritual world; therefore it can't be placed on the foundations which many traditional confessions are based on today. What do these traditional confessions claim? One thing they claim for instance, come quite naturally out of spiritual science: the indestructibility of the human soul, when the body is given over to the earth, the entry of man into the spiritual world, when man passes through the gate of death. However, it doesn't only depend on *that* such facts are being realised but it depends on *how* these results are presented. How then is the idea of immortality cultivated? By relying on selfish instincts originating from the ways of the human soul.

Just read the innumerable sermons, read the innumerable views on this theme — everywhere you will find how people speculate that the human being has an intense interest that he will not perish in death. Basically all the talk about immortality is a concession for spiritual egoism. The way the idea is represented, characterises it. Sharply denied against this half immortality is what Origen (Adamantius) spoke about, which the church certainly regarded as heretical: the pre-existence of the soul to which the unbiased spiritual researcher returns to again. What is basically offered in today's confessions? The conviction that two people come together in the world, conceive a child and that from the spiritual world the soul is newly conceived; that every time a sensual process takes place here, a spiritual process is added from the spiritual worlds.

My dear friends, this idea is not Christian. This idea is Aristotelian. Aristotle was the one who, out of the decadence of Greekdom, from the no-longer-understandable Platonism, taught about the development of the soul with the body and thus the one-sided immortality only after death. So Christian confessions, by denying pre-existence, do not represent something Christian, but represent something Aristotelian, something which in its depths certainly has nothing to do with Christianity. Now comes spiritual science, as it is meant here, and uncovers all the facts, along comes the "grapes" like the priest, the professor Traub (Traub means grape), and declares that spiritual science is merely copying.

No, it is not that. In truth, in relation to certain elementary things one agrees with old truths, like today one agrees with old Euclid about geometry. People like Traub have every interest in throwing rubble about that existed in older times, because if one then is able to study in an unbiased way, one realises it has its own wisdom. Their wisdom is just what is borrowed from what they want to bury so that one is unable to get behind it. As a result they make people dull; as if Anthroposophy draws from the gnosis and the like, so that people consider the gnosis as something dangerous and do not look for themselves how this gnosis has not flowed into anthroposophically orientated spiritual science, but certainly into the content of the modern confession as that part living in the gnosis which has been brought into decadence.

This spiritual science must point out how man descends from the spiritual world, how not a whim of the physical world causes the divine-spiritual world to create a soul that humans on earth bear witness to, but as the soul descends from the spiritual world with experiences it has had there; it must indicate just how the physical life is a continuation of a spiritual life. To the half immortality is added the whole, full immortality through spiritual science. If one goes this way then one recognises how the spiritual flows out of the spiritual worlds into single individuals. One can recognise how the spiritual flows in from spiritual worlds — but through man — into cultural progress, and how these cultural advances have very specific delimited epochs and periods of time. Today we stand in a period, in terms of culture and civilisation, which must certainly lead to something new. That is so.

When one peruses a book — it is rather thick — like that of Oswald Spengler, then one sees how he looks at individual cultures from a scientific viewpoint. He says: Cultures always develop: they have a childhood, a youth and a mature to dying age. That is the case with oriental cultures; they come into being, they grow, mature and die. The same with Greek culture. It is the same with our culture; it is now its time to die. Because, he says , we are required to look at cultures in this way like we look at the oak tree or the pine. An oak tree comes about, grows, ripens and dies away. Cultures are to be looked at in the same way. — Sure, we look at them in this way if we are completely vaccinated by a mere scientific way of thinking. If, in addition, we learn about spiritual looking and learn how to nurture it in the right way, then we know how to look at cultures in a different way. Then what comes into our souls is what I gave in my last sojourn in Stuttgart as a summary of the historical life of mankind, by me pointing out that once in primeval times people were instinctive beings, had instinctive spiritual lives, but something higher than what we can achieve with our intellectuality today. Compared to what was there in the beginning out of instinctive human wisdom, however, today we certainly are in a period of decline. However if we understand, as it is meant through spiritual science, how to open the source in our souls for a free, light filled thinking, for freedom which equals love, for social trust, for spiritual insight in general, that penetrates through our soul, through that which lives in us, that into this earth culture, in the earth civilisation, can in turn cause an ascent. If we are merely filled with what the scientific view offers of our observation of nature, that we can only believe what is presented today through this point of view, then there would be an inevitable decline.

There will be no decline when we become aware of this source of thinking which can loosen itself from corporeality, that in us this source is one of will, that one can just as much love the rise-into-the-spiritual world as one can love through physical love. Letting us lift into freedom the wisdom old mankind received as instincts and what today can be lifted only by what physicality can no longer give, letting us lift this into freedom, we present that which wants to descend with impulses of ascension. This is a fact that the question is put to mankind today: Is the world not in a descent? — Yes, it is in a decline if people want to only follow what is given from outside, if they are clamped down in an organisation, natural or social, imposed from outside.

The downfall will not occur if mankind creates a new world founded from within. The Lenins and Trotskys, who in all extremes want to build a new world based only on science, they take the quickest, most intensive route to decline. Whoever wants to create a new world based upon spirituality, moves towards social ascent — but only they do. For all those who today believe that the world can be cured through external institutions, through all kinds of external means, Marxism or the like, Oswald Spengler spoke about truly.

If only these people work with their power in the world, if only they direct the world's development, then Spangler's prophecy will be fulfilled, because he has only drawn consequences from where he must, filled with a scientific world view. Today the ways of life are serious, and it is necessary that the greatest seriousness seize the ways of the soul, but one must be serious about such great concerns. You need to get into the position to judge from the symptoms.

I told you that a good forty years ago, when as a young man, through the mediation of Schröer, I was able to understand Gervinus' way of thinking, and even then approached Gervinus. It made a deep impression on me how Gervinus demanded practice but had no idea about how to practice in the world in which those ideas were about which he alone knew how to speak, and wanted to find a conclusion in 1832 with the death of Goethe. It left a deep impression on me how he called people to do it, not to continue to lyricise, to dramatize, not to do fiction but be devoted to practical tasks of life, as he points people out to practice, with no idea for these practical tasks of life. That's how people behaved. The poets were there only for the school, at most in the concert hall; there they could sprout forth. What flowed from spiritual life could not intervene in the ways of life. A discord has come about between the way of the soul and the way of life. We have allowed this to develop. Now people like Oswald Spengler come and say: All that which is western culture, western civilisation, is finished, is doomed. — So, what can be done?

Now this is particularly interesting, and we want to take Spengler's own words to explain to our souls why he actually wanted to write his book, for which minds he actually intended it. He says himself: If, under the impression of this book, the people of the newer generation turn to technology instead of poetry, to the navy instead of painting, to politics instead of epistemological criticism, they do what I want, and one can't wish them anything better.

Now, my dear friends, I think that in the age in which one believes to have applied practice so wonderfully, people involved with technology instead of poetry, with the navy instead of painting, politics instead of criticism of knowledge, even before Spengler wrote his book — all that was there already, and of politicians, there were not too few of those either, up to today. To now make prophets of decadence regarding the decline of the western culture, to have to confess now that one wants to urge people to turn away from spirituality, to turn to a practice for which one has no ideas, yes, in principle does not want to have any ideas, to now proclaim the decline of the western world, because it is believed to be at an age of death — that is spoken out of the heart in the time of decline.

Perhaps I may, without falling into immodesty — because I have a wish, an attempt, to characterise a beginning — I may perhaps point out that which is brought forward from what is called anthroposophically orientated spiritual science, out of this spirituality, want to take on a practical form just here, from its centre, from Stuttgart, but from the opposite point of view. We don't tell people: Turn yourselves away from all spirituality, because that is in decline, and turn to the coming day. — We say to people: New spirituality has to be created; we need enter into new sources of spiritual life. We need to step into soul paths of spiritual seeing so that we can find just that practical life that is supported by real ideas. Admittedly it seems as if it can't go so quickly because what shows up in the bigger picture also shows up in the small details. However I only want to talk about that symptomatically.

The manner and way in which one can judge such an intention as it starts from here — had to be characterised in number 50 of our newspaper "Threefolding of the Social Organism" by Eugen Kolisko under the title "Theological criticism and Conscientiousness." It had to be characterised, based on the book of a university professor, Dr Philipp *Bachmann*, professor of theology at the University of Erlangen. This book "Death or Life" appeared here in Stuttgart. If you read the article by Dr Kolisko, you will see that he correctly summarizes his discussion at the end, in the following sentences, which are quite characteristic of those with diplomas and outer views given by external science, which is hollow inside and always develop those very forces that are derived from the alleged minds which have to lead into decline. Today one must have the courage not merely characterise in general, in abstract concepts of decline, but one has to throw a bright light on so-called spiritual life which acts even with the simplest things without conscientiousness that only parallels thoughtlessness and ignorance. That, my dear friends, must not be concealed if we want to speak today about the harmony between the ways of the soul and the ways of life.

So Dr Kolisko had to characterise what such an insignificant booklet is:

"It would not be necessary to study this book in such depth if it hadn't been written by a university professor. Such a person must know what the task of objective criticism is. The present criticism is frivolous."

It is particularly frivolous how the train of my thought in "Occult Science" is reproduced in this book.

"One can likewise proceed in the area of theosophy without damage, because here one isn't checked regarding the most absurd claims. Anthroposophy, Theosophy and Spiritism applies equally to many, and according to the saying that all cows are grey in the night, one can bring everything together with impunity and make snide criticism. If a critique is given in any other scientific area in such a reckless way, without sufficient knowledge of the area criticized, then only in one case instead of disfiguring in many cases, such senseless trains of thought of writers would appear, bypassing this way the literature available and mixing up opinions of various writers, so in scientific circles the decaying will be called to account, the reputation, and may lose its standing.

"For anyone who gives his readers the content of what is in my book "Occult Science — an Outline" about the members of the human being with the words: "The physical body dies, the ether body sleeps, the astral body forgets, the I (the sentient soul) is the memory" is either unable to reproduce a foreign train of thought or does it to maliciously disfigure it. Likewise, he is judged as a

181

critic. For today's educational system it is a sign of poverty that a university professor is unhindered by putting such a concoction in the world. What a theology professor has to say about Christianity and writes such criticism, I leave you to judge, you who can still summon up some indignation about such frivolously unscrupulous procedures."

This is namely what this Bachmann in his "Bachmanic adhesion" has found as the content of my book "Occult Science." This is how university professors read today. My dear friends, this is the one thing that today, from all corners, resists the desire for ascent; these are the ones who do not want to let anything come near them which can somehow lead to an ascension. These people are available to the broad masses, they educate our youth. Then there are the "Spenglers" who write that we must necessarily fall into a decline. Why do these "Spenglers" write like this? Because they are unable to focus their eyes on anything other than the "Bachmen" with their ignorance and frivolity. These things we must in all earnestness consider.

I now may, after having preceded three lectures, say in conclusion: After I tried to show in my first two lectures last week something about the ways that, in a cognitive sense, in a social way, the anthroposophically orientated spiritual science wants to proceed — proceed scientifically, not like these "Bachmann adherents" and "(grape) clusters" slander, having spoken also of what is to be artistically trained in Dornach, I may say today that those who strive in such a way for science and art be reminded of the beautiful saying brought across by Goethe and remain true forever: "Whoever has science and art, also possesses religion." Spiritual science and its art has religion but not a religion created from blind faith, but from a clear, light, real spiritual scientific knowledge, on a spiritually deepened striving of artistic will. After Goethe said: "Whoever has science and art also possesses religion" he continued: "Whoever possesses neither, has no religion!"

In our time it is perhaps possible for spiritual scientists and representatives of three-fold thinking, from their deepest affairs of the heart within spiritual science still say: Indeed, whoever has science and art, has religion also.- But today religion can only lead to an ascent if it creates itself out of a living science, not out of a science based on the dead; it can only lead to an ascent when it grows out of an artistic will connected to such spiritual knowledge so that one can say: Whoever today has a science rooted in spiritual seeing, whoever today endeavours, even if no matter how weak the beginning, to create an art connected totally in this spiritual seeing in the most intensive will, one should not reproach them for having given the religious element a chance on the way to life in the present. Because, in searching for the spiritual, in wanting to incorporate spirituality in art, one certainly also has the will to lead it over into social life, by connecting the value of human beings and human dignity in a social community, truly the insight into divine guidance of the world, to the divine primordial forces of life — a true perspective which does not only speculate on the egoism of people but in the context of people in the great eternal laws of existence.

A religion can only lead to an ascent if it does not want to speculate about egoism but point to the deepest harmony of individuals in relation to the whole cosmos.

To the same degree that such a religion, such a science, such art can permeate the human soul, to this extent will we advance socially. To the same degree, in spite of need and misery — but perhaps, if the resisting forces are too strong, still through much need and much misery — we will not face a decline in the culture of the western world, but an ascent of true human life — a life on the path of the soul and the path of life, the religious, the scientific and artistic can be done because through the spiritual, out of spiritually filled art, out of spiritually carried religion, work is done for humankind's present and for its future.

The Necessity of a Spiritual life.
Who can speak about the decline of the Western world?
A second lecture for the current time
Stuttgart on 29 July 1920

My dear honourable friends present here today! In my last lecture held here, I pointed to a significant literary, contemporary, publication, a literary publication which is referred to even by those who do not love it at all, which is generally called "literature," and which one meets far too often as the person has to do, who speaks to you now. He wants to involve the foundations of practical life, with the forces that shape this practical life; he wants to involve everything that shapes this practical life out of the spiritual, with everything that is direct, elementary in man, everything that approaches a human being's heart and soul and strengthens a person for life. He wants to have as little involvement as possible with what is today called "literature." Regarding the book — you can sense it from the title's formulation by today's relevant lecture — the book of Oswald Spengler, "The Fall of the Western World," may also speak to those who do not particularly love this literature as such. One can say that particularly those people who are not actually sleeping in their souls today can feel forces of decline, powerful forces of decay, working in terrible declining powers in our cultural life and civilisation and that this decline, these declining phenomena, are revealed in the language of Oswald Spengler's book which, firstly, is so characteristic of the whole spirit of our time, but secondly, rings out especially from the Central European, the German spirit.

In this book of Oswald Spengler there is nothing less attempted than to prove the necessity of the fall of Western culture, to prove by all means, one can nearly call it, with all refinement of today's scientific ways — yes, a science that has been proven by a brilliant man as a new science distilled out of the present one — so that Oswald Spengler's book, I couldn't call it a theoretical one, not literary one, but a book speaking about facts coming directly out of spiritual life of the present, also speaks in such a the way that the very thoughts of this book influences the deeds of the people who receive it. That many have absorbed these thoughts of Oswald Spengler's book comes from the simple fact that this book, despite containing 615 pages, has already sold widely; more than 20,000 copies have been sold. What the sale of a book reaching 20,000 copies means for the number of readers contemplated, even those know, who have dealt with such questions.

One can already say that among those ideas, in spiritual areas, with which one has to deal with today, if one wants to deal a bit with the undercurrents of the present cultural and civilized life there are two books which are the most important. The first is Oswald Spengler's book "The Fall of the Western World" and secondly, one which has perhaps not caught as much attention in literature, namely the book "The economic problems of the proletarian dictatorship." This book appeared for the first time in the Viennese cooperative publishing house "Neue Erde" (New Earth), written by the man who, as the supreme economic commissioner, i.e. as minister for the affairs of economic life at the time of the establishment of the Hungarian Council dictatorship, after his escape and his internment in Austria, summarised his principles and experiences in this book. One could say that both these books shed a terrible light on what is happening in the undercurrents of spiritual and even working life at present.

Oswald Spengler is a man who tried with his "Fall of the Western World" — that its kernel, so he says, lies in the year of 1911, thus before the start of the war catastrophe — to show how our western culture contains forces of decline, how just in its characteristic phenomena it proves that it is in a declining culture. For Oswald Spengler this culture shows itself as the culture of decline, so he must prophesy that at the beginning of the third millennium it must end just like the ancient Persian epoch once did, the ancient Egyptian, the ancient Babylonian, the ancient Greek, the old Roman culture came to their end. That, my dear friends present here today, doesn't prove he is a man coming with a superstitious prophecy, it doesn't say he is a man who submits to any kind of arbitrary fantasy, this says it's a man who masters the scientific spirit of the present in an excellent way. Precisely because of the genius of the author's personality, because of the universal mastery, one can say of twelve to fifteen contemporary sciences, because of the courageous penetration of all consequences of these sciences for practical and historical life, this book must be seen as a wealth of deeds, not just a single act. Everything I've expressed here can be said about this book on the one hand.

On the other hand it is a terrible book. Isn't it a terrible book which, with all the weight of the scientific tools that can be applied today, ingeniously proves that the signs of decline have led to the downfall of this western culture which already led at the beginning of the third millennium — these phenomena of decay within which we live, which expressed itself in the flaming, warlike world catastrophe and which now continues even if it goes unnoticed by sleeping souls?

In an introductory way we must really work for a bit with the whole manner and way in which Oswald Spengler arrives at his conviction about the necessity of the West's decline, if we want to answer the question which is actually the theme of today's contemplation: Who may now speak against the downfall of the western world? — One must not speak recklessly against the Spengler book. To speak recklessly against it would mean to also recklessly disregard the serious scientific tools of the author, would mean that one does not want to consider at all that which he has conscientiously taught us out of the phenomena of contemporary life. I believe many have already spoken out against Oswald Spengler's book who don't actually should not be allowed to do so.

Oswald Spengler first appears as a history writer in his book. He says it himself; he had noticed the signs of decline, as I said, before the world war catastrophe. He wanted clarity about the actual causes, about the nature of these declining phenomena. He was one of those personalities on whose souls the declining phenomena became a burden because the larger masses of the population, particularly the so-called intelligent people, still spoke about how wonderfully far we have come and how we want to spread what we have achieved everywhere, into all corners of the world — it was shown to us the power we actually had to have, in order to be able to do what we have believed in to carry it out into the world, to really spread it. Oswald Spengler describes to us how he came up with the idea of declining phenomena of the present, phenomena which in truth one can't speak about appropriately if one doesn't speak about the entire history of the West, namely about which thoughts live in the western culture and how we are able today, from a historic viewpoint, to enliven these thoughts in us, enliven it by taking action.

So Oswald Spengler continues his observations towards a comprehensive history book which wants to research the entire foundation of western thought, feeling and experience. Oswald Spengler realised that this scientific approach which has become common in the last centuries, will gradually and after also being applied to history, that this scientific approach — from the viewpoint of anthroposophically orientated spiritual science we have often heard highlighted here — that this scientific approach comes into consideration in all that includes thinking, feeling and willing in those parts of humanity that are responsible for progress in general. It became clear to Oswald Spengler that history, without a scientific approach, doesn't clarify the actual causes of historic events; how flawed the whole historical approach has become in the last centuries right up to the present.

That, my dear friends, is really also not without meaning in present practical relations because we will see after this, how in the widest circles, reality is made out of historical prejudices. We will, with a characteristic example of the Hungarian council commissioner for economic affairs, Eugen Varga, show that what Oswald Spengler pursues as historical thinking actually wants to become practical reality. If that which Oswald Spengler very clearly points out only exclude forces of decline then the way of looking and thinking which only come from thoughts and ideas emerging from this consideration of decline, even in the social organism, create only symptoms of decline.

In a person like professor Eugen Varga is incarnated, incorporated into the flesh, that way of thinking which Oswald Spengler is peeling off, it is only based on what must lead to the decline of the whole West at the beginning of the third millennium. If only declining phenomena are observed and added in an accelerated tempo with a socialist program and come before the world with the energy of a person like Professor Eugen Varga, then in a short time you will accumulate something that will lead to a decline. You accumulate this, that is, you create the germ of a declining social structure. Eugen Varga created such a social structure in the Hungary Council; such decaying structures were created by the comrades of Professor Eugen Varga, the Lenins and Trotskys in Eastern Europe. This expands more and more over Asia. That means nothing other than that one sees the cultural progress of the decline of the West, inoculating the social organism and then one doesn't need to be surprised when these phenomena — proven by a scientist as leading to the fall of the whole western world — when these phenomena are concentrated as socialist ideas in a short time lead to the decline of what one pretend to be building up. That's why these things are connected: Oswald Spengler's observations and Eugen Varga's experiences.

The time has come that whoever is seriously concerned with the affairs of the present should deal with them from a practical standpoint; it is time for this person, I would say, to go through the gates that lie in those public omissions and revelations, approach what makes a true realisation possible for actual deeds towards an advancement, to a resurgence of our declining western culture and civilization. Certainly it is so that at first the soul is sleeping in relation to phenomena of decline. Yet on the other hand it must not be concealed that it is a public frivolity if you do not want to look today at such phenomena as those mentioned here, but rather seek salvation with programs that are decades old and believe that you can achieve something other than decline with these programs and ideas. It is a cultural frivolity, a political frivolity carried on in the broadest sense, if you don't direct your glance to such phenomena.

Now Oswald Spengler became acquainted with what I've often called Goetheanism here; he came to know about Goethe's method of looking at nature as opposed to natural science which is maintained everywhere as official at universities from where it radiates to lower educational institutions and which, through the application of historic writing, has turned history into a caricature. Why did he find it necessary to become acquainted with the Goethean way of observing nature? He found it necessary to apply this Goethean method on history by applying it in such away, he believed, as it should be applied to historical phenomena. Goethe's method is very different from today's official natural scientific method of observation. Goethe looked at nature not from such a philosophic, mechanical, pedantic way as merely a connection between cause and effect; he looked at the rise of living beings in a living realm, how living beings emerge from birth, into youth, maturation, into aging and death.

One only need to read Goethe's treatise of 1790, his attempt to explain the metamorphosis of plants, in order to see how he views the development of the plant from the root, from leaf to leaf, in the ascent to blossom and fruit, to see how he looks at nature in its living, becoming, how every leaf is the symbol of the other, as the original form is only metamorphosed in the petal, in the stamens, even in the shoot. Inspired by this Goethean morphology, through this theory of the design of living beings, Oswald Spengler sets out to investigate the historical coming into being of humanity itself according to the pattern of Goethe's ideas about organic nature. So he realised he could look at cultures in the same way as one does the coming into being and growing of an organic life form, a plant, an animal or also a physical human being which is born, grows, ripens, ages and dies as it happens in cultures being born, grow, ripen, age and die, like the dying of the old Persian, Egyptian, Babylonian and Greek cultures, the Roman culture; he saw in the individual manifestations of these cultures what Goethe envisaged in individual forms of living beings. He takes

190

into account what the western culture has brought about so far — just as one who studies living beings and compares one living being with another — he compares the western culture up to now with what the Greek, the Roman and those further cultures of ancient times which, up to a certain point, have their development. He could calculate where present culture stood, while finding a corresponding point of view to the view of the Persians, Egyptians and Greek cultures and so on; one could, so he calculated, predict when the culture of the West would perish because one knows how long the old cultures needed before they perished.

All of this becomes useful because Oswald Spengler breaks with the philistine method of viewing history, and he has the courage to break with it, he has the courage to say what history has become in its connection to mere scientific ideas; he has the courage to say, for example: The previous form of the historical approach has kept the formal consideration of history at a level that would have been ashamed of, in other sciences. — Why does he think this? For the reason that he thinks it is necessary not to apply the dead method that is appropriate for the mineral kingdom and other lifeless things to history, but to apply a living method to history, where one cultural form is compared with another. One then has to be a man of such universal knowledge like Oswald Spengler; one must be able to use achievements in the most diverse fields of science, art and technology of different times and cultures and compare them with each other. One must, for example, be able to compare the style in the architecture of any cultural period with the methods in optics, chemistry, and so on — that is, one must have a comprehensive view of what really happened, and Oswald Spengler has it, and he has it as one who has a complete command of the current scientific spirit. In this way he can compare — like eyes can compare one plant with another, one animal with another — so he can compare for example the work of a mathematician in a cultural period with someone making music; he can compare what the physicist has done at the experimental table with what the socialist agitator at the same time calls a cultural form; he can compare what the chemist says, with what the painter conjures on the canvas. That

191

means he can really take and apply a morphological approach: he can compare, he can use a comparison, an analogy, he believes, to a scientific method and from this application of comparison, of analogy — which others only apply as a thread of fantasy — he finds strict methods of how to get out of superficial historical events which are usually considered isolated from one another, to deduce deeper causes.

This he does in his own way and it is interesting to see which results Oswald Spengler arrives at with his geniality, knowledge and boldness. He truly comes to transcend what history has actually become today in the hands of those who deal with history mostly from the point of view of one or other party without even being aware of it. How do today's viewers of history themselves scoff in front of their middle school students about the fact that in the time of Herder and Goethe, people described a Brutus, a Caesar, a Marc Antony, an Alexander, a Pericles, using them as an ideal, taking any ideal personality and applying them either in their excellent, angelic or even heinous nature. Today's history observers believe, in view of history, they are beyond all that which was there at the end of the 18th century and beginning of the 19th century, brought in from personal, human aspects into the historical perspective. Oswald Spengler rightly throws in their faces: "They sneer at historians of Goethe's era when they try to defend their political ideals by writing a history of antiquity, with names like Lykurg, Brutus, Cato, Cicero, Augustus, through whose rescue or convictions their own program is hidden through personal effusiveness; but even they can't write a chapter without betraying which party slant their morning paper belongs to." Often one has to take into account what is living in the consciousness of the people currently, especially in the intellectuals and even in those apparently at the pinnacle of science; one has to characterize it as Oswald Spengler has characterized it here.

Spengler points out something else. Spengler remarks for example, how little has been drawn out of the depths of events, what in recent time, I would like to say as absolute truth, has been felt about any phenomenon. Oswald Spengler for instance remarks on the whole hype that started over Ibsen's "Nora" at that time. Those good middle class people who believed they belonged in this very milieu and knew this milieu from which Ibsen's "Nora" emerged, they believed they could draw the entire problem of femininity into their sphere. Oswald Spengler said: How funny would it be with Ibsen's feminine problems if, instead of the famous Nora, one would replace her with Caesar's wife, for example. Don't they know that they are basically considering something sparse: those who did not cross over the middle class barrier between 1850 and 1950 — because then they will have disappeared — these ladies stepping out. It is quite a lot when a person of today must be taken seriously like Oswald Spengler who throws these things at people so eagerly — I would like to say out of sheer pleasure regarding their own education — how they often — unspoken or outspoken — occupy themselves in a strange way with self-praise and self-pleasure, how they know so delightfully much about the deepest secrets of the world and despite this, don't sense that these secrets are nothing other than the European superficiality between 1850 and 1950.

It would be terrible if in the present time, nothing can effectively work against the serious tools of Oswald Spengler. Now, my dear friends, it must be pointed out what in the course of several years — actually I can already say since a decade ago — has also appeared here in Stuttgart from the Anthroposophic viewpoint of spiritual science. You see, a significant fact has often been pointed out here, the significant fact that one actually looks at quite incorrectly, how natural science has acted on the western cultural process in the last three to four centuries. It is believed that this natural science coming from Kepler, Copernicus, Galileo and so on — all of this prevailing belief in the widest circles — especially the scholarly circles — that one can learn through this how to penetrate reality. It is believed that one must school one's thinking according to science, then in this way one would see what is actually being thought, what exactly is being thought, and as a result one must look at everything else coming about in life according to this pattern of observation.

193

Spiritual scientific observation leads to another kind of knowledge. This spiritual scientific observation does what, I would like to say, Oswald Spengler lapses from even in his superficial observations of Goetheanism, by doing it in a deeper way. Long before the name of Oswald Spengler was even mentioned, the most essential foundation of the entire western cultural development pointed to something else. It has been pointed out, certainly, that what happened in the development of western culture during the last three to four centuries, can only be understood from a spiritual scientific background, providing a real overview of the course of the whole history of mankind. In public lectures here, it has repeatedly been pointed out how totally different — one has to go back 7 to 8 Centuries if one wants to find it — the old Indian culture was, as I called it in my "Occult Science." I pointed out how different they were, different as an ancient Persian, ancient Egyptian-Babylonian, an ancient Greek-Babylonian, the ancient Greek-Latin culture they had and how. According to these cultures, they were born, became young, then matured and died, how our contemporary culture, the fifth cultural epoch after the great Atlantic catastrophe, emerged — our contemporary culture about which people talk about in the most diverse ways. Repeatedly it was shown how within this contemporary culture of ours, since the middle of the 15th Century, the intellectualist element, the element of mind, has risen and how in the development of mankind the emergence of this intellect — because before that the intellect did not mean the most cognitive power of the human being — how the emergence of this intellect for the whole education of mankind, means something special, especially in the West.

My dear friends, when one looks at the entire configuration — exactly what Oswald Spengler attempted, but did not manage — of the morphology of earlier cultural epochs in a spiritual scientific way, allowing it to go through one's vision, then one knows: Big, powerful, awe-inspiring things have been produced by these ancient cultures, by being born, being young, becoming mature, aging and dying. However, what our culture is called to do, what it has to carry from the deepest depths of human soul life to the surface of outer cultural life, is the maturation of the true force of freedom in mankind. For this reason I tried to find out what has emerged from the foundations of human soul life in the beginning of the nineties of the last century in my book "Philosophy of Freedom." After experiencing freedom, after the experience of freedom in the pure intellect, because in nothing else can freedom be experienced — although other things are also valuable in the human being — only in pure thinking can freedom be experienced and then radiate out to the rest of the human being. All that humanity found instinctively earlier in mysticism, in occultism and in theosophy as superficial knowledge, must be cast away. Today it is impossible for humanity to find what they absorbed from astrology, mysticism, theosophy, gnosis and what was useful for old knowledge, awaken it again somewhat, again wanting to warm it up.

What is incumbent upon us today is to bring out of the present viewpoint of development precisely that which leads to the consciousness of freedom: to grasp the being of the human being in touching it in pure thinking. If this human being is grasped in pure thinking, then a quite new spiritual world must be born out of this thinking. Out of the old cultures there was never anything born out of pure thinking that we have inherited as spiritual treasure, spiritual insights. Only in our time, out of pure thinking, can a true knowledge of the spiritual be born, because this knowledge of the spirit must be born out of pure thinking, because only in this way can a person simultaneously mature in the course of development of humanity towards freedom — to the real consciousness of freedom — which is then due to him in earth development. Everything that we experience in the terrible present, about phenomena of decline, come from this: Because mankind, from the lowest depths of its soul life, should grasp the crystal clarity of thought to conquer freedom and because mankind should mature to the strength that is necessary for this, old realities are omitted; they fall away first, drop into decline and the way must be sought as to how, from the crumbling debris of the old cultural life, the human will can rise, which penetrates thinking with full light, with which pure thinking can grow up in freedom.

195

In order to capture freedom, to find ourselves completely within, we must get out of the chaos, out of the ruins of outer life and give birth to human greatness from within. That's why mankind's view of what really could master outer life in its essence disappeared at first and it was precisely at the time when the consciousness of freedom awakened, but only a dead science was achieved. What came about as science was not something from which one could make actual progress in thinking but it overcame humanity as a weakness. What was to be achieved as freedom appeared as a weakness according to scientific observation. Science becomes weak because forces have to be diverted to the other side. Out of educational forces within the human being, science took on its own shape. How science has come into being is connected with the forces of mankind's development. It is not the case that these forces had to learn from what science has become.

Now Oswald Spengler found the following: a person can't penetrate the historical process of becoming with what science produces as ideas. It really depends on finding a necessary comparison in order to move from the outer appearances of historical events to deeper, inner events. However — and this we must keep clearly in view: Yes, Oswald Spengler noticed that today's historical observation, which is similar to the approach in which all of mankind is missing, he noticed this sharply and clearly, and he even noticed that what has come to the fore as evident in Goetheanism, could help the scientific approach out of all its limitations. However, Oswald Spengler is a spirit who himself — although he universally dominated contemporary sciences — was deeply ingrained, not in the way of thinking generated by natural science, but in the way of thinking that has been generated by science since the middle of the 15th century; he is unable to develop to that which from the depth of the human soul could now overcome his scientific viewpoint.

So Oswald Spengler ingeniously arrived at a negative insight: Yes, if we allow science to become our life of action then we only manage to bring about a decline. He comes to claim: What does today's

196

science give us? It gives us proof that what the western world at the beginning of the third millennium with its current culture was, must be over. — However, what has led from science is something he can't conquer. One must give him justice: With those ideas contained in scientific knowledge one can only arrive at unproductive social ideas for the present. One must rise up to comparison, to image, to allegory, in order to recognise the deeper historical forces. However when comparison and allegory become not merely an image of fantasy and the image not just a product of imagination, if image and comparison, allegory and symbol in the sense of Spengler, not just created from fantasy, then a real force must be created from the soul, which did not rise in Oswald Spengler. The real forces — methods of acquiring knowledge from Higher Worlds, should be sketched here — these forces should be developed if one uses image, allegory, symbol and symptom, as Oswald Spengler uses them, quite seriously, for the observation of world events.

This means, in other words, that Oswald Spengler is a person who strives from this way of looking at things because he feels the current approach to human development inadequate. He knows different ideas must be applied, above all things, to history. He doesn't want to apply these forms of ideas because they demand calling up forces within himself which can only apply to these forms of the ideas. It has to be said: When someone applies images, allegories, imaginations and symbols to the historic viewpoint then he continues, if he stays with the same point of view with which we are born — if he does not develop the spiritual forces of knowledge of which anthroposophically oriented spiritual science speaks — he continues to be a player of mere allegories, remains a fantasist in an historical territory. This means, what Oswald Spengler claimed as his method may not be applied from his spiritual viewpoint, but it may only be applied when a person has risen to what has already here been depicted as imaginative, inspirational and intuitive insight.

Oswald Spengler wants to apply methods to the historical viewpoint which are still permeated by the old scientific thinking, even if not by the scientific spirit. Oswald Spengler is one of those who goes red in the head when you mention what anthroposophical science speaks about is the only way out of the decline of the West. For Oswald Spengler it comes across, for example, in terms of social orientation from the anthroposophically oriented foundation, as salon communism and the like. Oswald Spengler shows genius in relation to his personal spiritual forces, shows universal thinking and recognition in the field of the most diverse sciences, but at the same time he also shows the utmost narrow-mindedness when it is about developing such mental powers in order for his methods to become fruitful.

My dear friends, only when one sees through this, only then can one speak against Oswald Spengler regarding the downfall of the western world. Only then can one say: Yes, you are right, the cultures that have come up in the course of historical development must be viewed in such a way that we look at their birth, their growing young, their maturing, their aging, their dying. — Yes, when we look at it this way then our culture reveals what we must ascribe to the downfall Oswald Spengler indicates. However, then we only see one culture beside another, like one plant next to another, and we derive nothing, which we can, when we observe through spiritual science.

When we study cultures through spiritual science and then glance back at the first culture, the old Atlantic culture — I have presented this in my lecture on the historical development of humanity — we find that what the human being possessed at that time as their own awareness, was primitive, quite elementary, simple. Yet, we find that at the same time, man could bring forth from his own powers of consciousness, an awe-inspiring primordial wisdom. We go back and find the most elementary stages of development in the first cultural epochs; but when we understand that the primordial wisdom lives in these cultures, then we literally kneel reverently down to what permeated these primordial cultures. If we go further, we find these first cultures replaced by other cultures. We find primordial wisdom less in what man consciously brings forward as higher, and so increasingly, until we reach our culture, namely since the middle of the

15th Century, we find a complete drying up of the primordial wisdom. This is even expressed outwardly. It is nonsense that it is believed people could have understood scientific thinking during the 10th or 11th century. No, they couldn't understand that because at that time quite a different language was spoken than today. You have to get to know the mindset of that time that has thoroughly changed. Therefore, what ruled in these earlier cultures had, albeit instinctively, dried out, so that one culture could bring about another culture. The primal Indian culture could supply the primordial germ of wisdom into the ancient Persian culture which in turn was able to send the primordial germ of wisdom into the ancient Egyptian culture, which in turn transmitted it to the Greco-Latin culture and so on. We have moved up — because of our consciousness of freedom — to an elaboration of the pure mind, of pure thinking, but we have lost the old instinctive primal wisdom.

Viewing nature only from the outside like Oswald Spengler does, we must speak like Oswald Spengler about the downfall of the Western world. We can only speak against the downfall of the Western world if we have the courage to say: The old, instinctive, spiritual knowledge has dried up, but in our hearts a new spark is already glowing. We are giving birth to a new spiritual life out of what we have acquired as intellect, which can penetrate our inner being to new cultural deeds. We don't only believe, but we know: within us is the germ of futures, not merely of a future, and so we learn to understand how differently we must look at what history has brought about, than how Oswald Spengler views it.

We see, for example, how the old Greek-Latin culture, which has come up from the south, is coming to an end; it brought Christianity over from the Orient, preserved the Mystery of Golgotha at first, then — what happened to this Mystery of Golgotha? Humanity still understood it at the time because the primordial wisdom was around; one understood what the origin of Christianity was. Then the Germanic peoples came from the North and took up what the ancient peoples had developed, which had come to maturity and died; they took it into their new blood and transformed it. These Germanic peoples were the last ones who could take up the primordial wisdom. In its bosom mankind developed, in which this primordial wisdom dried up and which would bring forth a new spiritual life from the power that must be generated from within itself. If this spiritual life is not brought forwards, then the western world's culture will pass over into barbarism.

Today it is not important to look at the outer world and say: I believe there will be enough forces to rekindle declining life. It's not a matter of standing there with a sleeping soul and waiting for this or that to happen in the outside world; that leads to decline. With proof Oswald Spengler is right, even if the historians he laughs at prove him wrong in so many ways, in the face of those who are allowed to speak out of a new spiritual life against the decline of the Occident, he ceases to be right. He ceases to be right to those who say: Yes, in the outer world everything may decline and will decline.

However, we can find something that had not been there: we can, out of our will, when we illuminate it with pure thinking, create a new world, a world which one can't see, but which one wills to see. One has the strength for such a will only if one wants to penetrate this will, wants to enforce it with that which can be won through spiritual knowledge as power, as giving impulses to this will — in ways which have often been described. Therefore one does not appeal today to the vague belief that, nevertheless, again and again there were forces which brought forth new cultures.

Today we have to agree with Oswald Spengler: Indeed, the facts prove a decline and Oswald Spengler only summarizes the facts to prove it. One has to agree with him if one doesn't have the certainty of this: the will is fuelled by the spirit, by Anthroposophically orientated spiritual science, it will not refute theories, or views, and not refute concepts and ideas that are false, but it will fight the facts of decline through its own sense of the facts. Today we don't need to refute theories or false views; today we need to conquer the facts to find the truth. Only this justifies speaking against the downfall of the western world. This shows us at the same time how people understood such an idea of Oswald Spengler's — the idea that the Western, the Central European peoples, with all that they have brought forward, are already at an end and that the Russian people — I have for a long time been repeating this before Oswald Spengler — that this Russian people hold the nucleus, the true future kernel to the future of Europe; that's right — Bolshevism, of course, offers the counterbalance, but it will destroy the Russian population. How does Oswald Spengler think of the process of the future?

He thinks to himself that this western world's culture will disappear and that which is rising in Russia will replace what is in Central Europe. — No, if one understands the kernel of Anthroposophically orientated spiritual science one would say something different, one would say: Just like Germanic peoples have received the kernel of Christianity in their way, as they could not develop anything out of their young blood if the Mystery of Golgotha had not appeared from the south, so from this Central Europe there must shine the culture coming from the East, what we ourselves are developing from a new spiritual life. It doesn't matter that Oswald Spengler's sense of the foreign Russianness is flooding the West and Central Europe by something young compared to what has died. No, it is a question of this Russianness having to find something that we ourselves generate as a new spiritual life, something that this Russianness has to receive in the same way as the Germanic peoples received the Mystery of Golgotha with their young blood. No, it is a question of this Russianness having to find something that we ourselves generate as a new spiritual life, something that this Russianness has to receive in the same way as the Germanic peoples, with their young blood, received the Mystery of Golgotha. The future of even the most future-minded depends on us not dying due to the decline of the Occident, but to bring the immortal part in us to unfold through a new spiritual life; only those who speak of such a new spiritual life may speak against the decline of the Occident.

It is obvious that where old thinking continues living and is conserved today is namely where socialistic theories come about, which shows that the decline is not only seen, not only allowed, but that decline is bred. In relation to this, it is extremely interesting to see how the Minister for Economic Affairs in the Hungarian Council, Professor Eugen Varga, has had experiences, which he describes in his book "The Economic-Political Problems of Proletarianism," just published by the Viennese cooperative publishing house "Neue Erde" — "The Economic-Political Problems of the Proletarian Dictatorship." There he describes how, according to his principles, he is more or less a Marxist in his principles, as Lenin and Trotsky are in an even more radical form, and with these forces, which are forming themselves to the point of bullishness, he now wants to establish an order, an economic order in Hungary.

In a few short lines I want to show how he is, on the one hand, a Marxist. He believes: If you make the world Marxist then it becomes real, so I first want to make Hungary Marxist and real. — He knows that it was the urban industrial proletariat that carried the Marxist ideas, and he knows that what he wants to establish can only be born from the ideas that the urban industrial proletariat swears by. Immediately he had to state one thing and says: Yes, the whole belief of this urban proletariat is that the future depends on the practical realization of Marxist ideas. If one meets such institutions, the first to become unemployed will be the urban population and next the urban industrial proletariat will run out of bread and become unhappy. The only ones who get off on the right foot are the farmers outside; they can, if you set things up the way we want them to be, they can fare a little better; the proletarians in the cities can expect only impoverishment at first and enormous inflation; the only thing that beckons them is ruin.

So what does this real Marxist, Professor Eugen Varga have to say? He says: The greatness of an ideal is shown by the fact that one can hunger for it. — But if the ideal promised to the people, that when the ideal is fulfilled, they will not have to go hungry, then it is questionable whether they really like to go hungry when it is it is not fulfilled. Varga would have had to wait and see whether it would not turn out, on internal reasons, that his Hungarian councillor would have perished. However, he has the excuse that it did not come to that, because he

202

can point to the Romanian incidents and other external reasons and so he finds all sorts of other things that he cites as his experiences.

It is in fact interesting to point out these events because one is dealing with someone who was allowed to become a practitioner, who could show how the stubborn theories, which one just thinks are practical, turn out to be reprehensible, pernicious, if one wants to actualise them. So the professor Eugen Varga also tells us many beautiful things about his Marxism. He also describes how he uses his councils, how everyone is elected from within the workforce, how the positions in the factories are filled, the supervisor positions and so on. He says: One must avoid the old bureaucracy. — What he is describing is bureaucracy. But he says: That which in the present is as thick as a stick will all become terribly beautiful in the future. — He relates: Yes, at present terrible things are experienced, because those who have been elected to supervise the factories are loitering around, just arguing, and the others, who are still supposed to work, think that they should all be elected to the supervisory positions themselves, because this loitering and arguing seems to them to be a very special ideal. — This depicts Professor Eugen Varga, the instigator of the soviet dictatorship in Hungary. He fails to notice that in a single sentence, on 47 pages of his book, he expresses a meaningful truth. I confess to you frankly and freely that his book is, to me, an extraordinarily interesting contemporary phenomenon, because in Professor Eugen Varga, what Oswald Spengler regarded as the phenomena of decline, is now transformed into socialist ideas. Already in his ideas there are forces of decline, so that through people like Professor Eugen Varga, people are inoculated with forces of decline.

If one leaves culture to itself; if one starts to doctor such ideas in these areas, as does Lenin and Trotsky and others in the East and in Asia, then destruction is forced in a concentrated way, so that history then rapidly goes into complete destruction. This is what the book of Eugen Varga is for me, a man who wants to be a practitioner of the theory of decline being put into practice — it is interesting to me in terms of cultural history, because this book is not just literature, it is something that expresses life in action.

What is actually interesting about it? I must say, as interesting as the book is — what actually is the most interesting is only one sentence which appears on page 47 of this book of Eugen Varga. This sentence even gave me a surprise. He describes how he structured his working councils, how at the top is the production commissioner and below, the individual commissioners, just as real Marxism imagines them to be. These production commissioners act as intermediaries between the works councils and the supreme economic office. Regarding these commissioners I found on page 47 of this book, a remarkable confession. You see, here he says: This system — he means his council system — meets all four of the above requirements, if the person who is the production commissioner is appropriate. — Now, my dear friends, if you put the appropriate personalities in all positions, then you do not need to implement socialist ideas in reality, because then all demands will be fulfilled by these personalities.

Out of the corner of this abstract theorist's reflections, eager to be a practitioner, jumped that which he consciously did not want to confess. Its four demands are: 1. that the councils be elected from among the workers, 2. that economic commissioners be set up, 3. that the whole should not be bureaucratic, and 4. that all people, including teachers, must be politically reliable. These requirements would be fulfilled — when? When the production commissioner is appropriate. — The economic system of the professor Eugen Varga will of course only be appropriate if the commissioner is as much a Marxist and Leninist as Varga himself. Here you see how these people reckon with reality. They do not merely depict — as historians portray the ancient heroes, an Alexander, a Pericles — according to the political terms contained in their morning paper. No, they want to shape people according to what their morning paper contains. You also have what Oswald Spengler considers as the main cause of the downfall, brought into the most direct practice, and the most important thing about practice is simply not seen.

What, my dear friends, leads to an answer of the question: Who dare speak against the decline of the western world? We live in a time when only those who feel in their souls that there is a spiritually oriented science which can ignite the will, can kindle the will so that forces arise which were not there before. Those who consider only the forces that existed before like Oswald Spengler, or that work on the outside like professor Eugen Varga, can either only see the downfall, or must cause it themselves. Who dare speak against the decline of the western world? Someone who may speak against the downfall of the western world is someone who demands that human deeds come out of the new-born spiritual life. — This is how the question must be answered clearly and this is what anthroposophically orientated spiritual science has been trying to do for years.

I observed towards the end of the Waldorf school year the results of lessons to the students in individual classes — and I have already mentioned some of this — how for example Dr Stein approached the 7th and 8th grade pupils with history from the perspective of the rising spiritual life as a will that is juxtaposed with the dwindling forces. I have mentioned other things that shine in the Waldorf School as good fruits of our spiritual science.

Today I would like to mention that people outside sneer particularly when it is spoken about — as it must be spoken about in spiritual science — of the soul and spirit, besides the body. One only has to see once, for example in Class 5 under the leadership of Fräulein von Heydebrand, how it is presented to the children — in the form appropriate to the children — what Anthroposophy makes of Anthropology, that it awakens in the children an idea of the real concrete form of the soul and spirit of man. There's a pulsating of life, there's nothing of the boredom of today's anthropological concepts that are otherwise introduced to children, because the knowledge is drawn from real life, real life is stimulated in the youth. It is only a question of the teacher's being able to transform, precisely for the corresponding age, that which emerges from anthroposophically oriented spiritual science.

It can also be said, then: the Mystery of Golgotha came as a strike into the earth's evolution at a time when it was understood with what remained of old instinctive spiritual science — I have often mentioned this in my lectures. Today people have to understand it with the rising, new spiritual science. Then Christianity will experience a new birth, then Christianity will again be understood because under the hand of the theologian, Christianity has degenerated into materialism. Instead of seriously considering how Christianity itself has to be found anew out of a renewed spiritual life today, theologians appear — forgive me for bringing this up as well — theologians who are against anthroposophically orientated spiritual science. If one wants to read all the literature against anthroposophically orientated spiritual science you will find nothing different, yet it is sometimes interesting to glance at the titles of publications. There is for instance — I don't know if any among you know about this beautiful sheet — "Die neue Kirche" (The New Church), published on behalf of the Hamburg People's Church Council by Pastor Franz Tügel and Dr Peter Petersen. In it is an article, in number 15 of the year 1920 "Theological Direction, Dr Steiner and the Devil." On page 232 we find the following sentence: "At most it is still conceivable that a Catholic could become a student of Steiner ..." — Such a thing is born out of today's culture; for once people should consider what the catholic clergy is throwing against anthroposophically orientated spiritual science, but here speaks a Protestant, and so the author thinks that this spiritual science, could, well, still pass for Catholicism and says — "there are relations which one can understand; but how a Protestant can join him, at least a conscious one, grasped by the spirit of the Reformation, is completely incomprehensible. In Steiner's school all faith is held as truth. Schaeder rightly points out, that all the exercises recommended by Steiner amount to legalism and morality. For me there is no doubt: Luther would have given the Steiner teaching in his language to the devil, he would also have strongly emphasized what is thoroughly un-German about it. He would have warned his Protestant church against the false prophet."

206

I would like to pose a question. Are the exercises I recommend meant to amount to lawlessness and immorality? What is emphasized here is something particularly bad, that the exercises recommended by me amount to legalism and morality. Well, many things are written in such a tone today.

However, there is also another tone in which one cannot say it is written. The already mentioned anatomy professor, Fuchs in Göttingen, managed with an ingenious distortion to say in newspaper articles that anthroposophy should not be scientific. He has proved nothing else with it than that he can currently regard as a scientist, only what just enters into his head as science, and what is not so, that he does not regard as science. That means, he does it in the same way as those who, when Copernicus appeared, considered Copernicus unscientific because he did not teach what they taught to the faithful in the church. In medieval times, grand inquisitors had come from the ranks of the church; today, they can come from the ranks of university professors and be called foxes; and their followers are prepared in such a way that they pull from their pockets all kinds of combat equipment, such as children's trumpets and ratchets, house keys with which to whistle, when a Dr Stein and a Dr Kolisko talk about anthroposophically oriented spiritual science. It cannot be said that these people first listened to the talks that were given; otherwise they would have had to conjure up the children's trumpets and rattles and whatever else they had, after they had heard the "bad" rationale of Dr Kolisko and Dr Stein. The rationale of Dr Stein and Dr Kolisko was not in the will of these people to be listened to; it was in their will to shout it down in the same way one would have done in medieval times by other means, according to what these people venerate as progress today. One must have the courage to look unreservedly at such sentiments. You don't need to do anything other than look at the numerous sleeping souls of people who do not want to look at the phenomena of spiritual life, who want to sleep in the face of these phenomena. Then you have to say — also about the supersensible — what a Viennese writes about his Vienna, what he writes about is what he loves there — even if it is not particularly well written, it is nevertheless something like self-knowledge. After this young Viennese draws attention to his own youth and brings it together with what is developing as a healthier spirituality — he says — writing in the Viennese 'Sonn- und Montagszeitung' (newspaper) No. 29 of July 19, 1920:

"The spiritual situation of the German Danube countries seems to me to be even less pleasing than the economic and political one. We possess pretty much the cheapest and shallowest variety of socialism, the oldest and long since vanquished variety of philosophy in free-spirited dissipation and banal historical terms; besides that, the most unedifying method of playing knowledge and faith off against each other; besides that, religiously dressed-up blanket intolerance; next to it, the most uncritical desire to fall for all the noisily dressed-up artifice, an admirable garrulity and a sentimental predilection for the self-evident; alongside this, genial traits, damped down by a tacitly agreed upon, warm-hearted lack of talent which regards the half for the whole and the whole for the half, and above it, finally, a respectable sort of vanity, which speaks to the other, blowing itself off: 'This tells me nothing! I'm dreadful and educated myself!'."

That, embedded in such a kind of spirituality, even the softest and most un-profiled brand of occultism is just the most popular here, seems hardly to be surprising. A wide, murky stream of smut flows through this city, and all varieties of truism flourish lushly on its banks. My dear friends, one may already say that there is a kind of spirituality, which lets the most stupid brand of occultism, the stupidest spiritualistic muck, just flow around — that, my dear friends, is at once self-evident!

Now I don't want — because it's already late — to point out that, other than Vienna, there might be this cuddly stream of frivolous shallowness with its audience, where one sleeps in the face of what is of the utmost necessity: the reawakening of those forces which need to awaken in the human breast if we want in the place of downfall, the place of the rising. However, if we can see the fallacy of how, on the one hand, geniuses like Oswald Spengler can prove the downfall of

208

what is present, how on the other hand people like Professor Eugen Varga show downfall currents through their deeds, then we will — if we have the ability to wake up in the soul — then we will still be able to perceive spiritual streams which as anthroposophically orientated spiritual science want to place in the will of people that which can be born out of the light of supersensible cognition. Then we will gain a new version of the Words of Christ: Heaven and earth may pass away but my Words will not pass away. — Then we will say: Yes, everything that is accessible to the eyes of Oswald Spengler and all that in which social reforms like Professors Eugen Varga would like to move, will perish.

What is born out of a truly new spirit, is what will dominate the future, because it does not only believe in some forces lying somewhere indeterminately, which will already help to bring about a new culture, as has helped before, but it wants to kindle one's own will, the deepest inner will of man himself, which one has in one's hand in freedom, to new forces. Then we speak against the decline of the Occident, because we do not only trust in the future, but because we want to bring about a future which we already see now.

Just as one sees the future plant in the germ of the old one, we want a future that we already see as a germ in us. The future will be, if we only want it, against all the forces of doom. It is to the Will that anthroposophically oriented spiritual science addresses itself; to the will, not to the inactive way of looking at things, and from there it wants to take the right to speak against the decline of the western world.

Today's great tasks in spiritual life, legal life and economic life
A third lecture for the current time
Stuttgart on 2 September 1920

My dear honourable friends present here today! The circumstances of public life in the civilized world, over the course of the last 50 years, cannot be overlooked, their reciprocal relationships have become difficult to see though and find clarity.

From what one could call the great economic upswing before 1914, today's misery has emerged, rising from the most complicated circumstances with the most diverse facts — facts, in turn, of a kind that is difficult to grasp. No wonder that people who have to live in this decline today, have to work, to strive, while from the depths of their souls they long for an ascent to a new beginning, that now questions can be asked in a small circle in the attempt to find betterment for this or that individual. As understandable as this might be, anyone who looks deeper into today's conditions must realize that nothing can lead from decline to reconstruction today, nor in the near future, if there is no understanding of the great tasks of the time. The great tasks of the time arise from specific sources which cannot actually lie within small areas. As well as I am able in one evening, I will try to give some reflections on some of these great tasks of our time in a modest way — I would like to say that one cannot do otherwise in the face of these tasks.

It seems that if anything obviously points to the way we must face the great tasks, it is to consider the great mistakes that have been made in this time. Two stages describe our whole public life in its immediate present development and it seems to me that these stages not only refer to external economic conditions but also to legal conditions, to moral and especially to spiritual conditions within the present civilization. If you name these two stages, Versailles, Spa and all that they have in their wake, if you remember all that they have brought to us, then it becomes somewhat difficult to characterize them, because today suspicions arise in the pursuit of a certain objectivity.

People's opinions harshly opposed one another: If a member of the Central European civilization wants to judge the West, it is quite sure that his objectivity will be doubted vehemently by the people of the West. I would therefore prefer not to pass my own judgment about what happened at Versailles, which is still reverberating in our present day; rather, I would like to follow the judgment of the Englishman John Maynard Keynes, who wrote the important book "The Economic Consequences of the Peace Treaty" which I already referred to in my Stuttgart lectures, from another perspective.

Keynes, after all, was a man who was present in a prominent position at the Versailles negotiations up to a certain point, until it became too much for him, and in his book he judges what had happened and also what he thought should have happened, in his opinion. One could say that in three punch-lines he summarised our present as so symptomatic of the Versailles facts, which are also so symptomatic of our present day. He, the Englishman, whom Lenin only a short time ago called the "English philistine," says quite simply: 'Nothing, but nothing at all happened at Versailles regarding a mastery of the great task, which those would have had if they felt themselves victors. What did Clemenceau do? He has ruined Europe's economic resources and has done nothing for the economy in France itself. What did Lloyd George do? He made some deals that allowed him to shine in London for a short time. What came from Wilson? Wilson has had good intentions about what is right and just' — thinks Keynes — but no way did it occur to him to somehow turn what he may have intended, with well-meaning, into reality. The three most important men, and they made huge mistakes at the time.

Now let us look at what actually come out of the terrible events that have taken place since 1914 for Germany. I do not need to describe it to you. Southeast of Germany, Czechoslovakia has become a relatively large empire. Born out of national aspirations, everything that governs there proves to be economically impotent in the face of tasks, which have been set for the economy in these areas. Northwards: Poland. Now, you only need to be reminded of the last few weeks to see, on the one hand, how what has been formed there has only contributed to the disquiet of Europe, and on the other hand, you only have to remember the perplexity of leading European figures in the face of what is boiling and simmering there. One only has to think of the tragic-comic in the transformation of the view from Polish "defeats" to Polish "victories," how one had faced, without opinion, without great guidelines, today this, tomorrow the opposite.

If one goes further East, it can seem today as if there are no longer any other guidelines than Leninism and Trotskyism, especially if one takes into account the disastrous conditions in Italy — no other guidelines than those forces that develop out of a phenomenal megalomania, forces which can serve for the destruction of civilization. The Germans of Austria are down, not to speak of Hungary, where the sad spectacle is taking place that when members of that party which a short time ago was at the helm, are led through the streets, captured and bound, they are then poked in the eyes with umbrellas belonging to pompously made-up ladies. This description could be continued for a long time, and one could see what has emerged for mankind from the circumstances since the year 1914.

If you look at what comes from personalities who are somehow active within this terrible decline — personalities who can often even indulge in tragic-comic illusions about an ascent that could be brought about by their intentions , one would like to say: In the short-sighted — monumental in its short-sightedness — lack of insight, was Lenin's speech at the second congress of the Third International, where he once again, in the old Marxist style, accused Western capitalism of all the banalities which have been heard so often. If one goes into it from a certain viewpoint of world history, of what is said in this large-scale speech about capitalism having grown into imperialism which tyrannizes five sevenths of mankind, then on the other hand the

213

question must be asked: What would have become of the whole of modern civilization if there had not been capital accumulation? Should one not ask: Is it not obvious that the forces contributing to our modern times show that such an accumulation of capital has not also been for the progress of mankind? In the face of our collapsing world, is it still possible to get by with such an abstraction which only proclaims the struggle in a very abstract form, or does one not have to ask: Isn't our decline, especially when this note is struck, also clearly based on something moral? Do not, perhaps, just such fighters like Lenin confuse the harmfulness of capitalism in general with the kind of morality, or rather immorality, with which capitalism has operated? Can we not also trace this spiritual note in the effects of capitalism? Also, does one perhaps not arrive at deeper impulses than those which are constantly proclaimed today, and whose declarations have nevertheless brought so few practical successes for the better?

One can already say: Indicative of today's intellectual, legal and economic situation is of course the counterpart, which again comes from Keynes, the Englishman, the sharp condemner of the Western powers, but it sounds somewhat different in Lenin's words. Keynes says for example: Yes, terrible things happened at Versailles. Instead of doing something towards the rebuilding of Europe, everything was done to transform Europe into a heap of ruins of civilization; bad things are there for the time being, worse things will still come about in the next years. — I am quoting these according to the sense of it, not the wording.

Even more curious is the way Keynes remarks on a few things which are there as underlying spiritual states, which have brought us to our current situation. It is interesting to note how this man, who sat in for weeks at the negotiations conducted by Wilson, Clemenceau and Lloyd George, how this man realizes how it actually came about that Wilson, who had beguiled so many people with his abstract Fourteen Points, had failed so utterly. A significant problem came to the Englishman Keynes, and something very strange comes to light.

Keynes constructs — as I said, from the view of the way Wilson sat there — how the others did everything they could to deceive him, just so that he wouldn't find out what they actually want. A strange psychological event that Keynes describes and dissects, which, I would like to mention, shines a profoundly significant light into the whole cultural condition of the present. Keynes obviously means: Had Wilson been told what France's wish was, that the Germans of Austria should not be allowed to unite with the Germans of Germany, if this had been clearly stated in such a way that Wilson would have heard these words, his sense of justice would have rebelled against it. Now one must see the struggle of such a dull mentality — if I may use that 'Entente' word — one must realize, how Wilson feels — as Keynes does — if you now visualize the following as a spectator.

Keynes said: Yes, the people around Clemenceau and Lloyd George did not say: 'It will not be permitted for the Germans of Austria to unite with the Germans of Germany' because Wilson would have rebelled against it, so that is why they said: 'The independence of German Austria is to be guaranteed by a treaty with the Entente powers until the League of Nations pronounces a different verdict.' This is what Wilson understood: the independence, the freedom of the German Austria had to be guaranteed. — Had he been told: They would be forbidden to unite with the Germans of Germany —, Wilson would have understood the same as he regarded for freedom and independence, as the ultimate constraint. Had he been told — this is how Keynes continues — 'Gdansk is to become a Polish city' he would have rebelled against it; this obviously contradicts the Fourteen Points. So he was told: 'Gdansk will become a free city, but all customs matters shall be taken care of from Poland as well as the supervision of all traffic matters, and the Poles shall become the protectors of the citizens living abroad.'

Oh, that sounds different than if one had said: 'Gdansk is to become a Polish city.' One can almost say: Yes, if one says it this way: 'Gdansk is to become a free city' Wilson's dull mentality gets excited. If, however, he had been told that Danzig should become a Polish city, it would have contradicted Wilson's view that every nation should be led to freedom. If Wilson had further been told that the Entente should have overall supervision of German rivers, he could have agreed, but this is how it was said: 'Where navigation passes through several states, it is an international business.' With this, Wilson was again satisfied.

If one wants to look at what moves in the world today as great powers, one has to look at what is happening between two aspects. I will now translate the word Entente into "Geistesverfassung" (frame of mind). Look what is happening between this "frame of mind" of leading personalities who have developed out of their former circumstances, to where they are now. Is uprightness and honesty still alive? Does a healthy sense and openness still exist? The opposite is mostly the case, and what is more, it lives in such a way that one is still convinced that one is an honest, open person, because what works has become an unconscious habit. How could Wilson become so deceived as he was in the style I have described Keynes? People who still cannot convince themselves that such an abstract, theorizing spirit like Wilson is a misfortune for Europe, sometimes say these benevolent words: 'This Wilson knew too little about European conditions' — admitting to it hypothetically, although I don't admit it, 'Wilson hardly knew European conditions.' In fact Wilson had written a comprehensive work of 500 pages about the state in which he describes in great detail the conditions of the European states, the state relations, the legal relations and so on.

We are faced with the fact: either it is untrue, that Wilson didn't know about European conditions or a contemporary authoritative figure writes an authoritative work for America, about European conditions without knowledge of these conditions. It is precisely the latter that would shed a bright light on the whole superficiality of our time, on everything that is in the spirit of superficiality and does not get involved in deeper foundations of things causing present events, the current developments living within the whole of human evolution. Still, something much more important lurks behind what I have presented.

216

Already many years ago, during a series of lectures in Helsingfors — at a time when Wilson was revered everywhere because two important literary works of his had been published — I drew attention to something that characterizes the whole nature of Wilson's frame of mind. Wilson once said: 'When one looks at the time in which Newton, the great physicist lived, one finds how for example, in the theory of constitutional law or in those who think about commercial and economic conditions, the same conceptual formations can be found for the economic and for the political conditions that Newton, the physicist, designed for the physicists.' Now Wilson says: 'From such dependence of the way of thinking and in relation to public, political or economic conditions we must free ourselves; today we must think in terms of the organic, regarding politics, world economy and so on.' Now he develops a kind of political idea about which one can say: Just as those whom he rebukes because they were dependent on Newton in their time, so he is completely as a politician, as an economist, as a man of law, the follower of Darwinism and thinking Darwinistically, as those whom he rebukes who thought Newtonistically. 'Darwin is in fashion' — is what Wilson, the world reformer, thinks as a Darwinian. At the time I said: We are now in a time when we must no longer allow our view of the real conditions of public life to be clouded at all by that which comes to us from the scientific side. What comes out of the scientific side — I have often said it here — is perfectly suited for the research of the surfaces of things but what involves forming ideas about human action, human coexistence, must go deeper into the foundations of the world than science has any need for. For this reason I say the dangerous thing in our time is to precisely have such a way of thinking as that of Woodrow Wilson.

That happened long before the war; that was in a time after which Wilson had for a long time been glorified as the world hero. What matters today is turning away one's gaze for everything which is outwardly perceived today. It is of necessity to deepen the gaze into deeper foundations of becoming and happenings. That, my dear friends, tries the direction of a world view which starts at the same scientific spirit, as natural science is on the soul-spiritual in human

217

beings. It is the anthroposophically orientated spiritual science which I have almost for two decades — every year more often — represented here in my lectures in Stuttgart.

What do we need to strive for in our spiritual life in the sense of the spiritual science that is meant here? I briefly want to point out that spiritual science does not arrive at results in an external way, but through the pupil firstly — intellectually meant — performing exercises. The pupil must again and again repeat what I have characterised in one of my last lectures here as a comparison. I said: If a five-year-old child picks up a volume of Goethe's poetry, he will not be able to do anything with it, and will do something quite different from what is intended with the volume of Goethe's poetry. If he turns ten years older, he would have undergone a development and attained a level of maturity that will enable him to do something with this volume of poetry. — The spiritual scientist as it is meant here, says: With that form of consciousness, which we use in ordinary life and which we also apply in usual science, with it we stand in the face of the higher world forces like a five-year-old child stands in the face of a volume of Goethe's poetry. Forces slumber in every human being out of which he can, in himself, develop and which then show him a different, spiritual recognition of the world and shows him above all that one can research the surface of things with natural scientific thinking, although grandiose, and that in this respect natural science has justly achieved the greatest triumphs. They show him that with the natural scientific way of thinking we do not get behind the innate things that play into the actions of man, if we do not reach for such methods and ways of thinking that are permeated by the spirit, and by which we can also understand man and the forces in him in a thoroughly scientific way. But then however we come from the kind of comprehension of human beings in general to a completely different comprehension of the world than the conventional spiritual life in which we find ourselves today.

In the face of this common spiritual life, one would like to remember the deeply heart-stabbing words Hölderlin spoke when his mind was still bright, not yet mentally deranged, but fine, sensitive to what was present in his cultural environment. Hölderlin, who had immersed himself in the harmonious humanity of ancient Greece and had come to love it, he saw, to a certain extent exaggerating, as such a spirit might do in his time, that the people in his environment, in comparison with the Greeks, had the following kinds of characteristics. He asked: 'Are there human beings living among ordinary Germans? Around me I don't see any human beings like the Greeks had been, I see officials, teachers, professors but no human beings; I see advocates, artist and scholars, but no human beings; I see young and sedate people around me, but no human beings. What I miss in my surroundings is a whole, fully developed humanity, which can also gain a harmonious relationship to the universe.' —

This kind of humanity lived consciously-unconsciously, sensibly-supersensibly in Goethe, and out of such a humanity, for example, streamed what Goethe himself cherished more highly than his own poetry — although it was, according to Goethe, so little understood: his natural scientific creations. In this Goethean scientific school of thought lived not only a one-sided physicist when he presents his theory of colours, there doesn't live a once-sided botanist describing his plants, there doesn't live a one-sided anatomist when he characterises human bones, but in this way of thinking the whole human being is alive; the whole human being grasps the individual parts of nature which can only be revealed when it is experienced, in its process, in the whole of humanity, from within.

In the course of time, this way of thinking has been increasingly contrasted with something that has been praised so much, but also sometimes criticized: specialization in all areas of life: specialisation which has entered our higher knowledge and from there has unfolded its effects, for example, down into elementary school education. This specialisation made people into physicists, into advocates, professors, teachers and so on, but drove out the human being. We must ask ourselves: Is it really a furtherance of knowledge itself if this knowledge has developed in recent times in such a way that the knowledge that led to a world view has split into those small parts from which even the human part has been lost and an eye for the world can no longer be preserved? Authoritative personalities are repeatedly portrayed as if they themselves are knowledge. If a person can look into the development of recent times, he would discover that it is not the case. He sees this knowledge and striving for the abstract unitary state as it has developed over the civilized world in the last three to four centuries. He sees that the unitary state, which absorbed everything that we want to re-divide today through the impulse of the threefold social organism structure, that this unitary state with its mingling of intellectual life, legal life and economic life into one fabric made of physicists and chemists, professors and teachers, in short specialized people, and with these it had to fill its staff positions if it followed its principles. It was this unitary state that sucked being human out of humanity which is what lived in Goethe and which Hölderlin so longed for, for his Germans. Spiritual science is that which can give the fully human element back to people, because out of being fully human alone it can happen that at the same time the cognition of feeling for everything human, a real legal and reasonable economic life can come about.

If one proceeds according to the methods of spiritual research, one does not get a superficial view of something or other brewed from single disciplines, but rather one receives fully living spiritual knowledge. This is like a light that can be cast over single areas. With it human beings are given the opportunity once again to place people above specialist positions; one gets the opportunity to put people first and the social entity afterwards — and not vice versa by putting the social entity first and then the human being next, thereby letting him wither away under a system template. Because spiritual science is something which in this way really comes from the fully human, but which must first be gained through spiritual research, it can also have a fertilizing effect on that which is fragmented in the world. What is fragmented in our world is for example our current legal science, the individual branches of our current economic life — everything is fragmented.

Well, whoever has listened to me over a longer period of time and is able to understand the actual meaning of what I say, knows that I do not say such things out of immodesty or silliness. I may as well point out that in February, in front of more than thirty specialists in Dornach, I tried to present the therapeutic element of medicine from a spiritual-scientific understanding of the nature of the human being in such a way that one really acquires a genuine therapy which is directly applicable to the human being. In this individual case I tried to show how stimulating a central view of the essence of the natural, the soul and the spirit can be for a single science. Whoever now considers the social effect of the striving of personalities imbued with our knowledge, will nevertheless reflect on the meaning of what I have said. It is a different matter if a physician is brought up in a closed circle and cannot see beyond the limits of his science, or whether he grasps his science in such a way that it becomes a light for him for everything of man's physical, spiritual and soul nature and that through this, at the same time, he acquires a true sense for all social interaction and coexistence of human beings, and thus, from his medical art, a lively, fruitful judgement arise on the treatment of major social questions.

In Autumn, beginning on the 26th September, more than twenty personalities, who have lived into the Anthroposophical spiritual science meant here, will hold a course of new university lectures in Dornach. In Dornach I have established our School of Spiritual Science, which we cannot open because it is not yet finished, but we will hold these university courses at the unopened Dornach School from September 26 to October 16. Personalities from the fields of physics, chemistry, political science, national economy and history, practitioners who are practical in life, in the factory or otherwise in life, artists in all areas, will first show in this trial course how that which specializes in individual fields, through living spiritual science, which is anthroposophically oriented, receives such a light that these sciences are no longer something theoretical, no longer something that one acquires and later has to peel away from oneself to a large extent, in order to then stand in a corner of life and from there survey nothing other than specialist things. No, it is shown how through this enlivening of knowledge which can come out of spiritual science, that specialization will be overcome and how through the new spirit, through a spirit which is as strictly scientific as that which is cultivated today in the universities, indeed "strict," even more rigorously scientific, that by this spirit the specialists are brought together so that they will not in their mutual incomprehension go alone in mankind's damaging ways but will work together socially and from the spirit lift our depressing time.

These university lectures are held in our Dornach Goetheanum in which every detail seeks such a style, such an architectural, sculptural, painterly style, as follows from the whole sentient conception, from the artistic conception, which arises from our spiritual science. Everything should work there, up to this framing as it were, like a symbol for what should happen from the spiritual side. For it must be the spirit that, following its true threads, comes back to the truth; to a truth from which goodness, from which morality and from which the healthy, strong will follow. It doesn't result from surface knowledge but it results from cognition in spiritual depths. Much more than being able to express mere characterisation, I hope these lectures of ours in Dornach will show how, from the spirit, the forces are to be sought for the building up of our depressed civilization. We don't want to logically discount remarks such as about the downfall of the Occident, as I characterized them last time here, but through action we want to create that which can be opposed to the forces of decline. I am convinced that we really would not be able to accommodate all the listeners in Dornach and its wider surroundings today, who would come — and hopefully in quite large numbers, despite the current sleepiness of souls today — if it were not for the fact that the traffic difficulties resulting from our decline were not so insurmountable.

If I may point out something closer to home, I would like to return once again to what is intended with our Free Waldorf School here. This Waldorf School, which we have opened up for the second school year, today, we have described here some time ago with reference to its achievements in the first school year. Through what it has become — it couldn't become more in its first year — it has become because our teachers were enlivened and inspired by those feelings towards the developing human being, the child — feelings that come from the research of spiritual science, that spiritual science which, however, has to behave in a completely different way with regard to certain spiritual things than many people have assumed up to now with regard to these things.

In our current time we have proclamations which speak about the eternity of the human being. To what end have all these proclamations come? If you really look at the world without prejudice and listen to sermons or theologies about the eternal in the human soul, it is not an appeal of the urge for knowledge, but basically an appeal to the finer instincts of the person. For those of you who have often listened to my lectures, you would know from which foundations the spiritual science meant here speaks about regarding the immortal part in man, how it gives certain indications about what happens when a person has passed through the gate of death and has shed his physical body. However, from another background it is being spoken about what one has for centuries become accustomed to hearing in Western civilization. What is appealed to again and again in this occidental civilization? To the finer instincts of the soul; man does not want his whole being to cease when his body crumbles to dust. It is about the desire for eternity. I ask you to go through everything that is offered along these lines in traditional proclamations, in sermons and theologies: it is the appeal to human egoism that does not want to die. While it is only an appeal to egoism, things are conveniently separated: knowledge for the sensual world and faith for the supersensible world. Of course, by reasoning only about the instincts referred to here, in relation to immortality, you only come to a belief, not to knowledge. However, by applying methods of spiritual science which are not easier

223

than chemical or astronomical methods but more difficult, in order to investigate the human being — more details can be found in my books "How to attain knowledge of the Higher Worlds" or "Occult Science, an Outline" or other books — then you find it isn't merely a matter of speaking about immortality, that means from the forms which the soul-spiritual human being assumes after death, but comes down to look at what the human being was before birth or conception, before he as a spiritual being descended through birth out of the spiritual world into the physical world and took on a physical body inherited from the father and mother. Something like this can become cognitions, but cognitions of such an inner power that it can penetrate our entire being.

If we, as educators, approach the child with such cognition then we look at the child in a completely different way. Then we know something about how the soul-spiritual forms out of the deepest human substrata, how the physiognomy, the skills, that appear from year to year, are formed in the body out of the soul-spiritual. By facing the human being as a teacher and educator, one gets a feeling without which there can be no fruitful education at all, the feeling: What you are coming into contact with in this human form has origins in spiritual worlds; you are entrusted with what the gods have sent down — so you stand before it with holy reverence.

My dear friends, just as there are forces that can only be explored through their effects in the external, physical world, for example, electricity or magnetism, just so there streams through, when you are a teacher or educator, what you acquire as reverence which has the effect of an imponderable force like something you only learn to believe when you see its effects, when you see what emanates from such holy teacher reverence, that it is something which surrounds the child's soul-spiritual growth in the same way that sunlight surrounds the plants to flourish into blossoms. A pedagogy out of the fully human, which is borne by feelings and sensations, yet by a sensibility that sees through world conditions and human conditions, a pedagogy that naturally becomes art, that does not talk abstractly about

224

education, such a pedagogy is the kind that can strive in the decisive generation over the next decades, to lead from our decline into a new beginning. We can say: What anthroposophically oriented spiritual science has been able to make of our teaching staff has at least borne fruit in the first school year.

Today there's only one thing in front of us, who have opened the second school year, that confronts the spiritual eye as a spectre to those whose whole heart and whole mind is with this Waldorf School. Out of the spirit we can bring Waldorf School after Waldorf School to life; out of the spirit practically — not theoretically — one of the great tasks of our time will be solved, step by step. However, we need understanding, understanding in the widest circles. We may hope for the spirit to be continuously supportive to us in our striving because to a certain extent it depends on us. Indeed understanding is what we need because the buildings housing the school need to be built; teachers are to live in apartments and also need to eat. All this is necessary. Already the spectre of destitution regarding such things and for what lies behind it, the lack of understanding in wide circles for one of the great tasks of our time, stands before our souls and impairs what we would like to do just in these days, for the second school year.

What we need most of all for the tasks of today is understanding in the widest sense of the word. Many people with idealism say: Ideals are elevated, they are not worthy to be brought into connection with mundane material relationships because the material world is something lowly; ideals are high, they have to find their own way — that's why we keep our hands on our wallets and spend nothing at all on our ideals, because why take idle money which isn't worthy of serving ideals, and give it to ideals? — This sounds trivial. However, if we want to do something that is necessary for the Waldorf School today, in this case it may be spoken about. Idealism today often manifests itself more through the enthusiasm to keep material things together and to cultivate ideals in them.

Now I am able to sketch something for you which connects again with something quite new in our spiritual life. For a long time already we have lost the direction and current of our spiritual life which looks at what I want to characterise regarding the prenatal human being. Our very language testifies to it: When we speak of man's eternity, what do we say? Immortality. — We only point to one end of life, towards where human egoism looks. We don't have a word for the other: "unbornness" for example, one could call it. Just as little as we don't lose our eternal essence when we lay down the physical body, just so, we don't receive it at birth.

When we speak about the eternal part of man, so we must equally speak about unbornness as well as we speak about immortality. We don't even suspect what we are missing in this direction. What we hope for in the time after death hardly inspires action in us. Should we know what lives in us, what lives in us as having descended from the spiritual worlds, as if it were only as a reflection of the spiritual world, then we can say we feel ourselves as — I would like to use the word — missionaries of the spiritual world.

In earthly work our feelings are moved, our actions inspired for our tasks as human beings in an earthly existence. From out of the spirit we must gain forces to really enter into what our tasks as human beings on earth are; it is not enough that we only remain in the nearest areas surrounding us in life. We must look at what surrounds us in spiritual life, what lives inwardly as spiritual life and even permeates all of life, right into the economic sphere. As far as this is concerned, people indulge in the strangest illusions. Whoever follows the historical course of mankind with a sense of reality, will see that the actual sources of spiritual impulses are not on the surface and can be looked for over in the Orient — actually not in the current Orient because today's Orient in this regard is decadent. The source of this very special spiritual life, as I have described it here in the lecture I gave on the historical development of mankind, lived thousands of years ago in the Orient.

There lived a humanity that understood nothing of what we call "proving" or "logical thinking" — a humanity that drew from the same sources as the spiritual science meant here, but in a different way, in the occidental way, and once open up to man, they knew that

226

something can live in a man's soul which reveals to him the spirit that permeates the world. Nothing that could be proved, or logical knowledge of the spirit, lived over in the Orient. Today, if we don't want to place ourselves in an antiquated time, we can no longer penetrate this oriental spiritual life, yet our ordinary spiritual formation still has something of it. There is a straight line from that spirit which shone forth in the Vedas, in the Vedanta philosophy, in the ancient Indian yoga system, which lived even in the Chaldean teachings and in ancient China; it is a straight line that moved in many currents through many channels to the Occident. In what we think in ordinary life as actually spiritual today, still have traces of Oriental spiritual life in it.

Even when you place the Mystery of Golgotha in human evolution as is necessary to understand Christ Jesus, it was oriental wisdom that sought to understand this event, which could only be comprehended through supersensible knowledge and then spread over the whole Western world. In this oriental wisdom something lived which today can't be experienced and felt in the right way, for which support is needed. What was present in the Oriental as its original soul-life had to, for centuries already, be anchored in dogmatic cohesive religious communities because the inner sources of spiritual life no longer flows in the same way and so people need such religious communities. This is what, to start with, sticks out like the first branch into our public life — a branch which is still has the Orient as the "lifeblood" in it. If one was to look impartially at our spiritual life, one would discover that today, what is thought, felt and sensed is still affected from what comes from the Orient, even in the sciences, physics, and above all, in religious proclamations.

Added to this peculiar oriental spirit which is little understood today in its entire configuration, it flows through the Occident — taking the way more over the South and pouring into Central Europe, but also fertilizing the West — a completely different school of thought. There came into, what I could term a comprehensive sense the legal-, the state- and the political thinking.

In the wonderful Greekdom we see a strange blending of what sounds from the Orient, what still lives in the Greek as having come over from the Egyptians, in which Greece is not yet fully revealed, now already the juristic thinking, which brought the peculiar proving art into the conception of the human being. In Greece, we see life only sparsely permeated by logistical, legal, governmental thinking that was not present in the Orient. If for example there were commandments presented in the Orient, they were something quite different there than commandments were in the Western world. We then see the judicial spirit essentially rising from ancient Rome. We see how the proving, using logic, the combining and separating of concepts, develop into a special art. We notice how a second element mixes into that which streams over from the Orient, as the judicial, the political pours into the spiritual current, the "state machine." Even the spiritual-religious, the spiritual-scholastic we see permeated by this juridical element.

It would have been quite impossible for the Oriental to have found in the original thoughts of his world view, instead of the concept of "karma," something like "guilt and atonement" or "redemption." What lived in the Orient in the idea of "karma," or in world fate, was something quite different. Then, however, the juridical element made itself heard in the world view; it put itself into the religious world view. The human being was seen differently at the turning point of time, than in the Orient. Now he is thought of as being "judged" by the world because he has loaded "guilt" on to himself. One spoke differently about "guilt" and "judgement" in the Orient. These judicial-proving and separating-judging elements of the Western world have even crept into the religious element.

If we go for example to the Sistine Chapel in Rome and consider Michelangelo's painting of "Christ the World Judge" in front of us, where He passes judgement on the good and evil, then we see for ourselves how the judicial, world-political spirit is carried into the religious conception of the world, even there. This is the second branch in our civilization, which still has an effect in Fichte, in Hegel, and which saturates what still emerges at the turn of the 18th, 19th century in German intellectual life. It is not in vain that Fichte and Hegel started their thinking literally from the roots of law, from the political, the state relations, and the way in which these minds think of mankind's development is to be understood in a "state-powerful" sense compared with earlier times.

More recently a third stream was added to the second one, which developed in the West out of the western folk systems and instincts of the people. In the East, in the times when the East had its greatness, nature gave what man needed in such a way that he made the distribution of the products of nature, as well as the distribution of what man produced, out of his spiritual life. There was no economic thinking; there was not even legal thinking. If we go as far back as the 18th century, we still find a low level of economic thinking in Central Europe. However we find everything dominated by an increasingly legal thinking, by a state-, political thinking.

In the West, this economic thinking had been developing for a long time and it evolved more and more out of the natural instincts and dispositions of people. The conditions developed in such a way that where one thinks essentially "western," now also for what was grasped earlier from the viewpoint of logic — for science, for truth — economic thinking is applied. It came out of America. There one had the teaching of pragmatism, which roughly says: '"True" and "false" is something that is only illusion; we have taken this from the legal world view. Our view is this: If something proves useful in practical life, it is right, it is true, and anything that proves to be not useful is harmful, is false.' According to this world view of life everything was judged according to whether it is "useful" or "harmful."

These ideas came into human habits of thinking and live also in the philosophers. If for example you really want to understand philosophers like Herbert Spencer and others, you will only understand them if you say: This Herbert Spencer thinks out philosophical systems, but he has ideas which as such only stand in the wrong place; instead of thinking out philosophical systems his way of thinking should be used to build factories, set up trade unions and help the economy get on its feet; for this, his ideas are useful, but not in the philosophical field.

If we thus trace what our humanity is going through in its historical development, we see: First a spiritual life is formed, which refers back to an inheritance from earlier millennia in the later time, then gradually a state life, a political life, a juridical thinking comes up, later the economic life develops to it, and this life develops differentiated over the earth. Added to this, as we approach the newer times, we see how the spiritual life that has come over from the Orient has died away and the dry pedantic and philistine nature of today's teaching and education comes particularly from the death of that old spiritual heritage. This points out with all vivacity that we should not wander back to the Orient but through ourselves we must develop a free and original spiritual life by opening ourselves up to the sources of this spiritual life.

The old legacy is over. A new spiritual life is wanted in our time, and such a spiritual science now wants to proclaim it from Dornach. With such a new spiritual life it will penetrate pedagogy, permeated education and through something like the Waldorf School it will make it fruitful for modern life. Even for the old legal spirit, little is left over today.

I recommend you read about characteristic, symptomatic phenomena of the present, such as in the small booklet on jurisprudence by the Mannheim teacher Rumpf, then you will see: Just as religious world views today have to borrow from the outside, because the inside no longer bubbles, so jurisprudence and political science borrow from economic conditions, because they no longer have anything bubbling alive from the inside. So when we look today, we see a mixture of economic thinking and legal thinking spreading chaos over our lives. For anyone who really sees through things, will know how much of this chaotic confusion within our public life has penetrated right up into the sphere where social upheavals, social trials and tribulations manifest in outer deeds. We can only move forward if we seek a new spiritual life in the way I have described. The old spiritual life has passed away as an inheritance. We will find the new spiritual life only if we do not hand over the school to the state, but if we position the whole of spiritual life on its own, for then alone can we lift spiritual life out of what it is now.

From the human individuality and personality the human being brings, when he enters the physical world from spiritual heights, some real spirituality and something new with him. This is what we want to uplift. We don't want to dictate to people how they must develop according to some or other set of rules, but we want this real spiritual aspect to develop powerfully through love from the teacher, from the educator to the child. This spiritual life can only be maintained by those who are active in it. A new spiritual life will bring the living spirit, which our social life needs so much, back into the present; it will make the deep source, which man brings with him when he enters physical existence through birth, fruitful for human coexistence. This is one of the great tasks of our time.

A second task is how we get back to living — not regurgitating old Roman or, for that matter, old concepts and logistical fabrics, but originally, through the living together of one person relating to anther in the democratic structure of the state — how we can again come to live in the human sense of a social community with the pulse between right and duty. No dictated law will ever develop a sense of duty. Only that law which arises between equals, between one person who has become mature in living exchanges with another mature person, only this law will also make people eager to work and this law will include the regulation of work in itself.

Spiritual life, as I refer to it, is described in my "Key Points to the Social Question" in such a way that it must become the regulator, especially of capital. Then that which is needed for modern development, the accumulation of capital or means of production, is through the spirit — which will illuminate it, when the spirit is freedom, in its proliferation, in its progress from generation to generation will recreate itself anew — then capital, through the spirit, will also carry within itself what for example Keynes and others miss: morality. As a result economic life will not be set on egoism and only self-acquired capitalism but live with spiritually imbued capitalism — even out of insight into the necessities of the world — the new capitalism will work in the sense of people who have been educated in the new spiritual life. Then labour, too, will no longer be a commodity, but will be included in the independent constitutional state which is developing for itself; then labour will come into its own in that social fabric in which man who has reached maturity works with every other man who has reached maturity on the basis of an equal right. Only from the feeling for the duty to work in freedom can the upswing in our life arise, not from the demand of being in barracks and doing duty, which must suffocate every feeling of justice in man. From an independent spiritual life, from an independent legal life we must grasp the great tasks of our time. If we go into economic life, we see that if we separate out everything that is in it today and has to be separated out — the right to own land, for that belongs to the constitutional state, labour, which today is paid for as if it is a commodity, for that belongs to the constitutional state, and the means of production, insofar as they can be capitalized, for they belong to the spiritual limb of the social organism — if we take all of this out of economic life, commodity production and consumption remain in it.

A commodity, as a human product, does not only involve one human being; goods pass from one human being to another. It is not only the one who has something to say about the commodity, who has experience of its production, but also he who creates the traffic conditions for the things or who has to judge the needs. All kinds of people are involved in economic life and everything in economic life is a commodity. If we thus have within economic life, on the one hand, the administration of capital in the spiritual sphere and the administration of labour in the legal sphere, then what remains for the administration of economic life is that which is solely justified: the price situation, the mutual price value of the goods. If price is to be discovered between chance and reason, it can only be determined through associations.

In associations different groups of people must be involved with goods from the point of view I have characterized, and because people are involved with a commodity from different points of departure, in order to establish the price of one commodity in relation to another, money can only be the external indicator of the commodity's value. Only through economic associations will it be possible to find the true price of an economic product — that's what matters. This can't be determined through dictates and so on, but only from experience of one association with another.

For example, if a person is employed in an industry and works in it, the price of his work product must be determined in such a way that it is neither too expensive nor too cheap. When I have finished making a pair of boots I must receive all kinds of goods to satisfy my needs until I have again completed another pair of boots. This can't be calculated, it can only be experienced in the living interaction between associations. In order to understand that the problem of prices is at the centre of the whole economic life, a more detailed study of my "Key Points" and those that point to it, is necessary, especially my essays, for example in the *Dreigliederungs-Zeitung* which will soon be published together by the publishers of 'The Coming Day' (Verlag des Kommenden Tages). In these publications is what is needed to allow the spirit we require for our ascent.

To solve this one great task of the present time, we must have a new spiritual life to cultivate individuality; we must extract human self-importance and human abilities which can only be placed correctly in a human context through the correct understanding of the human personality and human individuality. In order to make spiritual life effective in the right way, we need state, or legal, or political life in its parliamentary structure left to itself — not encompassing spiritual life but letting it live from out of itself — which can never be in intellectual life or in economic life. From this then morality and mutual assistance will be brought forth, therefore everything that must play out between people, so that a humane existence can come about. In the economic life as well, we need to solve the price problems as one of the great tasks of the present. We can only solve them if we first let the economic life be on its own, existing on the basis of association.

We can only move forward if we let these three independent members work together in a free way and are not afraid of a possible "division" or "cutting up" of these three members. You only need to think a little about the human organism and you will no longer have this fear. In my book "Riddles of the Soul" I have indicated how the human organism also consists of three independent parts: the nervous-sensory activity, the rhythmic activity and the metabolic activity. From these three activities — as activities — the entire function of human life is structured. Just as little as one can't breathe with the eyes or see with the lungs, just so the state should not determine the spiritual life, just so the spiritual life should not interfere with the legal life. Just as little as one can't think with the stomach, just so one can't from the basis of economic life give political dictates or determine laws. Just by the fact that the lungs breathe, that the head sees and thinks, and that the stomach digests, the three independent members in the human organism work together in a unity; this unity does not exist abstractly, but it arises as a living unity from the three independent members.

Thus, the true unity of the social organism will emerge when we grasp the three great tasks of the present in spiritual life, in legal life and in economic life. These three great tasks are certainly a Utopia for many. Even to the people of the thirties of the 19th century, what has developed in Central Europe from 1870 to 1913 would have been a Utopia in terms of economy. We can just think that in 1870, thirty million tons of coal were mined and processed in Germany, that in 1913, 190 million tons were mined and processed — truly, for a man of the 1930's, that would have been Utopia if he could have spoken about such an increase in coal production and processing at that time. One should not be afraid of such an accusation of Utopia or phantasmagoria. Even if what is presented as Three-folding could not be realized immediately, let us remember words once uttered by

Fichte to his listeners when he was talking about the nature and destiny of the scholar. What he meant was roughly the following. 'We know that ideals can't be realized in practical life immediately but we also know that in such great ideals, great impulses and great forces exist which can bring humanity forward. When the so-called practitioners don't recognise this, then they testify to nothing other than that during the development of the world they were not counted; and so may a benevolent deity grant them light and sunshine at the right time, a good digestion and if possible also a little understanding in due time!'

He who is a real practitioner counts on the real practical forces of life and does not let himself be put off by those objections which are quite in the style characterized by Fichte and which then say: 'What shall the prostrate Germany, what shall mankind in Central Europe do alone if all the others do not cooperate with the threefold structure?'

My dear friends, if we work with all our strength — even today, when it is almost too late — on this threefold structure of the social organism so much that it enters as many minds as possible, and really put it before the world in a living way, then the others, even if they are the victors, will see it as something fruitful and salutary for the world and for mankind. When my "Key Points" were translated into English, you could see how almost every review of this book began with the words: 'You can't help but read this book with prejudice' — but even then, they approached the content with a certain objectivity. There is only one thing missing: the people who help us make these ideas fruitful for life. We need people in whom the spirit of progress lives — but a progress spirit — not a progress phrase. The more we acquire such people, the less we will have to fear the reproach that we in Central Europe are unable to compete against. Another objection that is often made is this: What is the individual capable of even if he has sussed out the fruitfulness of the threefold impulse? Oh, may he as an individual not be troubled that the "others" can't suss it out, may he look at it as an individual and therefore set the example for others to enter the path, where single individuals may add up to many. Nor should the other reproach be a source of vexation to us when people say repeatedly: 'If you seek ascent along such a path, it will take a long time.'

We don't want to waste time about how long it might take; we rather want to be clear: The more intensely we want it, the faster it will come! We do not want to "contemplate," but we want to think and act in such a way that it must come as quickly as possible through our actions, our willing and thinking.

When, in your soul, you enliven the right ways for correct social community living, when you fire up your soul through these thoroughly experienced impulses which show you in what way, out of the spiritual life, out of the legal, state or political life and out of the economic life, an ascent is possible, then you can work from a single earth territory against the prejudices of the whole world in such a way that many individual territories come into being which take up the impulses and carry them on for the progress and salvation of humanity.

In this way a long period of pain can become a short one; in this way space and time and a multitude of obstacles can be overcome, if from the independent consciousness of what is right and out of the correct economic consciousness of the present, you really want to find true salvation for humanity towards a new ascent.

The Spiritual Crisis of the Present and the Forces for Human Progress
Stuttgart on 10 November 1920

The serious crises which current civilised mankind is undergoing is not only something noticed by everyone, but it is something that is actually being experienced by everyone. Recently there are two of these crises that have emerged, I would like to mention, quite clearly outwardly and explosively.

The one more sneaking crisis has already been noticed and mentioned by many people at present, but its essence is only noticed by very few. This crisis, which initially brought such severe misery and hardship to mankind and which we can describe as a state crisis of the present day, this crisis can probably evaluate 1914 as an explosive year. We know how the most terrible battles took place in the European state system and how mankind is still suffering from the terrible after-effects of these battles today. One can say that within the course of these battles, but especially after these battles, an apparent end was reached in 1918 but it became apparent then, how little of it was basically delved into in order to search for the source, the actual causes of this state-legal human crisis.

From two sides one could hear something like a motto, as it were, which should indicate the direction according to which the terrible crisis should develop. Some said — I do not want to go into the characteristics of the individual parties, this doesn't belong here, but I just want to mention it — they thought that out of the turmoil of war, another state system should emerge for civilized humanity; at least, so many thought, the existing states would have to change their borders, erect safeguards here or there. Others again, not less numerous, wanted to make for themselves, from the most divergent points of view, the motto: 'Neither be victors nor vanquished!' — That would mean the state systems of civilized mankind must emerge from the turmoil in the same form as it was before. It has to be said that both those who thought of conquests through the change of state borders, as well as those who pronounced the slogan 'Neither victors nor vanquishers be', actually realized that this terrible confusion in the second decade of the 20th century had arisen simply from the fact that the states, in their mutual relationship, with their borders, could not remain as they were, and also, neither did they contain within themselves the power to reshape themselves in any way so that a tolerable relationship could emerge between them.

That the outcome 'be neither victors nor vanquished' could not have been accomplished is shown by the outcome of the war. That it was not done with "victory" either, is shown by what has developed since then because if you look at what has arisen from the way of thinking, from the way of observing of those who are among the victors, then one must say: At Versailles, at Saint-Germain, at Spa and so on, everywhere there were those who thought with the same kind of thinking with which the states were set up, which had become mixed up and created confusion. They wanted to continue with the same way of thinking, the same way of looking at things. They wanted to establish some new state territories, which we have also seen come into being — at first outwardly — but what they hoped for has not happened.

Whoever takes an unbiased look at the conditions of civilized mankind today will have to admit that what has been set up, especially in Europe, already clearly shows that it cannot have an inner existence. From the disorder of all that has come out of the peace treaties, the unprejudiced person must recognize that one simply cannot continue the old way of thinking, the state way of thinking, which has risen up through modern history. It has asserted itself in the peace treaties; it has proved its impossibility by the facts.

The second crisis — one could perhaps more adequately call it the explosion of the second crisis, because it had been in preparation for a long time — is to be registered approximately in the year 1918 and the years that follow. It can be called the economic crisis. Out of the turmoil of war arose that longing of mankind which one might call the aspiration to arrive at such economic conditions which are present instinctively in the needs of many members of today's civilized humanity. What have we seen emerge from this economic crisis so far? If we look to the West we see the absolute helplessness, we see the continuation of economic activity as it has risen up out of modern history; we see a perpetual experimentation without guiding ideas; we see those who think about this economy until now, in the highest apprehension of the outcome of this experimentation.

When we look to the East, we see that purely economic thinking, insofar as it has asserted itself in the minds of Proletariat, has taken on a strange form. We look in the European East — and we see the same thing continuing deep into Asia — we see the effort to create, one might say a militarized economic state structure. That which has suffered such a shipwreck from the old constitutional states, the purely militaristic principle, we see applied in the East. I would like to say: we see the purely militaristic principle applied to an economic organism that is to be created.

Today, the facts also are sufficiently clear regarding these efforts. Who would claim today that anything else could be accomplished by this militarization of the economic life in the East of Europe, than merely robbery of the old economy, the destruction of the old economic fabric? Illusions are created about what is supposed to come about for mankind, but it crumbles more and more with each day, each week. Then again, we see how thoughts, views, as people formed them, especially in the second half of the 19th Century, as so-called thoughts of economic reforms, social reforms, how from these thoughts — where one wants to apply them radically — nothing remotely fruitful can emerge.

To all of this it can already be said: two crises, the governmental crisis and the economic crisis, stand before civilized mankind today, without any prospect of a way out. One does not have to develop lengthy spins to recognise that this is what it is, as I mentioned here in my introduction, one merely needs to devote oneself to the observation, in an unbiased way, of what is happening. Out of these observations, which one could already have made for decades, if one links the spiritual attention to the way in which these two crises were clearly preparing themselves, out of these observations, is what gave rise recently in Dornach to the undertaking of anthroposophical university courses. Certainly, these anthroposophical university courses, held in September and October of this year in Dornach by thirty lecturers from the various branches of science — their importance for today may not be overestimated; they are the very first and perhaps a weak beginning, but a beginning driven by a definite, purposeful intention. In Dornach, these thirty lecturers were to show that the anthroposophically oriented spiritual science, which I have been presenting in Stuttgart for almost two decades, has the inner strength and the inner scientific methodology to enrich a wide variety of subjects so that they can take on a form corresponding to the demands of the present, and life in the future.

In any case, in order for something like this to be undertaken in a purposeful way at all — what is necessary? It is necessary to see through what is most important in the third crisis, a crisis which is basically only the outer expression of the other two crises mentioned before. This third crisis is not yet considered, in its essence, by nearly the whole of mankind: it is the crisis of our entire spiritual life.

I know, my dear friends, that this is an expression of something that is being met with the most serious doubts in the widest circles today. I also know that this is uncomfortable to hear. It shows in the example that many admit to the governmental crisis and many admit to the economic crisis, and that this admission has led them to demand fundamental changes in the conception and institutions of state and economic life, but that extremely few are convinced that spiritual life must bring about a transformation right into the individual sciences. In many circles today, it is thought that spiritual life must provide the sources for further prosperous progress of mankind, to get out of hardship, misery and social turmoil. But people think of the participation of the spiritual life in such a way that they simply take only those "spiritual goods" that have been so-called "safe sciences" which are now being disseminated into the widest possible circles through the most diverse channels, through national and adult education centres and so on.

However — I have mentioned this here before — people are not impartial enough to thoroughly consider the following fact: When it is recognised that particularly in those circles which have so far participated in the spiritual life as it has developed in modern times in mankind's evolution, and that these educated circles are the very circles which have essentially become the bearers of the turmoil, if one recognised this, then one must admit that the same confusion cannot be eliminated by popularizing those thoughts which have led to disaster and which were brought up by this spiritual movement, because the same confusion would then have to emerge from the widest circles which has already emerged from the narrow circle of the bearers of this spiritual life.

Therefore, the aim of Dornach, where these anthroposophical adult courses have taken place, is not merely to popularize extensively, in a conservative way, that which we now have in so-called 'safe science' or in other spiritual goods, within which the confusions have asserted themselves, but to fertilize this spiritual property anew, to give it an impact by which it can be the carrier of a different government, a different economic life. The renewal of spiritual life, not the spreading of spiritual life, is the goal of the anthroposophically orientated spiritual movement. The impulses, the thoughts, the views which have led to the confusion of government and the confusion of the economy, already existing in the old spirituality, is to be recognised within the anthroposophically orientated spiritual movement. However, few people today make the effort to really look at the origins of our misery and our life, at the crisis in our spiritual life. That is uncomfortable. Surely something must be "safe" somewhere or other; one must be able to stand on firm ground. It is believed that everything would falter if one were to work with reform on spiritual life oneself. That is the reason why anthroposophically orientated spiritual science has such difficulties to speak to people of the present day because basically, the interest that they derive from their inner world historical sense of duty must be asserted in the broadest circles which are not at all active. The sources of the crises are sought everywhere, in the economy, in the state, but one is afraid to look for them in the spiritual life. Until they are sought in spiritual life, nothing at all will improve — not even in economic life, not even in state life.

What is external reality in the life of the state, even if people today don't want to realize it, is only the expression of what people think, what they have learned to think through the spiritual life that has emerged in the developmental history of mankind in the last three to four centuries, especially in the 19th century and at the beginning of the 20th century. The state and economic crises are too noticeable to be denied, that it should not be concluded that both the state and the economic development must be given new impetus. That something must also happen in spiritual life, many admit to. That just such a thing has to happen, as anthroposophically oriented spiritual science wants, is very often opposed by those people of the present who also often admit to the former.

Today there are enough examples to use — examples that can be taken in the present time both from world areas suffering from terrible cultural pressure, which belong to the defeated ones, and from those cultural areas that belong to the victors.

After the warlike turmoil had found a temporary, but only apparent end, after the revolutionary spirit had dawned, we noticed within Germany the call to separate the ecclesiastical, the religious element from the state. I would like to say, taken in an abstract way, this is the first of all the dawning calls for a part of what the threefold social organism wants: It wants to detach the entire spiritual life from the state and economic life and place it in its own self-administration, built only on its own principles. Today only the most inner part of spiritual life is understood so that one can only in a purely abstract sense strive for its separation from the life of the state.

However, other phenomena have also emerged in this domain in Germany. From one particular side, a decidedly anti-religious, anti-Christian sentiment was making itself felt, and that which asserted itself was associated with the war cry: separate of the Church from the State. It became particularly difficult for Protestantism to find its way into what had come about as a result of the war and the revolution. On the one hand one had to see how the Catholic Church, through their ancient constitution, would not lose much by separation from the state, for it has so many political and administrative and also traditional impulses within itself that it could indeed only gain by this separation from the state, especially if it still intriguingly circumvents the separation from the state. On the other hand, the connection of the Protestant churches with the powers of the state was so close — the Protestant churches were designed to see ecclesiastical power exercised by state powers — that they felt as if they were at the mercy of the state because of their separation from it. This became a certain mood that led to the emergence of a kind of battle cry for the gathering of all who could still direct their gaze from the religious point of view towards the spiritual. The different confessions need to be organised so that they don't achieve a separation but a unity through a kind of self-government.

Something else appeared which is highly characteristic. Those who were the bearers of this "gathering" of the various ecclesiastical confessions, they openly said that it was good that the separation of ecclesiastical, religious affairs of the state should be as trustworthy as possible vis-à-vis the state authorities, that the detachment — as they put it — should take place "benevolently," so to speak. They said openly that at least religious education is to be still provided by the state and so on, that the church is not simply dismissed from the power of the state, but be compensated in a certain way — well, and what can be more than a "benevolent detachment from the state."

243

One can clearly see that religious denominations are accustomed to being directed by the state: they can't find their way into a certain independence from the state. This is not based on economic circumstances only; it also comes from the way people think. So we see how the churches, which are supposed to achieve independence, in a certain sense, even if half-heartedly, still look towards the state for leadership, to which they have become accustomed through centuries. This is what we can say, roughly, about Central Europe.

Let's look abroad. It is extremely interesting that in Switzerland, for example, we can now hear speakers from America who are ecclesiastical representatives of religious confessions. What do they have to say? In their speeches they say something like the following — I can only briefly summarize in a few sentences what is set forth in detail — they say something like, from the American point of view, of course: Mankind is striving, they say, for the League of Nations. The League of Nations is to lead mankind out of the old, militaristic conditions; it is to bring the longed-for peace and a newness of human culture and human civilization. What statesmen have achieved so far, they say, what they have accomplished so far, can't bring about a viable League of Nations — and they attach Woodrow Wilson, whom they describe as a good-natured, but actually somewhat foolish idealist. For such a League of Nations would be forged together by external, state relations which have actually outlived their usefulness, which no longer have any load-bearing capacity for human civilization. That which is the true League of Nations — so say these American pastors — must be rooted in the hearts of the people. But, they say, this could only be rooted in the hearts of the people, if Christian feeling, religious vows are found all over the world. So these American speakers would actually like to join the Europeans in constituting the League of Nations from the religious point of view; they want to win the hearts of mankind religiously.

What I'm telling you, dear friends, is something that arises from spiritual life. Whoever hears the speeches of such American pastors, says to himself, when he is able to see without bias what is now raging economically over Europe: No matter how beautiful the words may be — they are at times very beautiful, these words that are spoken there — no matter how beautiful the words may be, they do not find the way to the hearts of men; they are powerless to constitute an inner League of Nations. From those people whose drives and instinctive battle cries sound as social battle cries, they no longer have an ear for these beautifully spoken words; they demand something else, because their hearts are not open for these words.

Here it shows — how from the very basis from which the call is sounded, to detach oneself benevolently from the state, to gather together that which is scattered — everywhere it is evident that one can already notice the insidious spiritual crisis of the present. One must be really quite biased if one can believe that on the one hand through the beautiful words of the American pastors, the World Federation can be established in the hearts of the people, or that, on the other hand, that spiritual renewal can be brought about through an assembly of the various confessions existing in Central Europe — a spiritual renewal that is now really powerful enough to bring forth strength for the social progress of mankind, strength to bring forth power that can reform in the state and economic spheres.

Only if one is biased, one can believe this. Anthroposophically oriented spiritual science, studies from its insights, from its way of looking at things, what is actually taking place, and it observes: Yes, the will is there to make spiritual life powerful again among people, so that the state and the economic life can emerge from thoughts rooted in a fruitful spiritual life — there is no other way to reform the economic and state life. The will is there, but something is missing: it lacks creative power. Today it does not matter that American pastors repeat the old-fashioned words — no matter how beautifully they are forged, they have lost their value for the hearts of men. Today, it is not important to collect the confessions from the past; today, it is important that a new spiritual life comes among people through a new creation. Someone who actually understands the spiritual crisis is someone who does not merely want to repeat the old but who develops a will for a new spiritual creation.

We need to ask ourselves: Why do the most beautiful words turn out to be powerless? Why does a collection of religious confessions lead nowhere? We notice that in the course of the last three to four centuries throughout civilized mankind, what we call the state life and what we call the economic life, have become more powerful. These two have so completely taken spiritual life in tow, that those in Central Europe who are to be separated from the state in regard to their religious creeds, are in turn longing for the state and its leadership. Spiritual life has been taken in tow to such an extent that today the most beautiful words that can be spoken out of this old spiritual life can no longer find their way to the hearts in which the inkling for today's reforms arises. This proves from external historical facts that we need not merely a new fertilization of the old, stimulation for the old, but we need a complete new creation. Anthroposophically oriented spiritual science supports these standpoints. Anthroposophically oriented spiritual science wants to fertilise individual sciences which will give ideas to the state and to the economic life of mankind. Anthroposophically oriented spiritual science should also fertilize state life itself and economic life in such a way that both receive new impulses which are created in spiritual life itself.

With the larger part of the sciences we have at least for a beginning, succeeded — we can emphasize this after our successes, after our results during the Dornach higher education courses. Historical, physical, chemical, biological, legal, even mathematical, philosophical, psychological — all these fields have already taken shape through our higher education courses, through which it becomes clear what these branches of science will become when they are methodologically, strictly and scientifically imbued with what the spiritually scientific research intend, as they also have been represented here in Stuttgart for more than one and a half decades.

Anthroposophically oriented spiritual science wants to specifically point out the necessity for new spiritual creation in this crisis.

Why, I say, do the most beautiful words turn out to be powerless? Why do people long for state leadership to return? Because, in essence, one has gradually achieved a spiritual life which was completely and utterly only an appendage of the state life or economic life, which was completely and entirely established in accordance with the educational and teaching institutions through the will of the state which was completely supported by obsolete economic forms. What the state and economic life in the last centuries have made up out of old creeds, has today become something powerless if it wants to assert itself in the way the American pastors want to establish a League of Nations.

Yes, my dear friends, this is the powerlessness by which spiritual life has been educated by the government supervision, by the economic superpower. The spiritual life which anthroposophical orientated spiritual science aims for, must, as I've often explained here, arise from the innermost soul experience of the human being itself. This experience of the soul, however, cannot be under any supervision or supreme power, but it can only be developed in full freedom, through the completely free development of the human individualities, in the free self-administration of this spiritual life itself. When this spiritual life is under self-administration, if it can bring forth precisely the kind of science that has been shown in Dornach and shown every day in the Waldorf School in relation to pedagogy; when this freely administered spiritual life can really unfold individuals' abilities, born or conceived in every human being, brought from the spiritual worlds into the physical world, then the fruits of such a free spiritual life can blossom and augment state and economic life. The life of the state and the economy came into crises because they were deprived of what must be supplied to them from a free spiritual life. By taking the spiritual life into their own hands, state life and economic life have suppressed the fertilizing effect which can only become theirs if they release the spiritual life, so that from this freedom the spiritual life can work over into the territory of the state and into the economic sphere.

What I am suggesting here can certainly also be substantiated by an unbiased observation of the course of the history of civilization. I only want to point to this evidence in a broad outline. We see how since the 15th, 16th, 17th centuries, especially since the 18th century, economic life has become more and more complicated and intricate. We see how the necessity to develop this economic life which in former times had been more instinctive even into the city culture, into the guild system, now must be redirected out of unconscious thinking. One only has to look at people who are to be named among the intellectual founders of the newer economic sciences, at minds like the Frenchman François Quesnay and the Englishman Adam Smith, and one will find, how, in the period of world history in which it has become necessary to grasp the economy from a spiritual point of view, scientific thought itself has become powerless to express any points of view about economic life.

Both Quesnay, the Frenchman who founded a theory of economics, who wanted to establish a theory of economics based more on political economy, as well as Smith, the Englishman, who founded a similar theory of economics, they both basically developed a few axiomatic principles such as "the validity of private property" and "the economic freedom of the individual" upon which to construct the whole economy.

If one looks in particular at the founder of modern economics, at Adam Smith — and his thinking is only the outflow of the thinking of his whole age, of the 17ᵗʰ and 18th century — one finds that this thinking of Adam Smith, which haunts economic life, is basically a faithful reproduction of the thinking which at that time asserted itself as scientific thinking, especially in the West of civilisation. It is very interesting to follow how, for example with Newton, using the physical-astronomical thinking as a method, as a way of looking at things, how that entered in a general way into science as the way of dealing with problems which one then encounters again with Smith in his treatment of economic tasks.

As mathematical physics wants to derive everything from a few principles, so, a man like Adam Smith would like to derive the entire national economy from a few principles that can be grasped abstractly by the intellect. It is interesting to follow how unbiased minds, even Bulwer in a novel, scoff at that which now asserted itself as thinking in economics. Bulwer says in his scoffing: 'In the past, it was believed that anyone who wanted to get involved in the national economy had to have extensive knowledge of what people were doing between one another in their business relationships. Today, you only need abstract principles, and the whole economy is derived from them.' — Before that, Young, an unbiased thinker, already said: 'Until now, he had thought that a person who wants to talk about economics must know the virtues and vices of people, the way people communicate in economic life, what they do there — in short, that such a person must have extensive knowledge.' Adam Smith showed him, Young said, that all you needed were a few thoughts, and that with a few strokes of the pen you could assemble from experience all the economic knowledge that you have, into a few abstract thoughts.

As economic life became complicated — what happened to economic thinking? My dear friends, something has happened to this economic thinking, which first asserted itself in the West, which originated in the newer economic life and is modelled on modern economic life and which, in its final consequences, whether one admits it or not, now appears in the few abstract thoughts of Lenin and Trotsky as the last consequence in the East of Europe. This is what you need to consider. What it is about will only be understood if one doesn't only adopt a few abstract thoughts about it — which people today love very much — but if one gets a thorough overview of the course of mankind's development over many centuries, as I have indicated several times already, and as I will now indicate in a few words from another point of view.

My dear friends, just like the kind of view initiated by Newton was taken up by other thinkers as a soul doctrine and through this human doctrine of the soul it has become mechanised just like Newton mechanised astronomy, just as this mechanical-mathematical science was drawn into the national economy of Adam Smith, likewise, even the popular world views have adapted to it. Today, in the time of the newspapers, the popularising of science, basically there is hardly anyone who is not in some way, even if they don't know anything about it, seized by the spirit of this scientific direction. This kind of science lives on the one hand in mathematics; mathematics is the only thing which rises from within the human being because all of mathematics can't be accessed through observation as it is something which springs up from within the human being. In this scientific direction which has mathematical thinking, as with Smith for example, also with Ricardo, the later editor of the National Economy, it is clearly noticeable — this mathematical thinking is one side of modern science. The other side is the sensual observation of the external world and the formation of all kinds of abstract theories, of atomistic or other materialistic theories about this sensual external world.

These two currents actually exist: sensual observation of the external world and mathematized thinking. One has to be fair to what appears on the one hand as mathematical thinking, even in the field of national economy, and on the other hand, as conscientious observation of experimentation in the outside world. One must be fair to that, because that has brought up the great triumphs of modern, Western science. I have also emphasized it many times: From anthroposophically oriented spiritual science, these triumphs of modern science are by no means opposed, but fully acknowledged. However, one has to recognise that within mankind's development there was a time when this kind of scientific attitude was not present at all. Today only the last decadent remains of what existed in this field of mankind are there.

Now I'll refer to the Orient. If you want to see the things that matter in their actual form, you must not look towards the Orient of today, where everything is already in decline, in deterioration; what was once a primordial wisdom of mankind, what was even greater than it has later become — you can read about this in my book "Occult Science." It was even greater in the time before the Vedas, before the Vedanta philosophy came into being; but what still shines out artistically from the Vedas, from the Vedanta-philosophy only in last echoes; the unbiased discoverer can still see in the whole oriental development. There's a lot of greatness, a lot of powerful wisdom in there. There is nothing in it of the special way in which the western science of more recent times works. The way of thinking, the way of looking at the world, was quite different there.

The scientific methods which we venerate so much today, and rightly so, which we must emulate, they were not found in the ancient oriental thought. For this the old oriental wisdom had, what I would like to call, a world-view — in contrast to science: a world-view without science. This was basically the characteristic essence of the ancient Orient in its wisdom.

This worldview is meaningful because it stretches over the whole human being; it is significant because through this worldview the human being grasps himself as spirit, soul and body. However, this worldview appeared in the ancient Orient in such a way that little attention was paid to the body and to what belonged to the external, physical world. This life was more an understanding between soul and spirit, in which man knew himself rooted, but it was a worldview. That means that what a person thought and experienced, he established for himself in his situation firmly, through his relationship to the world of his senses and to the world of the spirit. He didn't do this scientifically but through soul intuition. What the soul acquired through spiritual perception lived in its original form in the ancient times of the Orient. But the legacy of it lived on and basically one senses this oriental worldview of life right up into our recent times.

This worldview of life, it has given up that by which, for example, the first Christianity — in which this ancient Oriental wisdom and worldview was still alive — understood the mystery of Golgotha as giving meaning to the earth. Instead of looking in the way the ancient Orient had, the intellectualistic element became more and more established and since then remained as an inheritance. In our more modern time, before the non-ideological science of the West arose, which also gave shape to soul doctrine and the national economy, as I've mentioned, there formed in the middle, already beginning with ancient Greece, clearly developing in ancient Rome, then establishing itself over central Europe, that which, I would like to express it as: putting man into an inner struggle. He grasped an event that can only be grasped with the spirit, the Christ event, still through the inherited echoes of ancient, oriental wisdom. Besides this, more and more, through the special dispositions of Western mankind, that which is mere human intellectuality, which is the entire cosmos, shimmered into this Central Europe as well, above all our earthly environment and the human himself, basically wanting understanding only through mathematics and observation of the outside world.

So, on the one hand, there lived in Central Europe precisely that which one could call a leaning towards the old Oriental heritage. Everything that lived in the Middle Ages and more recent times in the content of the Christian doctrine and still lives in it today, everything that lives in it in terms of worldview — even if it has almost faded away, even if pure rationalism has taken hold of modern theology — is for the most part old oriental heritage, because only a few approaches are present towards new creation. Connected with this is what man first of all creates out of himself, through mathematics and observation of nature, but which he does not bring to a worldview. So in the Middle Ages, in the time when Albertus Magnus and Thomas Aquinas were active, we see occurring in a conscious way this dichotomy between what human reason can achieve through observation and through mathematics, what is limited to the outer sensual world, and what is to be revelation, the Mystery of Golgotha, which was not called that at that time, but which according to its content, not according to the fact, was ancient oriental heritage. Basically this dichotomy is still alive today in all pubic life, in Central Europe, even in the state and economic life, arising from the Middle Ages — this dichotomy between non-idealistic, scientific thinking and the old, inherited worldview without science.

The Middle European is since the time of the Greek epoch called to this inner battle. This inner struggle in particular produced the highest spiritual blossoming of the mind in the period of German culture around the turn of the 18th and 19th centuries. What lived in Herder, Schiller, Goethe, in philosophers of German idealism, in Fichte, Schelling, Hegel, was only alive in all these minds, because the spirits of these souls had deeply, inwardly condensed the struggle that exists between science without a worldview and the inherited worldview without science. One can see in Goethe's individual sayings how he tried to bring together that which science gives on the one hand, and that which lived in him according to feelings, imaginatively as an old heritage of the Orient. Yes, in Goethe's case it goes even further; he experienced this dichotomy within himself until the eighties of the 18th century. This drove him to the south, because in the south he could at least feel the echoes of what had remained in the south of Europe, of what had been the ancient oriental worldview without science, which, however, was very, very much on the wane in Greece. From this worldview void of science, what has come from the Arabs and spread across the European south, into the West, is nothing other than mathematics, dry mathematics. It is basically Europe's last remnant of that which, as comprehensively universal, emerged from the science-less worldview of the Orient. There, everything that was available as wisdom was rising from within the human being just as with us, in our civilization, it is only found to be the case with mathematics. It is basically Europe's last remnant, albeit a lasting remnant of what had originated in the Orient as comprehensive universal worldview void of science. There, everything present in wisdom was welling up in the human being, whereas in our case, in our civilization, only mathematics does this in us. This is what Novalis in particular felt towards mathematics and expressed it in a stammering way.

The civilization of the West has newly acquired what I would like to call the observation and experimental system, from which the actual science of the West has emerged, from which everything that man does not initially gain from his inner being, but rather what he obtains by letting the world of the senses act on the senses. What first became of the scientific spirit is what has become the scientific spirit through which all leaders have obtained their education, their scientific character, and which, my dear friends, has revealed its powerlessness in the face of economic life, in the face of state life, in the minds which I have mentioned and to which many other names could be added.

This is how we see our modern life approaching us. I would like to express in symbolic terms what has actually asserted itself in the last three to four centuries as our emerging modern life. Outwardly it is characterised by what we notice, on the one hand, from what is developing in terms of the essential spirit of science dominating schools and universities. We see that what is done in schools and universities as something partly leading to an existence estranged from the world. We see how the universities stand as lonely islands of education. We can see, however, how something else is happening, how the new scientific approach, the unworldly scientific approach, stops at the human being. Characteristic of this is the Darwinian doctrine, which with such scientific conscientiousness researches the development of the living beings from the simplest being to the most perfect, which, however, places the human being, so to speak, at the head of this animal organization and only comes to explain the human being, in so far as he is animal. From this and many other things one could show how the mathematizing and purely externally observing science stops with its findings before it comes to the human being. So we have a scientifically orientated education system without a world-view, an education system which lives in abstractions and doesn't attribute to human beings what the science-free worldview of the Orient had — a sense of one's position to the world — which only satisfies the head, the intellect, and doesn't grasp the whole human being. That's on the one hand.

On the other hand something comes up that I would like to symbolize by using the example of the factory with the modern practitioner. What is the relationship between the factory and the college? Yes, there is a relationship, but this relationship has taken on a very one-sided character. What shines from the modern universities into the factory is mechanical science. This illumination by mechanical science has brought about for the factory, and for everything that belongs to it, that great formation of technology which has founded modern civilization. Up to the formation of the technology in the highest sense that science could work, it stops with its cognition before it gets to the human being.

In the factory as well, the practitioner stops at the human being. He extends his routine — because it is nothing other than routine — only into the technical and into that which is connected with the technical. He cannot establish a human relationship between himself as an entrepreneur, as a leader, and those who work on modern civilization out of the broad mass of people.

Science stops with its knowledge when it is faced with the human being; practice stops short of the human being in action, in social design. A boundary indicates this stopping. One has taken into the area, which has this boundary, all that could come out of the modern mathematical science into the technology which could also stimulate commerce, trade, traffic and so on. But from science, which stops at the knowledge of the human being, from this science no social life could be obtained which could have satisfied the great demands of the newer times on this purely human side.

So, beyond the boundary stood all of mankind, which now demanded its human dignity in recent times; so stood that humanity to which one had not found the way in practice, just like the human being himself and his essence had not found the way in the modern worldview-less scientific knowledge. This is the tragedy that has led to the modern crises, because what is written in the books of modern practical life, what is written in the ledger, in the cash book, has nothing to do with what lives outside in the souls of those who stand beyond the boundary, in front of whose humanity one has come to a stop. They appeared with their mental demands and out of these mental demands the counter-image of the present mental crisis arose in the present.

Thus we see these universities, these colleges, schools of education which reach into the technical — I could call it, reaching into what is free in the human — opening the way to the factory, to industry, to modern money economy but which will not penetrate as far as man himself.

So, on the other hand we have the emergence from imperfect sense observation which at first was the cognitive, unworldly science, the experimentation sense of modern practitioners who are not interested in leading ideas but who limit themselves to the experimentation of the mathematical-mechanical-technical, engaging people in work without caring about the social structure of mankind. We have seen the advent of the practitioner who today has a prim hatred against all leading ideas, a formal hatred against everything scientific, of everything cognitive, who, however, is right on the one hand, that this modern, unworldly science has nothing of what can shine in practice where the human heart is involved. However these practitioners are wrong when they attribute this scientific direction to all spiritual life. So they remain in their routine, this is how they want to continue, I could call it in a spiritless, merely experimental management.

This is what makes it so difficult for the bridge to be drawn which could reach from anthroposophically orientated spiritual science into the most practical aspects of life. The only thing to blame for this is the reluctance of the practitioners, who want to remain in routines towards what for example is an impulse for the three-folding of the social organism emanating from spiritual science. We increasingly see this rise of hatred for practice in all that is spiritual life. So in the West today we see a confused bustle of experimental economic activity, of experimental state activity. In the East, we see this economic activity, this state activity, culminating in a militarized economic state, which must paralyze everything human.

So we can see how in fact, out of the spiritual crises, the state crisis and economic crises have arisen. From this clear insight, what has been represented here for more than one and a half decades as anthroposophically orientated spiritual science, the forces of progress for humanity can develop. The anthroposophically oriented spiritual science would like to develop out of the same scientific spirit that has developed in the West without a worldview, from the innermost knowledge of the innermost experience of the human soul — knowledge that in turn becomes a worldview that does not rehash the old words — the words that no longer find their way to the hearts of the people; knowledge that does not merely collate the old confessions, that also wants to spread light over an outlook that opens up when looking at the most powerful event of the development of the earth, the Mystery of Golgotha.

There's opposition against such a renewal of the spiritual life, which wants to look at the basic fact of Christianity, which can be rightly grasped and looked at only in the spirit, from the spirit of modern mankind. We can't return to the Orient. We can no longer strive for a worldview that is not scientific. We are beyond the time when a science-less worldview could be sufficient for mankind. Today we are faced with the great task of developing a worldview through science and with the inner development of human beings. This we will be able to do if we really see into the true character of anthroposophically orientated spiritual science. As long as there are still people who claim that what is achieved through the method of cognition — an inner, but strictly scientific method, even modelled on the strictest mathematical methods — is gained by the spiritual-scientific method, that it could be as much vision as any vision or hallucination, as long as there are people who claim such, because they for example, in fact could not read at all what is written in my books "Occult Science" or "Knowledge of the Higher Worlds"; as long as there are such people and as long as people believe that, spiritual science will have a difficult way to go. I will still have more to say about this. Such people do not see that what is understood with spiritual perception, what is grasped through it is that the human being awakens himself inwardly to spiritual sight and that it teaches him to distinguish between fantasy and reality. It is basically a very simple factual logic which underlies this distinction that our opponents are unable to grasp.

How do I know that when I lift a kilogram of weight, for example, I'm not subject to a hallucination but that it is an external reality? How do I recognize that? I can tell by the fact that I simply have to strengthen my sense of self when I lift the weight. I need to strengthen myself inwardly. If I have a mere vision or hallucination my sense of self remains unchanged in its intensity: I am absorbed in the vision, because I don't have the experience of having to make my sense of self more intense. I notice the resistance by the fact that when I lift the kilogram of weight, I have to use the strength that is in me, which I don't do when absorbed in a vision. Neither do I, when I have spiritual experiences, hallucinations in fantasy, in which the sense of self is not increased.

You will find everywhere in spiritual-scientific writings it is described that those experiences, through which one enters the world in which man is before birth or conception, in which he will be after death, in which his eternity is rooted, that those experiences through which one enters the world of the supersensible presuppose that the soul must be made more awake than it is in ordinary life, that is to say, it must be made inwardly more intense, inwardly more strongly experiential.

In this, however, is expressed exactly that which guarantees the scientific nature of that which is asserted as spiritual perception. And if

258

one asserts what I have only hinted at here, what I have often discussed in lectures here in Stuttgart for many years, if one asserts this, then, yes, only then one attains the correct view of what has seized modern humanity like a crisis in spiritual life. One can see, for example, how mathematics came to the West as an ancient inheritance via Arabia, but how it was powerless to conquer the complicated economic and state life of the West, as it is shown, for example, by Adam Smith. One makes the observation that this mathematical thinking, this mathematical view is acquired entirely from within the human being and by awakening the soul inwardly, one develops precisely that which is inherent in this mathematical thinking. Precisely that which lives in the spirit of mathematical thinking, is what prepares man for a higher perfection towards inner, spiritual methods. This way one acquires quite a particular spiritual perspective.

Through the inner experience of mathematics which is limited only to the world between birth and death, through inwardly enlivened methods of spiritual science applied to mathematics, one can learn to recognise that which enters the soul through inspiration. It comes in such a way that it opens up our outlook for what the human being experienced supersensibly in spiritual worlds before birth or conception. Mathematics is that which has scientifically preserved for us a last point of departure to get to observe our prenatal human life.

What the western worldview-less science acquires in its external observation, if it is developed here (spirit-scientifically), it first of all provides something that doesn't remain abstract observation — for the worldview-less science it remains an abstract observation — but what rises also to the moral, as I have proved in my "Philosophy of Freedom," what rises to the moral imagination thus arises in the foundation of the moral life of the human being. Everything that we gain from the outside world in terms of thoughts, leads to images, to imaginations, which finally connect with inspiration. This we experience. And as imperfect as that is which we can observe from the outside world between birth and death, if we process it inwardly, if we also experience what we observe externally in the soul by means of the

259

method of spiritual science, then from our imaginations we can also see the life we enter after our death. From the mathematizing, from the observing and experimenting of science, when the spiritual science is applied to this science, it will in turn give rise to a worldview — but now a worldview that can give modern civilization the power for the progress of mankind.

The worldview has the characteristic — it shows in the oriental, science-less worldview — that it has an effect on the mind and will of the human being, that it has such an effect that man establishes a legal life according to these particular views and through which he brings about an understanding for what happens between one person and another in the human community, in other words, he builds a state life for himself. A worldview stimulates the will that determines economic life. A science without a worldview merely speaks to the head, to the intellect; it leaves the mind and the will uninfluenced. While intellectual science in the beginning of the 20th century reached its highest blossoming, we see feelings remain uninfluential in an attempt to give warmth to the state, and the will, unable to shape economic life. Feeling and will are given over more and more to the animal instincts with a grand training of the intellect — we would be heading for this barbarization if head and intellect were to train the instinctive life more and more and leave mind and will untended, as is already so terribly evident in the East of today's civilization.

To seize the feeling and the will in turn and thus generate a new force for the progress of mankind, this can be done by anthroposophically oriented spiritual science, which in turn elevates itself to a worldview — this could not be done by the Science which has no worldview. Anthroposophically oriented spiritual science penetrates into feeling, that means into the life of the state; it penetrates into the will, that means into the economic life. In this crisis and in the healing of this crisis it is necessary to notice which the two other crises are.

Science without a worldview only grasps the intellect, my dear friends. The emotional life is unaffected which should lead to the legal understanding between one person and another, which is the decisive thing in the state, and it leaves likewise the will uninfluenced, which is supposed to have a formative effect in economic life.

So we see how the threefold crises have come about in recent times. We see how people thirst for a renewal of the spiritual life, but how they do not want to admit that this renewal of spiritual life can only come from a new creation. As a result we see in the idea of the "collection" the impotence of the old spiritual life, in the beautiful words of the American speakers who address the Swiss and speak to the Europeans in general. The necessity of a renewed creation of the spiritual life must be pointed out.

Only through a recreation of the spiritual life can something new emerge, something that was not there before, which does not prove its impracticality like the modern state system which in 1914 entered into a catastrophe, not merely into a crisis, because it had no free spiritual life beside it to prove its impracticality as it did in the economic life, which turned into a catastrophe in recent times because it was not fertilized by a free spiritual life.

In recent times we see the rise of an intellectualistic science which can't induce people who have grown up in the life of the state and in the life of the economy, to find fruitful ideas for the state or economic life. We see people in state institutions, who, instead of creating an understanding for the feeling of relations between one person and another, their feelings are only for the satisfaction of their egoism and thus they gradually undermine the structure of these state institutions. We can observe how through the merely intellectual science which involves only the head, the will is uncared for in the purely instinctive life which also flows into the deeds of egoism. We can see from the worldview-less science the rise of un-brotherliness, which aims only at the elevation of the existence of one's own being.

New forces for the progress of humanity we will find in anthroposophically orientated spiritual science, and from this modern science we will once again find a worldview. It will engender the kind of thinking which is not merely intellectual thinking, a thinking illumined through feeling, the kind of thinking that empowers the will. We will see people of action springing from this thinking, people who, instead of mere satisfaction of their egoism, will seek human understanding in a community orientated state. We will see people who through their associations, connect with others with different economic needs, with various economic abilities. Out of the will, fructified by true spiritual thinking, we will see the creation of a sense of fraternity that works in associative community in such a way that a person, together with others, will work with the understanding for all and thus also for himself. We will see the emergence from the thinking person of action, a person with a feeling for the law, a brotherhood minded person with an economy orientated will, and thus from an anthroposophically oriented spiritual science a new power for the progress of humanity can emerge out of the spiritual crisis.

COVER ARTWORK

Title: **Chakra Dance**

Artist: **Hanna von Maltitz**

Year: **2011**

Material: **Oil on canvas board**

Dimensions: **50 x 70 cm**

Where: **Artist's Collection**

Notes: **Price: ZAR 3,000**

Artist Bio: **https://go.elib.com/Hanna**

The Future of Anthroposophical Publications

The Internet is about choice, and choice means the freedom to choose. The Rudolf Steiner Archive & e.Lib believes this is what the future of publications — the dissemination of knowledge — is all about.

This publication absolutely falls in that category: the freedom to choose whether to just use the information we present on-line, or use that information and purchase one of our other offerings, like a hardcopy of the book, or a softcopy version, like a CD or something for your Kindle. Proceeds from your purchases help us to continue these efforts to bring newly translated material to researchers and Rudolf Steiner aficionados all over the world. Freedom is a gift ... it is a gift of love. And as John Lennon wrote, "Love is all there is!"

ON-LINE RESOURCES

- Rudolf Steiner e.Lib. *Healthy Thinking*, Bn/GA# 335, translated by Hanna von Maltitz.

- Rudolf Steiner e.Lib. *Der Weg zu gesundern Denken un die Lebenslage des Gegenwartsmenschen*, GA# 335, original German.

- Rudolf Steiner e.Lib. *Healthy Thinking*, Bn/GA# 335, Side-by-Side Compare.

- Fine Art Presentations – e.Gallery. *Hanna von Maltitz* (see more of Hanna's paintings)

- Rudolf Steiner e.Lib:
https://rudolfsteinerelib.org/

- Rudolf Steiner on Social Issues:
https://rudolfsteinerelib.org/SocialIssues/index.php

- Toward a Threefold Society
https://wn.rudolfsteinerelib.org/Lectures/GA023/English/SCR2021/GA023_index.html

- The Renewal of the Social Organism:
https://wn.rudolfsteinerelib.org/Lectures/GA024/English/AP1985/GA024_index.htmll

- The Inner Aspect of the Social Question:
https://wn.rudolfsteinerelib.org/Lectures/GA193/English/RSP1974/InnAsp_index.html

- The Social Question
https://wn.rudolfsteinerelib.com/Lectures/GA328/English/eLib2017/SoQues_index.html

- Art as Bridge between the Sensible and the Supersensible
https://wn.rudolfsteinerelib.com/Lectures/GA190/English/eLib2021/19190330p01.html

These on-line resources are wonderful for research … and buying the book to read and study at home is even better! It not only enhances your understanding, but it also helps our being able to continue providing Steiner's never before translated into English offerings. Pass it on!

OTHER BOOKS

translated by Hanna von Maltitz

All titles available at Amazon.com

THE FOUNDATION COURSE

(by Rudolf Steiner, translated by Hanna von Maltitz):

This is a First Edition English translation of a series of eighteen lectures. In this course, *The Foundation Course*, where over one hundred people interested in the questions of a renewal of religious life and activity attended, Rudolf Steiner speaks about the ways in which, through spirit knowledge, religious activity can be fertilized and led into new forms of cultural organization. This text includes the reproductions of blackboard drawings and inscriptions, notebook entries, etc., in-line with the text. It is subtitled, *Spiritual discernment, Religious feeling, Sacramental action*. **ISBN: 978-1948302371**

THE IMPULSE OF RENEWAL FOR CULTURE AND SCIENCE

(by Rudolf Steiner, translated by Hanna von Maltitz):

This is a First Edition English translation of a series of seven lectures, entitled *The Impulse of Renewal for Culture and Science*, and published in German as, *Erneuerungs-Impuls für Kultur und Wissenschaft* (Bn/GA/CW Number 81 in the Bibliographical Survey, 1961). This course was organized by the Federation of Anthroposophical University Work and the Berlin Branch of the Anthroposophical Society. **ISBN: 978-1948302043**

THE SOCIAL QUESTION

(by Rudolf Steiner, translated by Hanna von Maltitz):

This book is a First Edition, never before translated into English, series of six lectures. Rudolf Steiner gave these lectures early in the year of 1919 at Zurich, Switzerland. Here Steiner proffers ideas to solve the social problems and necessities required by life, by studying the life sciences and social life, and the living conditions of the present-day humans. **ISBN: 978-1791660536**